AI Afterlives

Bloomsbury Studies in Digital Cultures

Series Editors
Anthony Mandal and Jenny Kidd

This series responds to a rapidly changing digital world, one which permeates both our everyday lives and the broader philosophical challenges that accrue in its wake. It is inter- and trans-disciplinary, situated at the meeting points of the digital humanities, digital media and cultural studies, and research into digital ethics.

While the series will tackle the 'digital humanities' in its broadest sense, its ambition is to broaden focus beyond areas typically associated with the digital humanities to encompass a range of approaches to the digital, whether these be digital humanities, digital media studies or digital arts practice.

Titles in the series

Ambient Stories in Practice and Research, Edited by Amy Spencer
Digital Humanities and the Cyberspace Decade, 1990–2001, Claire Warwick
Drone Cultures, John Muthyala
Hacking in the Humanities, Aaron Mauro
Listening In, Toby Heys, David Jackson & Marsha Courneya
Metamodernism and the Postdigital in the Contemporary Novel, Spencer Jordan
New Directions in Digital Textual Studies, Edited by Christopher Ohge, Kristen Schuster
Representing the New AI in Film and Television, Graham Allen
Resisting Big Tech, Niels Niessen
The Trouble With Big Data, Jennifer Edmond, Nicola Horsley, Jörg Lehmann and Mike Priddy

Forthcoming titles

The Generic Person, Sophie Day, Celia Lury, Helen Ward
Cultural Institutions and Digital Inequality, Indigo Holcombe-James
Provoking Online Drama, Crystal Abidin and Jin Lee

AI Afterlives

Digital Memory and Synthetic Pasts

Jenny Kidd and Eva Nieto McAvoy

BLOOMSBURY ACADEMIC
LONDON • NEW YORK • OXFORD • NEW DELHI • SYDNEY

BLOOMSBURY ACADEMIC
Bloomsbury Publishing Plc, 50 Bedford Square, London, WC1B 3DP, UK
Bloomsbury Publishing Inc, 1359 Broadway, New York, NY 10018, USA
Bloomsbury Publishing Ireland, 29 Earlsfort Terrace, Dublin 2, D02 AY28, Ireland

BLOOMSBURY, BLOOMSBURY ACADEMIC and the Diana logo are trademarks of Bloomsbury Publishing Plc

First published in Great Britain 2026

Series design by Rebecca Heselton
Cover images © Alhontess via Getty Images

A catalogue record for this book is available from the British Library.

A catalog record for this book is available from the Library of Congress.

ISBN: HB: 978-1-3504-3752-4
ePDF: 978-1-3504-3753-1
eBook: 978-1-3504-3754-8

Series: Bloomsbury Studies in Digital Cultures

Typeset by Newgen KnowledgeWorks Pvt. Ltd., Chennai, India

For product safety related questions contact productsafety@bloomsbury.com.

To find out more about our authors and books visit www.bloomsbury.com and sign up for our newsletters.

Contents

Figures

Tables

Acknowledgements

This book largely emerges from the *Synthetic Pasts* research project and has been made possible by the generosity, insight and support of many people and institutions.

We are grateful for project funding provided by the Leverhulme Trust and for the institutional backing of the School of Journalism, Media and Culture at Cardiff University and the Department of Digital Humanities at King's College London. Special thanks to our colleagues and collaborators whose questions and feedback sharpened our thinking; and to researchers and practitioners in the wider field, whose exchanges in conferences, seminars and workshops pushed our ideas further. We also want to thank the institutions, cultural partners and artists who engaged with our work and expanded its scope, often in unexpected ways. The careful attention of anonymous reviewers strengthened the arguments and structure of the book, which the editorial team at Bloomsbury supported with thoughtful guidance and care.

Finally, we thank our families and friends for their patience and encouragement. Their support has carried us through the long and uncertain process of research and writing.

1

Introduction: Deep learning technologies and the future past

AI Afterlives explores how automated and algorithmic processes are changing the structure and behaviour of media fragments from the past, in-so-doing, offering them – and the memories we produce with them – new kinds of 'afterlife'. These developments – for example, creating 'holographic' resurrections of celebrities, generating deepfake historical figures, animating photos from archives or powering voice assistants with our deceased relatives' voice data – connect viscerally with urgent discussions about what futures artificial intelligence (AI) heralds, and what impacts it might have on what and how we remember and commemorate. While there have always been myriad and competing narratives about the past produced from personal and institutional archives, recent advances in machine learning technologies that change, manipulate or create new media objects present unprecedented challenges, as we explore.

For the first time – building on an extensive multi-method empirical study carried out between 2021 and 2025 – this book investigates how the production of what we call AI afterlives (1) affords new networked, technological, temporal, spatial and affective realities for archival materials and (2) impacts individual, collective and cultural memory work as a consequence. It asks what values and cultural assumptions are embedded in the systems that produce AI afterlives, and what ethical challenges they present, for example, in relation to datafication, exploitation, bias, deception and (often posthumous) consent. In doing so the book speaks to human concerns that reach beyond the digital, such as how we grieve, how we express and understand identity, and the impacts of disinformation. By centring such ethical ambiguities, our approach treats algorithms as 'more than cold mathematical objects' (Airoldi 2022), recognizing the ways they intervene within and are shaped by society, culture and (geo)politics, including how they mediate our processes of memory and memorization. Across a range of case studies – from genealogy sites, cultural institutions, the creative industries and the digital afterlife industries – the book argues that AI afterlives will transform how we remember and mourn, offering new possibilities for storytelling, but risking the distortion and commodification of memory and personhood. Its analysis highlights the profound ethical, cultural and personal stakes of AI's role in shaping memory, and the ways we understand life, death and legacy.

Our perspective on these issues is informed by the work we do as media and digital culture scholars who work with the past: exploring cultural heritage, memory and archives, and how they interact with the digital environment. We find thinking about AI afterlives is a helpful way of crystallizing concerns that have been expressed more generally about how materials from the past are made use of in our networked present. For example, concerns about how, what and who we remember, debates about ownership of the past, rights, sustainability and potentials for distortion, exploitation and exclusion. These are longstanding issues in relation to heritage and memory, but they become more – or differently – complicated in the digital environment, perhaps especially now in the context of AI and automation, where revival, reinvention and reworking become normalized, and often invisible.

AI Afterlives is interdisciplinary in scope and methodology, bridging insights from (digital) memory, heritage and media studies, and bringing them into dialogue with critical work on algorithms. It participates in a 'detaching' of archival media from what Wolfgang Ernst refers to as the 'dominance' of 'histori(ographi)cal discourse', a process which suggests new ways of thinking, researching and writing as a result (Ernst 2013, 30). In doing so, we advance debates about how AI systems interact with the archival past, which we now experience in myriad physical, digital and hybrid forms. The book introduces – and tests – a series of experimental methodologies for these disciplines, offering deep reflection which can inform the research practices of others. Our work is evidence of an urgent turn towards algorithmic and data cultures within the arts and humanities, demonstrating intellectual curiosity – as well as critique – in response to these developments, and offering inspiration and conceptual tools for researchers who find themselves working in – or adjacent to – this growing research area in the coming years. The book's novel contributions matter given the creeping personalization, popularization and commercialization of machine learning technologies, and the elasticity and pliability of media texts – and our memories – in digital environments. This is where *AI Afterlives* intervenes.

To set the scene we begin with four illustrative examples of AI afterlives. Working across a range of practices, platforms and services, these vignettes begin to suggest what is at stake in our analysis.

Example 1: In October 2024, the *MyHeritage* genealogy service added *LiveMemory* to its suite of AI tools.[1] *LiveMemory* can be applied to users' family photos, enhancing them and turning each into a five-second video clip animated with AI. Whereas previous *MyHeritage* services only animated faces, and in limited pre-defined ways, *LiveMemory* can animate whole scenes within photos, including those featuring multiple people, and is much more versatile. Like all the AI tools provided by *MyHeritage* the framing of *LiveMemory* is explicitly mnemonic; these short videos are promoted uncritically as 'the ultimate way to reminisce' (MyHeritage 2024). *MyHeritage* encourages users to share these short videos widely via social media, where outputs assume complex personal, public and commercial significance (as we explore further in Chapter 3).

Example 2: Within the creative industries, debates about what are called 'synthetic media' have picked up pace, connecting with questions about copyright, labour rights and (often posthumous) consent. A range of developments – for example, creating 'holographic' resurrections of celebrities, deepfakes of movie stars or AI-generated voice 'clones' of singers – demonstrate these tensions well (as we explore in Chapter 5). In 2024, in partnership with publisher Hachette, ElevenLabs – a voice technology research company – launched a series of synthetic 'Iconic Voices' which could be used in its app. The voices of a range of high-profile cultural figures were licensed and synthesized ('cloned'), so users of the app could have those stars give voice to content. For example, Judy Garland could read you a book or Burt Reynolds might talk you through a company's latest annual report. On its launch in 2024, Dustin Blank of ElevenLabs reflected

1 Including *Deep Nostalgia*, which we introduce in Chapter 3.

that adding these new voice profiles to the app's list of narrators marked 'a major step forward in our mission of making content accessible in any language and voice' (in Leatham 2024).

Example 3: Images created using generative AI have become highly visible in the digital environment. Large Language Models (LLMs) trained on text-image pairings scraped from the internet, surface (often unsettling) representations, including of 'the past'. Through these processes historical images and their descriptors are sedimented into composite renderings in the present, but not straightforwardly. These systems are open to accusations of bias and are a product of the techno-cultural environments within which programmers produce them (a theme we return to in Chapter 4). One example that shed light on these tensions was the launch of Google's Gemini AI in 2024. On its launch the system had to be taken offline for a period after it started overcorrecting bias problems in its training data, resulting in unsettling and at times deeply problematic representations of the past; for example, ethnically diverse US founding fathers and a female Pope (Shamim 2024). Jack Krawczyk, Senior Director of Product for Gemini at Google, reflected that the system needed further 'fine tuning' to recognize the 'nuance' of historical context (BBC 2024).

Example 4: An installation featuring a deepfake recreation of Salvador Dalí, developed in collaboration with advertising agency Goodby Silverstein & Partners, was opened at the Dalí Museum in Florida, 2019. Built from over 6,000 archival video frames and comprising 125 videos (totalling forty-five minutes of footage), the system can generate 190,512 possible combinations to respond to visitors (Sen 2021). In these videos Dalí greets visitors, quoting both his original writings and newly scripted lines, and even requests to take a selfie with them, which he shows to visitors and offers to send to their phones, encouraging social media sharing. The installation also roots Dalí in the present, featuring scenes where he carries that day's *New York Times* or comments on the local weather (Lee 2019). In 2024, the Museum extended this synthetic resurrection through *Ask Dalí*, an LLM-powered chatbot allowing visitors to converse with Dalí about his life, art and even contemporary events through a lobster-phone. This system was trained on transcripts of Dalí's interviews and translated writings, including *Diary of a Genius* and *The Secret Life of Salvador Dalí* (Solomon 2024). The use of such approaches in the heritage sector is something we return to in Chapter 6.

Through these vignettes we can begin to chart how AI systems present new possibilities for interacting with materials from the past. But we can also start to imagine – and perhaps even feel viscerally and instinctively – how discomfort and even distress can follow. What kind of pasts do AI systems imagine, or 'hallucinate', and how do these representations interact with our memories, both individual and collective? How do audiences for this content feel, experience and make sense of these pasts? What ethical and regulatory considerations should inform this work where it includes digital human remains (e.g., in relation to consent)? And what kinds of 'work' is it appropriate for deceased persons to take on? This book builds from these concerns through four guiding research questions:

RQ1. How do different kinds of users – from members of the public, to artists, to heritage workers – use deep learning algorithms to automate and remediate media fragments of or from the past (creating 'AI afterlives')? What kinds of representations do they produce?

RQ2. How does individual, collective and cultural memory-making operate in and through such materials? What affects, thoughts, beguilements, deceptions or diversions (for example) might they produce?

RQ3. How is the design of these tools shaped by corporate interests and logics? (i.e., business models that rely on data accumulation or extraction, and are often optimized to operate in the orbit of social networks and platforms.)

RQ4. What challenges do these practices bring into focus for everyday users, developers or for those working in the cultural and creative industries? What ethical considerations do they suggest?

These research questions have underpinned a rigorous and extensive multi-method enquiry which we introduce later in this introduction. Before that though, we locate the book's original conceptual work and key arguments.

Situating *AI Afterlives*

Digital environments offer a multitude of ways for us to interact with the past, to the extent that we might now say technology is where the past lives (Kasket 2019; Sisto 2020; Savin-Baden and Mason-Robbie 2020). Indeed, as Wendy Hui Kyong Chun reminds us, the very ontology of digital media 'is defined by memory' (2008: 154, see also Graham 2023). The introduction of automated processes which classify, rank and sort the past (in social networks, for example) has been subject to increasing academic enquiry (Jacobsen and Beer 2021a, 2021b; Sisto 2021), but there has been less focus on how computational processes are inserted (or seemingly insert themselves) into the very 'fabric' of personal or institutional archival assets, 'remediating' (Bolter and Grusin 2000; see also, Erll and Rigney 2009) them – and the memories we attach to them – through recursive and mechanized algorithmic logics. In studies of digital heritage there has been some exploration of the emerging intersections between algorithms and archival practices (Murphy and Villaespesa 2020), but there have been very few studies of what we would call 'synthetic media' within those contexts (although see Kidd and Rees 2019).

Our use of the term 'synthetic media' refers to a suite of emerging practices including the creation of deepfakes, AI-generated artworks and virtual performers (Kalpokas 2021); content either generated or altered by AI, often with minimal human intervention (Ufarte-Ruiz et al. 2023). As our vignettes earlier demonstrate, we are concerned with synthetic media in our own work, but more specifically in a subset of issues raised where content being generated or modified concerns the past and its uses in the present – personally, collectively, culturally, politically. This has been the focus of our recent work (2021–present), and we are grateful to a range of funders for supporting that enquiry. The Leverhulme Trust supported the Synthetic Pasts project (2024–6),[2] and we are also grateful to the UK Arts and Humanities Research Council (2024–5) and the Security, Crime and Intelligence Innovation Institute at Cardiff University (2025) for additional funds.

Through our focus on the AI afterlives of archival materials we explore what mnemonic, epistemological and sociotechnical concerns flow from our increased uses of synthetic media to interact with the past. In doing so we centre burgeoning questions about responsible and ethical practices where algorithms meet our desire to remember, and we pay particular attention to how these issues play out in the context of synthetic forms of 'algorithmic afterlife' (Lambert et al. 2018). In this book, we are careful not to treat AI afterlives as mere 'technological curiosities' (Vaccari and Chadwick 2020: 10),

2 More about the Leverhulme Trust Synthetic Pasts project can be found at www.syntheticpasts.com.

instead seeking to understand their richness and ambiguity, and we resist any compulsion to deride these practices simply because they are 'unfamiliar' or 'artificial' (Elder 2020: 80). Indeed, we would concur with Alexis Elder that *resisting* artifice in and of itself is unhelpful given it is such an important human device (Elder 2020; see also Zylinska 2023; Bajohr 2025; Hall 2025). Instead, the chapters that follow earnestly explore whether and how AI afterlives might be considered new expressive creations, derivations or deceptions, or whether conversely, their formulaic and repetitive qualities mark them as banal.

To do this, as we go on to detail, we have created expansive original datasets to explore varied stakeholders' experiences of AI afterlives with depth and richness, embracing the 'nuanced and oblique' impacts of these technologies (Natale 2021). We have also immersed ourselves in a range of programmes, platforms and services as researcher-users; prompting, generating, manipulating and circulating our own AI afterlives (see Chapter 8, our 'Data Coda' for more on this). Creating these outputs has prompted us in return; to consider what kinds of representations or 'predictions' (Manovich 2023) AI systems conjure, and where their blind spots are. Our work in this area continues to be a rich critical-creative enquiry benefitting from a range of collaborations; with cultural institutions and artists, developers and designers and with other researcher-users like us.

We are clear that technology has always been intertwined with our desire to connect with the past, and to the afterlife. The invention of the phonograph in the nineteenth century, for example, which meant users could hear the disembodied voices of (often deceased) people, was behind the rise of spiritualism, séances and necromancy – the art of conjuring the spirits of the dead (Kapcár 2015; Gruvæus 2023). In this book, we study a range of technologies being used in the present day to create such afterlives; perhaps with a view to support grieving, education, commemoration or entertainment, and sometimes with a view to capitalizing on continuance. In almost all cases, a primary motivation is to foster, or maintain, connections. This connective impulse reflects our deep individual and familial need to create stories about ourselves and about those that came before us. Where do we come from? Who are we connected to? and ultimately, who are we? This is a strong instinct of genealogists and family historians, for example. These approaches also reflect our collective desire to understand our pasts as communities, societies and nations. What stories and peoples do we choose to remember? How do we remember them? And what might be the function of forgetting? These are crucial questions in the work of heritage institutions, for example, and their complexity is difficult to overstate. In the book, we make connections across this range of contexts – the personal and the collective, the private and the public – and we challenge those distinctions.

In exploring a series of 'mnemotechnologies' (Stiegler 2009, 2011; Prey and Smit 2018) we showcase how AI afterlives emerge or are situated at the interstices of the socio-cultural and techno-material world. Bridging interdisciplinary perspectives we interrogate the ambivalent logics (Davis 2012) of the platforms and processes that make AI afterlives possible. We highlight the critical importance of charting the past's adaptive and pervasive qualities, not least where those intersect with corporate interests and narratives, as is so often the case (Amazon, Meta, OpenAI and genealogy companies, for example). We pursue a critical perspective on platforms that facilitate and encourage the creation of AI afterlives, showcasing how, within these contexts, memory is increasingly encoded within a 'machine habitus' (Airoldi 2022), where algorithmic systems 'as socialised agents' 'recursively' interact with users.

AI Afterlives explores what AI means for memory and where it is situated. Andrew Hoskins has written extensively about what the impacts might be for memory as digital infrastructures and connection become the norm (Hoskins 2011, 2018), proposing that digital media usher in a 'new grey' of memory; a locatedness of memory that exists beyond the self (Hoskins and Halstead 2021; Hoskins 2024). This is not to say that memory can be externalized digitally such that it will persist indefinitely through time. On the contrary, our digital remains and access to them are precarious and fragile. Some digital assets persist while others are lost, and some are in the hands of a few companies that we cannot say for certain will still be around in fifty, ten or even five years. Indeed, we already need data archaeologists to help us access some content, that is, specialists who can recover computer data in now obsolete media or formats. Notions of persistence and permanence are intensely problematic in digital environments then, and this raises philosophical and practical questions when it comes to memory. So too do notions of physicality and materiality. Like Tonia Sutherland we 'reject the tendency to associate virtual experiences and digital technologies with an escape from the body, challenging the notion that the digital sphere is any less "real" than our analog lives' (2023: 6). Instead, we understand work with AI afterlives to be situated on a rich 'continuum of materialities' (Galani and Kidd 2020), which we explore in this book.

Our use of the term 'ethics' – which crops up time and again in this book – is itself something we have reflected upon at length as we prepared this manuscript. The term's embrace within the AI community has been heavily criticized in its vagueness, for its prioritization of industry interests and for its superficiality in practical application (Bode and Goodlad 2023). Joshua Gellers makes the case that AI ethics discourses currently lack 'complexity, interdisciplinarity, and epistemic humility' (2023: 2, see also Dietrich et al. 2021). As Dal Yong Jin notes, ethics has become 'a potential solution often pushed by the industry hoping to emphasise the individual choices of designers over the scrutiny of critics calling for more regulation and accountability around AI development' (Jin 2021: 136). Ethical discussions, Jin (2021) contends, are too often coordinated with digital platforms' efforts to swerve legal regulation, and Luke Munn argues that AI development takes place in an '"a-ethical" space', that is, 'a realm where ethical dilemmas never even enter the frame' (2023: 871). Notwithstanding these concerns we have chosen to commit to the term 'ethics' given it allows for a structured, theoretically grounded and inclusive discussion on a range of issues: from datafication to bias, exploitation and access (Véliz 2023; Nyholm 2023). It also helps us to situate technology within complex structures – and negotiations – of power; structures that are shaped (variously) by values (Hare 2022; Stark 2023).

Our use of the term 'AI' also needs some unpacking here given that, as Luke Stark notes, the term 'is a leaky discursive umbrella sheltering heterogeneous and often contradictory ideas and practices' (2023: 66). AI is clearly not a monolithic entity but a diverse set of technologies and algorithms that utilize data to perform tasks; from prediction and simulation to the creation of content that can mimic human abilities and artistic styles. AI systems are deeply dependent on human inputs and data, and profoundly entangled in social, cultural and economic contexts. The uses of AI we are interested in here largely sit within the subfield of machine learning where computers learn from data and make predictions or decisions without being explicitly programmed, a field which has been supercharged by the availability of big data and the internet. We will talk in the book about uses of generative AI, natural language processing, deep learning and (less so) about computer vision, and we commit to being clear about how AI afterlives are being powered in each of the cases we explore. It is evident to us that AI is 'a key sociotechnical institution of the twenty-first century' (Bareis and Katzenbach 2021), but we largely avoid tripping into debates about artificial general intelligence (the 'singularity') which extend well beyond the remit of our study. We do appreciate however that such debates circulate around the activities and moments we take as our case studies, impacting – in subtle and not so subtle ways – how users and commentators feel about the creation of AI afterlives. What is of interest to us is not debates about whether these technologies are *actually* intelligent, but what mnemonic and socio-cultural impacts flow from those assessments. In this sense it is the lived, performed, embodied and material aspects of AI that occupy our efforts; what Minna Ruckenstein (2023) calls 'the feel of algorithms', and Garnham and Smith (2023) refer to as their 'social life'.

The concept of 'afterlives', as we conceive it, moves beyond spectral metaphors of haunting or resurrection to encompass the digital and material remnants of human life; traces that are reanimated, repurposed, remixed or remediated through computational systems. While the term evokes notions of posthumous persistence, revival or immortality, we understand AI afterlives equally as practices of handling what remains: the data, memories, images, voices and narratives that are recycled and recontextualized after their original purpose has expired. These afterlives are not just about representing the dead, but about how the living engage with, reconstruct and assign meaning to the residues of presence; often shaped as much by technological affordances and logics as by cultural rituals of mourning, memory and care.

In constructing our argument, our focus is not on the impact of digital or technological change on individual cognitive processes of remembering and forgetting. We focus instead on studying the 'emergent, relational, and contextual' qualities of articulations of memory 'in the wild' (Fawns 2022) – that is, how memory is performed and experienced across different (digital) media and contexts. No one study can cover all aspects of the problem, and our conceptual contribution can be summed up as follows. First, it draws together, builds on and extends interdisciplinary work (in memory, heritage, media and critical algorithmic studies) to make sense of AI afterlives. It pushes these fields forward with a new conceptual vocabulary which can aid future analyses of AI-driven memory systems. Second, the book participates in a more robust confrontation of synthetic media not merely as a technical novelty or cultural trend, but as a force reshaping epistemological and ontological boundaries. This book's contributions are timely – and urgent – arriving at a moment when technological capabilities are accelerating, but our regulatory, cultural and ethical responses remain underdeveloped. By critically examining both the promises and the risks of AI afterlives, the book charts a developing field of study but also offers a broader imperative: to resist the flattening of memory's complexity and to imagine and pursue more sustainable futures for our digital personhood and societies. Futures rooted in care, nuance and interconnected, multi-directional world-making. Our hope is that the analysis presented here stimulates further empirical and conceptual work on this key aspect of everyday life.

Key debates in the book

A series of critical debates permeate this book, centring the ethical, social and cultural implications of using deep learning technologies to create synthetic representations of the past.

As has already become clear, one central concern with AI afterlives is the blurring of lines between what we might call authentic and artificial memories, raising questions about potentials for deception and the reliability of digital content purporting to represent the past. We explore whether algorithmic processes which blend, abstract and 'make images from math' (Horning 2025) will ultimately serve to homogenize, flatten and distort memory; undermining our confidence in the stability of the 'real', and our perceptions of memory's durability (despite its trickiness and instability in practice). In the book we analyze how digital technologies – in particular the creation of synthetic media or 'synthetic pasts' – shape memory creation, storage and access in the context of genealogy sites, cultural institutions, the creative industries and what has been called the 'digital afterlife industry' (Öhman and Floridi 2017; Öhman 2024).

In the last of these contexts, the use of 'deathbots' raises questions about how we engage with loss in the digital age and what it means to archive and remember a person. Indeed, it challenges us to revisit what we mean when we talk about personhood. As we demonstrate, these complexities are not adequately considered by developers of these technologies, who challenge themselves to entangle biology (bodies) and information (data) in ever more intimate ways. Can a body or a life (and death) be reduced to data? What are the implications if it can? and how can we understand the materiality of AI afterlives? These revivals are not 'non-material', not least given the real and raw emotional reactions they provoke. We consider the future of what Adam Buben refers to as the 'thin me'; the person that 'survives' death in increasingly intricate digital assemblages (Buben 2015: 31). We note the desire for those who are becoming (or being made) 'immortal' to recreate a younger self; the ABBA-tars of ABBA Voyage for example, preserved in aspic in their 'prime' of 1979. In the book we note how these practices play with the temporality of memory, creating a sense of parallel pasts and (sometimes simultaneously) a multiplicity of possible futures.

The use of digital systems to 'revive' cultural icons raises questions also about the endurance of cultural memory, and its manipulation and exploitation by algorithmic intermediaries, or, more accurately, by the companies and institutions providing these services. Each year Forbes publishes a list of the highest-paid dead celebrities (in 2024 Michael Jackson made $600 million), and there are now even agents that represent dead clients. Evidently there is much to gain from personality rights, and the emergence of generative AI has reanimated debate about who owns them. The Digital Replica Contracts Act which protects actors' voices and likenesses from being copied or used without specific permission in New York state was passed in June 2024, and there will no doubt be further legislation to follow. In the book, we consider concerns about the displacement of creative labour by AI, and about whether the embedding of AI systems (even as 'co-pilots') will mean an unravelling of our very definition of creativity. The commercialization of digital assets emerging from and about the past is a central theme in the book, with touchpoints suggesting new regimes of accountability and care might be necessary.

The role of cultural institutions such as museums and historic sites in relation to AI afterlives is also a central aspect of the book's inquiry. It is easy to see why the creation of AI Afterlives is intriguing for institutions wanting to communicate about the past in engaging, playful or personalized ways. There is some hope that these approaches might enable new kinds of storytelling and interpretation, offering opportunities to explore alternative histories or represent marginalized voices and perspectives. There is also excitement about AI's potential to facilitate more accessible and inclusive exchanges, for example, providing compelling interactions in multiple languages or enabling more extensive and creative uses of assistive technologies. In the book we are keen to acknowledge these potentials, while also making the case for caution. Cultural institutions' custodianship role is clearly an important one, as is safeguarding the trust that people continue to place in them.[3]

Key to the debates in this book is a consideration of ethical issues brought about by the algorithmic turn, and in the 'platform society' (van Dijck et al. 2018). These concerns are nowhere more urgent than in debates about how new technologies mediate our experience of death and grief. There have been similar concerns about analogue data of course, but the regulatory and ethical frameworks for digital data are less clear. This is in part due to the scale and spread of our digital footprints, but also the pace at which technologies change, the blurred boundaries between private and public spaces online and the extractivist compulsion of technology companies. There is now more talk about our 'born-digital' remains; remains that are born *of* the digital environment in pretty much every moment of our existence (in many, not all societies). These include, for example, our social media posts, photos, emails, voice notes, playlists and our fitness and sleep data. Such data are of an unprecedented scale, and scattered through multiple platforms, services and servers, connected in ways we might not have anticipated, or might not yet be able to anticipate. Concerns about 'data harms' (Redden 2022), extractivism, privacy and consent permeate this book's interrogation of ethics in relation to AI afterlives.

The debates recounted in this section and explored in this book are underpinned by rapid advancements in technology, regulation and the

3 Recent reports including Museums Association (2020), American Alliance for Museums (2021), NMDC (2022) and NEMO (2023) continue to report high levels of trust in museums and museum professionals.

evolving nature of digital memory practices. But it is important to remain mindful that they are not new debates. Technology has always been indelibly a part of how we tell stories, understand ourselves, communicate our desires, connect to the past and hold onto those we have lost. It is no surprise then that AI's ramifications are felt so keenly; in our ethical, personal and public lives, in our culture and politics and in how we remember. *AI Afterlives* seeks to understand these complex phenomena through varied approaches, emphasizing the need for inclusive discussions about how these technologies are shaping our understanding and experience of the past.

Research design and methods

The book presents an innovative interrogation of AI afterlives building on and expanding methodologies from different disciplines, combining and testing them to develop new insights in response to our research questions. The empirical work moves creatively across a range of contexts and approaches, making sense, for the first time, of AI afterlives and their complex sites of study.

Our empirical work was carried out between 2021 and 2025 as follows:

- Social media analysis of 6,935 posts on X, alongside a platform analysis of the *MyHeritage* genealogy service (underpinning Chapter 3).
- User walkthroughs of four 'deathbot' services, alongside qualitative and quantitative textual analyses of those platforms' policy documents (ten documents, ~35,000 words) to reveal how values and data practices are articulated (underpinning Chapter 4).
- Content and textual analysis of news reporting around nine historical case studies spanning more than a decade (2012–23), amounting to 793 international news articles (underpinning Chapter 5).
- Thematic analysis of nineteen interviews with cultural professionals in the UK, alongside analysis of discussions from three workshops with a further thirty-five cultural professionals (underpinning Chapter 6).

Our datasets are briefly introduced in the relevant chapters, but a more complete list of data sources and reflections on each approach can be found in our Data Coda (Chapter 8). The Data Coda details and evidences how we have prioritized responsible design, transparency and ethics as sincere commitments guiding our approach.[4] We wanted to make it clear in the book how these values have shaped our work, and felt it important to dedicate a fully reflective chapter to this. We refer to this chapter as a 'coda' to highlight its distinct role: an essential addition to the book's main structure, but an addition none-the-less. Our Data Coda provides an in-depth overview of our diverse approaches to AI afterlives, offering readers the opportunity to understand and assess them. This more reflective account, informed by the work of Bonini and Treré (2024), also represents a novel interdisciplinary contribution, and we hope it will pave the way for methodologically curious, creative and similarly reflexive studies in future.

Most chapters in the book have both qualitative and quantitative dimensions to the analysis they present, responding to Manca's assessment that to fully understand digital memory practices there is 'a need to use mixed-method approaches that combine quantitative tools and qualitative instruments' (2021: 14). Samuel Merril (2025) has pushed this observation further, arguing for the use of 'hybrid methodologies' in the study of social and cultural memory, and we have embraced this approach also. According to Merrill, 'Hybrid methodologies' usually involve combining methods from different fields, but should go beyond that by relating to 'ontological assumptions' about the subject of study. For example – as Merrill notes – adopting a hybrid methodology for digital memory studies might involve: embracing its temporal, spatial, technological and agentic complexity (even messiness); studying how mnemonic objects move or travel through 'processes of remediation, translation, translocation, or transduction'; and enlisting computational collaborators. These forms of hybridization have characterized our approach throughout, as we outline in the Data Coda. We find this notion of hybridity appealing, not least because hybrids, according to Maurizia Boscagli, 'refuse to occupy their assigned space in the grid of meaning and value' (2014: 11). Hybridity draws attention to 'flux', 'in-betweenness' and 'liminality' (Chadwick 2013: 5), and suggests new assemblages, power relations and dynamics (Galani and Kidd 2020). Following Nick J. Fox and Pam Alldred (2017) we have used

4 Where appropriate (including in our creative and collaborative work) we have used UKRIs AREA Framework for responsible innovation (UKRI 2023), which we have found to be a rich and enabling resource.

a mixed methodology in this study in order to produce 'research-assemblages' that recognize and mitigate the micropolitics of methods.

Our use of humanities and social science research methods has been coupled in our work with other kinds of investigation. We have employed 'making' as a creative practice and as a method, for example, in producing a number of video essays to illustrate our findings, and a highly visual web presence (www.syntheticpasts.com). These outputs are a reflection of our critical-creative approach, and are inspired by the work of scholars in adjacent and overlapping fields. Jenna Ng and Oliver Tomkins, for example, whose video essay and work on 'The New Virtuality' has been so instructive to our approach (Ng and Tomkins 2023), Lev Manovich's artistic and foundational work in new media studies,[5] and Joanna Zylinska's 'hybrid' enquiry, combining philosophy and artistic practice.[6] Throughout the project we have created many generative AI images and videos as researcher-users of platforms and devices, and as a way of visualizing our findings and concerns in relation to AI afterlives (using AI content generators like Gemini, Magic Media, Dall-E4 and Stable Diffusion). We have created deathbots, virtual avatars, online installations, a Twine game and even a digital Ouija board as a mechanism for visualizing our research themes and concerns, and we have done extensive desk research, interacting with publicly available chatbots and avatars, and exploring the varied ways others are using these technologies. We have also collaborated with artists to further our creative endeavour. In 2024, we worked with Mark Stuart-Smith[7] on an installation of *Black Box* on The Strand in London as part of King's College London's *Fake or Real?* Exhibition, and we worked with creative studio yello brick[8] who produced a series of playful encounters for use in our workshops as a way of generating discussions amongst participants. Use of these creative approaches has produced different ways of thinking about and through the issues we foreground in this book, and we are continuing to develop these partnerships.

As researchers attuned to critiques of digital infrastructures and data power, we have our own reservations about using some of the platforms we analyse

5 More about Lev Manovich's work can be found at https://manovich.net/.
6 More about Joanna Zylinska's work can be found at http://www.joannazylinska.net/.
7 More about Mark Stuart Smith's work can be found at https://markstuartsmith.co.uk/.
8 More about the work of yello brick can be found at https://www.yellobrick.co.uk/.

in this book, and we are aware of how dramatically some of these services (most notably perhaps X) have changed during the timeframe covered by our study. Reflecting on our positionality, we recognize that our behaviours and experiences on digital platforms shape the way we study and attribute value to them, and that, as users, we are equally influenced by the algorithms, echo chambers and personalization processes that govern broader access to digital content, by our own 'digital habitus' (Romele 2024). As such we are also acutely aware that our own engagements with these technologies cannot fully capture the diversity of experiences they generate for others. As researchers based in predominantly English-speaking regions of the Global North – specifically Wales and England in the UK – we have remained conscious of our positionality throughout this research. Our interpretations are inevitably shaped by the cultural, economic and social contexts we inhabit, which will have influenced how we interact with our data and have engaged with outputs produced in non-Western or non-English-speaking contexts. We acknowledge that our own values, assumptions and biases will have shaped this work, potentially leading us to overlook important nuances in global perspectives on AI afterlives – particularly those presented in scholarship not written in English. The many hours we have spent reflecting on our positionality in relation to our field sites have underscored the limitations of our study, while also sharpening our sense of its genuine contributions and areas of strength.

Our exploration of AI afterlives opens diverse pathways for future research at the nexus of synthetic media, digital memory and AI-mediated forms of posthumous presence. As the technologies in question continue to evolve, so too must the critical and methodological frameworks through which we engage them, and our work points to innovative possibilities for how such research might be conceptualized and conducted.

Overview of the book

AI Afterlives is structured across eight interrelated chapters. Following this introduction, Chapter 2 'Synthetic media | Synthetic pasts' offers a detailed theoretical framework for our exploration of AI afterlives in the book. We examine three key themes suggested by the book's title and our research questions. Firstly, we define and discuss synthetic media (with a particular emphasis on generative AI, deepfakes and virtual performers), raising questions about remediation, authenticity and truth. Secondly, we expand the notion of digital memory (how digital technologies shape memory creation, storage and access), including how it impacts our understanding of the past and selfhood. This section highlights concerns about the manipulation and commercialization of memory, particularly in the context of death and grief. Thirdly, we explore algorithmic culture (the pervasive influence of algorithms on our lives and memories), addressing concerns about bias, lack of transparency and the exploitation of data within algorithmic systems. Chapter 2 also gives an overview of methodological considerations for studying these complex phenomena, acknowledging the challenges of researching digital data and the evolving nature of digital memory.

Chapter 3 examines the ethical and social implications of AI-driven afterlives in the context of genealogy platforms, focusing on a case study of *MyHeritage*. By interrogating the *Deep Nostalgia* feature – which brings *MyHeritage* users' deceased ancestors 'to life' by animating their photographs – the chapter investigates how technology remediates and re-scaffolds personal memories, fostering what we call 'algorithmic nostalgia' as a result. The discussion is supported by a quali-quantitative analysis of 6,935 tweets related to *Deep Nostalgia*, as well as an exploration of key public documents from *MyHeritage* and relevant third-party sources. We explore in detail how these algorithmically augmented outputs emerge from semi-automated data collaborations and behind-the-scenes mashups which, through the layering of driver videos and additional information, become increasingly distanced and disconnected from their original source materials, even as they present the illusion of immediacy. The chapter argues that while *Deep Nostalgia* is marketed as a tool to revive ancestors for nostalgic purposes, it risks homogenizing and distorting memories through its reliance on pre-programmed movements and facial expressions. It also introduces the concept of 'deceptive genealogy', where the line between authentic and artificial memories becomes increasingly unclear, and makes the case that these approaches, heavily reliant on data extraction and social media sharing, raise significant ethical issues.

Chapter 4 offers a critique of the 'Digital Afterlife Industry', analysing four platforms – *Almaya, HereAfter, Seance AI* and *You, Only Virtual* – that use

AI to story and archive personal memories, including through the creation of what have been termed 'deathbots'. It examines how these platforms enable users to curate and preserve the memories of individuals, the types of mnemonic resources they generate, and the user experience of engaging with them. The chapter also investigates how corporate entities conceptualize and manage care and responsibility in relation to these practices, particularly given the context of remembrance and grief that they operate in. Supported by a series of sociotechnical walkthroughs and a thorough quali-quantitative document analysis (ten documents, 34,967 words), the chapter argues that the platformization of memory in digital afterlife services operates with a critically over-simplified understanding of memory, and of connection. This significantly de-emphasizes the extensive suite of ethical considerations associated with these digital practices, and the role of emotion and social context in memory formation and recall. Use of these platforms prompts reflection on what aspects of a person might be considered indispensable when preserving their 'essence' in digital form, but, in their current manifestation, highlights the huge gulf between the promise of these services and their actual outputs. Extending our discussions from Chapter 3 here we draw on Poell et al.'s (2019) definition of 'platformization' to draw out the combination of infrastructural, economic and governmental dimensions which 'reorganize' cultural practices – including mnemonic ones – around platforms.

Whereas Chapters 3 and 4 zoom in on memory practices that are largely personal, in Chapter 5 we turn to practices of cultural memory. We explore constructions of the past through cultural and media artefacts and events (Assman 2010), with a focus on synthetic media 'revival' in the creative industries. Building on an analysis of 793 English language news articles covering a series of nine historic case studies – from the Tupac Shakur 'hologram' (2012), through to the voice 'cloning' of Polish actor Milogost Reczek (2023) – we explore public narratives about uses of AI to 'revive' cultural figures; in particular singers, actors and celebrities. We explore the implications of these developments for our interactions with mainstream media output, and for the processes of cultural memory-making they are associated with. We demonstrate that writers, actors and musicians increasingly fear being replaced by cheaper and (infinitely) more 'productive' AI agents, raising concerns about job losses and a diminishing sense of artistic control. These anxieties are heightened by forecasts of rapid technological progress, compounded by the dominance of voices from the tech industry in the discursive spaces these creative practices inhabit. While such recreations may foster a sense of connection with cultural figures, we argue that they risk distorting the interpretive processes surrounding their death and legacy. The capacity to endlessly manipulate and repurpose digital likenesses threatens to erode the value of an artist's finite body of work, potentially fostering – or reinforcing – misleading or false cultural imaginaries. In the chapter, we also explore the concept of 'magic' in relation to these technologies, and the role this plays in obscuring their more problematic aspects. We caution against uncritically embracing the 'techno sublime', urging a more nuanced and critical understanding of the potential consequences of reducing individuals to digital data. The analysis raises questions about what it means to remember cultural icons healthily, authentically and respectfully, and demonstrates that norms are still very much in flux; there is currently no consensus on many aspects of digital 'revival' within the context of the creative industries.

Chapter 6 turns to an examination of AI afterlives in the heritage sector, and in so doing, connects with complex negotiations about collective memory and the power dynamics that shape it. We argue that the deployment of synthetic media to create immersive and interactive representations of historical events and figures holds the potential to radically reconfigure memory practices – blurring the boundaries between storytelling and simulation, emotional resonance and historical accuracy, and innovation and commodification. Drawing on participatory research and workshops conducted with fifty-four heritage professionals, the analysis reveals a cautious optimism surrounding AI's potential, tempered by significant concerns regarding disinformation, sustainability and the influence of third-party platforms. The chapter interrogates whether AI-generated interactions risk flattening historical complexity, particularly when curated avatars privilege emotional appeal over uncomfortable historical truths. High-profile examples such as *Hello Vincent* and *Dalí Lives* are critically contrasted with the more ethically attuned *Dimensions in Testimony* initiative and the experimental work of artist Nora Al-Badri. The chapter situates AI afterlives within broader traditions of archival critique, postcolonial memory politics and ongoing debates over the ownership and curation of the past, revealing tensions between innovation and ethical stewardship, authenticity and emotional connection, and AIs flattening and speculative compulsions. It also exposes the ambiguity of 'responsible AI' discourses.

The book's conclusion presents our closing reflections on memory, mourning and meaning-making in the digital age. It argues that AI afterlives are reshaping how we remember personal and collective pasts within the logics of platform capitalism. These approaches shift memory from a fluid process to an automated and commodified one, often prioritizing visibility and profit over authentic preservation. Synthetic media offer illusions of connection but often involve distortion, data abstraction and manipulation, obscuring their dependence on reductive templates and extractive logics. Our conclusion argues that AI afterlives offer opportunities for innovation and engagement but, given the challenges, necessitate critical reflection and the creation and use of context-sensitive resources. Reflecting back across our findings we urge technologists, policymakers, archivists and researchers to critically examine the design and governance of AI-driven memory systems, emphasizing the importance of preserving the richness and plurality of memory, while resisting its reduction to computational logics or simplified narratives.

The book then closes with our Data Coda (Chapter 8). Here we detail how – and why – we have tested an expansive suite of humanities, social science and creative research methods, offering our reflections on the amalgam of approaches which we characterize as 'hybrid' (Merril 2025). Chapter 8 details these investigations providing a fully comprehensive overview of data underpinning each chapter, as well as a reflection on research ethics informing this work.

As the promotion of deepfake and voice-synthesizing technologies intensifies, the ethics of working with AI afterlives is likely to become an increasing concern for scholars across a range of disciplines, and this study furthers our understanding of these issues. In this book, we critically explore synthetic pasts in new ways, offering, for the first time, an expansive exploration of their significance and implications. We offer a critical, interdisciplinary examination of AI afterlives, analysing how synthetic media are reshaping memory, mourning and presence across personal, cultural and institutional contexts. We trace how AI systems – through platforms, deathbots, avatars and synthetic revivals – mediate memory and reconfigure the dead through processes of commodification, automation and algorithmic design. Rather than treating these technologies as novelties, the book shows how they challenge core assumptions about authenticity, authorship and consent, especially as memory is refashioned into data-driven, emotionally resonant, but often reductive forms. A key contribution is the theorization of AI afterlives as sites of epistemic tension and contested presence, where remembrance is shaped by infrastructural inequalities and historical legacies. By surfacing the ambivalence of these systems – their simultaneous intimacy and extractiveness – it calls for their study as cultural artefacts that demand critical scrutiny, creative disruption and cross-cultural re-imagination.

2

Synthetic media | Synthetic pasts

As we noted in the book's introduction, digital environments offer a staggering array of opportunities for people to remember and interact with the past, to the extent that we might now say digital infrastructures – and increasingly we must include algorithmic systems – are where the past lives. In order to interrogate this proposition and its implications throughout the book, this chapter introduces and connects scholarship on three key sites of study relevant to our inquiry: synthetic media, digital memory and algorithmic culture. We set out a series of dynamic trans-disciplinary debates before, lastly, turning our attention to methodological considerations suggested by those key foci.

Synthetic media

The emergence of synthetic media is a key underpinning development given the concerns of this book. The term 'synthetic media' refers to content generated or manipulated by artificial intelligence (AI), and encompasses varying textual, image, aural and video outputs. Examples include deepfakes, AI generated art and the creation of virtual performers (Kalpokas 2021). Synthetic media can now be produced with minimal human intervention (Ufarte-Ruiz et al. 2023), contrasting with traditional media which continue to rely heavily on human content creation and post-production. As such, according to some scholars, synthetic media present 'a newfound popular power' for almost anyone to create outputs (Ananny 2024). Auli Viidalepp (2022) distinguishes between fully synthetic content (which is completely generated by AI) and synthetically *enhanced* content (such as deepfake videos), and Raphaël Millière (2022) does similarly, referring to partially synthetic approaches which modify archival media and totally synthetic media which are entirely generative. These categories provide helpful distinctions when it comes to understanding the different ways in which synthetic media can be created and used, as well as their implications.

There are now many published works on synthetic media emerging from a range of disciplines, much of which we will introduce in the sub-sections that follow. Deepfakes, for example, have been written about extensively (Chesney and Citron 2019, Ajder et al. 2019, Rini 2019; Vaccari and Chadwick 2020; Lees et al. 2021; Lees 2023; Oscar 2023) as have virtual performers and influencers (Stanyek and Piekut 2010; Harris 2013; Ng and Bax 2023; Matthews and Nairn 2023). As digital technologies create ever more realistic simulations, literature suggests that a blurring of boundaries between the real and the virtual will follow, raising questions about the nature of authenticity and truth. John Fletcher proposes that this constitutes a 'paradigm shift' given that 'seeing is no longer believing', and that when 'old verification procedures fail … traditional mechanisms of trust and epistemic rigor prove outclassed' (Fletcher 2018: 457).

From these observations, we can begin to discern some of the challenges for memory that synthetic media produce or at the very least exacerbate; in relation to false memory, for example (Liv and Greenbaum 2020; Murphy and Flynn 2022; Schincariol et al. 2024), questions about personhood (Leaver 2019) or about the commercialization of synthetic content featuring the deceased (McLeod 2015). Studies discuss potentials for harm such as the spread of misinformation, the exploitation of personal data and myriad legal and intellectual property issues. These concerns are amplified given the lack of regulation in many countries when it comes to synthetic media, and the fact that developments in AI tend to outpace the ability of governments and regulatory bodies to create the necessary laws and frameworks. This means there are currently gaps in governance allowing for the misuse of synthetic media.

Despite these concerns, studies are keen to point to a suite of potential benefits suggested by synthetic media should the ethical and regulatory contexts be strengthened. These include enhancements to education, training, advertising, healthcare and entertainment (Westerlund 2019; Millière 2022; Kaur et al. 2024; Arora et al. 2024). It is hoped that uses of synthetic media might lead to more versatile digital content, including new possibilities for personalization, translation and the creative use of accessibility tools (Kamble and Chaudhari 2024). It has even been suggested that deepfakes might serve as a form of 'digital camouflage', protecting identities for whistle-blowers or targeted individuals (Gramigna 2024).

Given this swathe of potentials and pitfalls, there have been calls (for example, from Nightingale and Wade 2022) for more interdisciplinary studies of the manipulation of digital assets. Our own research into AI afterlives is one such study.

This section introduces a series of debates relating to synthetic media that will variously permeate the chapters that follow. First we explore debates about generative AI, before discussing forms of synthetically enhanced content through the theoretical prism of 'remediation'. We then briefly explore literature about two increasingly high-profile examples of synthetic media: virtual performers and deepfakes.

Generative AI

Generative AI refers to a class of AI models and systems designed to create new content or data that mimics real-world information, based on patterns and structures in large datasets. These outputs can include text, images, videos and music – what we might call *fully* synthetic media.[1] Generative AI differs from more 'conventional' uses of AI focused on analysing data for tasks like classification or recommendation (Nguyen et al. 2023; Garon 2023). Tools like ChatGPT, Midjourney and Dall-E are becoming increasingly familiar, and there is much anticipation of their disruptive impacts, not least within the creative industries where they offer unprecedented possibilities for artistic expression, content generation and the personalization of entertainment experiences. These tools – in theory at least – require less time, artistic skill, technical expertise and computational resources to produce outputs (Millière 2022), but their use provokes a great number of concerns which these industries are only beginning to grapple with (Kidd and Nieto McAvoy 2025). Literature examining these contexts is helping us to move beyond an

1 These distinctions are of course flawed given how these systems might themselves be said to remediate extant digital data.

understanding of generative AI merely as a tool, prompting us in addition to consider the complex interplay between human values, technological advancements and the evolving nature of creativity (De Cremer et al. 2023; Epstein and Hertzmann 2023; Jiang et al. 2023). The ability to manipulate and fabricate digital content with increasing realism evidently necessitates a re-evaluation of our epistemological frameworks (Horning 2025; Nieto McAvoy and Kidd 2026).

In relation to creativity, scholars have begun to explore the extent to which authorship is being complicated by generative AI (Fenwick and Jurcys 2023; Abbott and Rothman 2023). Some argue that these systems produce nothing but an echo of the vast datasets they are trained on, and lack genuine creative intent. Massimo Airoldi (2022) emphasizes the fact that any creative potential in generative AI is always and inevitably tied to the data it is trained on and the algorithms that govern its operation, raising questions about the extent to which it could ever be considered to exhibit genuine, unpredictable creativity (Mitchell 2019; Crawford 2021). Lev Manovich (2023) understands these outputs as 'predictive media', a term that is 'figurative and evocative', but also 'scientific' in that it references generative AI's underlying mechanism which predicts the most useful outputs based on prompts which have been inputted by a user. For example, in text-to-image AI models (such as Dall-E), the network attempts to predict images that best correspond to the text input. The role of prediction in these processes is profound, but we are reminded that 'probabilistic vision is not the same as understanding' (Manovich 2023: 15). Eryk Salvaggio (2023) writes about the predictive qualities of AI image-generating in particular, proposing that 'AI images are data patterns inscribed into pictures' and as such can be read as 'infographics' that tell 'stories' about their underlying datasets. Pinpointing these storied qualities is helpful as it begins to suggest the registers of 'feeling' and emotion that are ingrained in everyday engagements with data visualizations (Kennedy and Hill 2018), and by extension, with generative AI outputs.

Some scholars have proposed that generative AI's creative potentials are strong, anticipating that these advancements could unlock 'new frontiers' in creativity, innovation and value creation (Safavi and Ghazinoory 2024). Gelayol Safavi and Sepehr Ghazinoory anticipate the advent of an 'Industry 4.0', where the integration of 'cyber-physical systems' – such as AI, cognitive computing and cloud computing – marks a new era of interconnectedness, efficiency and agility in production systems. Several studies have examined how AI systems challenge and perhaps in time evolve conventional notions of creativity (Magni et al. 2024). Emerging perspectives highlight the importance of practices like co-creativity and collaboration between AI and humans (Wingström et al. 2022; Bender 2023; Vinchon et al. 2023). Joshua C. Gellers (2023) proposes that the 'iterative loop' between human input and machine output in generative AI systems complicates traditional notions of authorship, leading to the concept of 'hybrids' where human and machine are creatively intertwined (Gellers 2023: 1; see also, McLeod 2015).

When it comes to assessments of generative AI's potential mnemonic impacts, the issue of deception looms large. Scholars have raised critical questions about the potentials for deception where generative AI systems mimic human behaviour or evoke emotional responses, especially given that deception is not a mere by-product of generative AI but a fundamental component of it (Natale 2021). AI systems often incorporate deceptive elements such as human-like appearances, voices and language, to produce specific effects and affects in users. Simone Natale (2021: 7) introduces the concept of 'banal deception' to describe the mundane, everyday situations where AI technologies employ (or 'domesticate') deceptive mechanisms, in-doing-so exploiting users' perceptions and psychology. These mechanisms, while often subtle and imperceptible, have significant consequences as they contribute to the seamless integration of AI into our lives. Those who are critical of AI's deceptive tendencies advocate for transparency in AI development and deployment, ensuring users are aware of any potentials for manipulation (Mitchell 2019). They emphasize the need to develop new tools to discern real content from fabricated content, and argue for improved digital and data literacy as well as critical thinking (Fenwick and Jurcys 2023). Others have been calling for the development of explainable AI (XAI), that is, algorithms that can explain their reasoning in a human-understandable manner (Bryan-Kinns et al. 2023). Concerns about deception often stem from the 'black boxing' of AI models which makes it unclear how decisions are made, and XAI allows humans to see inside a model and understand more about why it took a certain action. The hope is that such transparency helps detect intentional or unintentional manipulation, reducing fear and suspicion and providing reassurance about a system's alignment with human values. XAI might prove especially important in relation to how generative AI interacts with memory, allowing users of a system to interrogate how a memory has been accessed and interpreted, whether it has been inferred, misfiled or fabricated, and whether it should be accepted, rejected or corrected as a result.

Generative AI clearly complicates the relationship between media and memory given its ability to simulate and 'recreate' experiences and moments in time, but we must remain mindful that no media technology is a neutral conveyor of memory (van Dijck 2007; Bond et al. 2016). As Joanne Garde-Hansen et al. noted in 2009, how human memory (matter) and silicon memory (information) converge in the coming years may well have a profound impact on how we understand the very nature of memory (Garde-Hansen et al. 2009; see also, Hoskins 2024). This becomes a more charged observation when we consider how intertwined the development and deployment of generative AI are with structures of power and control (Crawford 2021; Bonini and Trere 2024). The concentration of resources and expertise in the hands of a few powerful technology companies makes it likely that these technologies will further entrench existing inequalities and serve narrow corporate interests (Mitchell 2019; Stark 2023; Barassi 2024). What this will mean for generative AI's role in memory work is an open question, and one this book responds to.

Remediation

A key theme in this book is the dynamic and changing relationship between old and new media. Jay David Bolter and Richard Grusin's work on remediation, defined as 'the representation of one medium in another', helps us to understand and articulate this relationship, supporting an analysis of how new media technologies often incorporate, reinterpret and even transform other older forms of media (Bolter and Grusin 2000). Processes of remediation are not simply a matter of technological evolution however, but complex cultural phenomena that shed light on how our understanding of the past shapes our experience of the present (Erll and Rigney 2009). As such, remediation offers a valuable framework for understanding AI, particularly its visual and cultural dimensions. By tracing the lineage of AI through earlier media forms, we can better grasp its assumptions, limitations and potential impacts.

There are a number of key aspects of remediation theory which inform our analysis of AI afterlives in the chapters that follow, beginning in Chapter 3. Firstly, remediation involves a complex negotiation between the old and the new, with varying degrees of fidelity to an original medium. Some new media forms aim for high fidelity, seeking to faithfully reproduce the experience of older media, while others embrace a more transformative approach, reinterpreting or even subverting the conventions of media past. Secondly, remediation theory gives us a way of talking about how new media technologies create a sense of immediacy for users or viewers (Bolter and Grusin 2000). This is frequently connected to a desire for transparency, where the technology in use attempts to erase itself, letting the viewer interact with the content as though they were experiencing the original medium first hand. This sense of transparency is typically deceptive however, as the technology always influences the experience in some way, subtly yet profoundly shaping our perception (Bolter and Grusin 2000). Thirdly, as we noted earlier – and importantly for the practices we explore in this book – remediation's technical processes shed light on varied social and cultural practices. The ways in which new media incorporate and reinterpret older forms reflect prevailing cultural values, historical narratives and social dynamics. Studying remediation can reveal how our understanding of the past shapes our engagement with the present, and how new technologies contribute to ongoing processes of cultural memory. Taylor Annabell's (2023) study of how young women on Instagram perform digital memory work is a great example of this. Social media platforms like Instagram, with their ability to capture, store and resurface past content, can be seen as remediating older forms of memory preservation, such as photo albums or scrapbooks. Exploring how individuals perform digital memory work through these platforms can reveal the complex interplay between technological affordances, cultural practices and personal narratives in the construction of digital memory (Annabell 2023). Fourthly, remediation theory highlights how new media technologies can challenge existing power structures, norms and ways of knowing. AI clearly poses new ethical questions about knowledge, and is suggesting changed structures of power and authority as was noted in the previous section.

As will become clear in the chapters that follow, practices of remediation can also be strategies for AI developers to make their technologies more relatable and acceptable to users, and to heighten user engagement. By framing AI systems as extensions or remediations of familiar media forms, developers can seek to mitigate anxieties and encourage adoption. Deathbots, for example, are often marketed as a way to 'chat with the dead', drawing on existing cultural practices of communication and remembrance. This framing can obscure the ethical implications of interacting with deathbots however, as we will explore in Chapter 4. AI technologies thus reshape and redefine established practices, industries and human experiences, while simultaneously drawing on and interacting with existing systems and forms of knowledge. Through the prism of remediation theory, AI can be understood not just as a tool for automating tasks but as an evolving medium that reshapes how we produce, receive and interpret knowledge. AI shifts the boundaries between authorship, creation and distribution, which echoes the way television and radio remediated the printed word. AI in these contexts doesn't just replicate what humans do but remediates creative processes, reimagining (for example) the role of the artist and creator. As noted previously, Lev Manovich has suggested that AI, particularly in the context of visual media, operate through processes of prediction (2023). This would seem to set it in contrast with earlier forms of media creation which rely on recording or simulation. The predictive capacity of AI systems however, while seemingly novel, can be understood as an extension of earlier media's efforts to represent and interpret reality.

Remediation theory thus provides a valuable framework for thinking about AI as a force that both draws on and reshapes older systems of knowledge, culture and technology. It allows us to recognize AI not as a radical break from the past but as an evolution of ongoing human and technological practices. By understanding AI through the lens of remediation, we can see how it interacts with, challenges and refashions existing norms, institutions and human roles in ways that are both novel and familiar. Two examples of algorithmic remediation that we deal with at some length in this book are the creation of virtual performers and the production of deepfakes. In the following sections we introduce each in turn.

Virtual performers

Given our focus on AI afterlives we have found work on virtual performers and virtual idols (Liu 2023) to be informative (see especially Chapter 5). A virtual performer is a digital or computer-generated entity that simulates the role of a performer, often in entertainment contexts such as music, theatre or dance (Ng and Bax 2023; Matthews and Nairn 2023). These performers can take many forms, including avatars, animated characters or 'revived' persons (often referred to as 'holograms'), and they may be used in live or recorded productions. Scholarship focuses on the ethical, social and philosophical implications of virtual performers' creation and reception, and is insistent on treating these practices as more than technological novelty. Instead, these outputs are understood to be complex cultural artefacts that challenge our understanding of identity, authenticity, liveness and even the boundaries between life and death (Ng 2021).

Virtual performers can be read as a form of remediation as they incorporate elements of live performance, recorded media and digital animation to create a hybrid experience, blurring lines between the real and the virtual (McLeod 2015). Ken McLeod (2015) suggests that the appeal of virtual performers lies in their ability to evoke a sense of wonder and awe; what he terms 'technological magic'. This 'magic' is often associated with the creation of a convincing illusion of presence, where the virtual performer appears to possess a degree of autonomy and agency. Of course, this 'illusion' is a construction, and we mustn't underplay the role of human programmers, designers and (often living) performers in crafting it. Elsewhere in this book we reflect on the work done by the term 'magic' where it is used to talk about these approaches and about technology more broadly – concluding that it often works to obscure and to decentre the more problematic aspects of these systems (echoing McLeod 2015; Kopelman and Frosh 2023; Recuber 2023).

Ng and Bax argue that virtual performers, as externalized computational code, can be owned, transferred, copied, shared and therefore inserted into a 'capitalism of immateriality' (2023: 2). This suggests important questions about control, ownership and consent, particularly where virtual performers are based on the likenesses of real individuals, living or dead. Where the latter is the case (i.e. the individual is deceased), and 'resurrection' for commercial gain is under scrutiny, there are clearly additional questions about dignity, exploitation and the potential to distort or manipulate the past (Stanyek and Piekut 2010; Cull 2015). As we will demonstrate in Chapter 5, such practices can push at the boundaries of acceptability, evoking a sense of unease or discomfort, particularly where they approach a level of realism that triggers the 'uncanny valley'. This discomfort stems from the dissonance between the human-like appearance of a virtual performer and our awareness of its artificiality (Matthews and Nairn 2023; Lou et al. 2022).

The emergence of virtual performers raises questions about the future of live events and the evolving expectations of audiences. While it can be tempting to view them as a threat to the authenticity of live performance, it is possible they will expand our understanding and experience of 'live'-ness, incorporating new technologies and seeding innovative forms of engagement (Cull 2015). Some scholars highlight the role of fan-created content – such as fan art, cosplay and remixes – when it comes to shaping the reception and evolution of virtual performers, blurring the lines between producer and consumer. This participatory aspect of virtual performance is particularly evident with vocaloids like Hatsune Miku, where fans play an active role in creating and disseminating new content (Bell 2015; Jørgensen et al. 2017). Virtual performers are provocative as they nod to an uncertain future for identity including the intriguing possibility of hybrid identities, raising questions about authenticity, ownership and the nature of embodiment in a digitally mediated world (Black 2008; Prior 2017). They also raise questions about the 'puppeteering of pastness' which are pertinent to our study of AI afterlives (Ng and Bax 2023).

Deepfakes

Discussions about the ethics of deep learning technologies, and in particular deepfakes (Fletcher 2018; Chesney and Citron 2019), have often centred concerns about authenticity and disinformation. Scholars consistently highlight the capacity of deepfakes to undermine trust in audio-visual media, proposing that the increasing realism of AI-generated 'fakes' makes it challenging to discern real from fabricated content. There are suggestions that deepfakes will lead to widespread scepticism about the fidelity of content, and eventually to what Aviv Ovadya terms 'reality apathy' (Ovadya, in Warzel 2018). Relatedly, Rob Horning writes about what he calls 'deep reals'; real images that conform to a 'grammar of fakeness' to the extent that they activate peoples' generalized anxiety about deepfakes (Horning 2025). An erosion of trust in audio-visual content has profound implications for our reliance on video and audio as evidence, impacting journalism, legal proceedings and social interactions. Regina Rini, for example, cautions that deepfakes could lead to 'epistemic chaos', gradually eroding the credibility of media fragments to the extent that they no longer serve their function as reliable evidence (Rini 2019: 12).

There is also concern about the potential of deepfakes to be weaponized for political purposes, to create false narratives or to manipulate public opinion (Fletcher 2018; Westerlund 2019). In time, the ease with which deepfakes can be created and disseminated will likely amplify their potential to trigger reputational damage, harassment and emotional distress (Chesney and Citron 2019). It is no surprise then that deepfakes have been understood as 'trouble' (Chesney and Citron 2019) for their 'threatening' and 'damaging' potentials (Westerlund 2019; see also, Silbey and Hartzog 2019). Some conclude that citizens and consumers need to be protected from them, and that their effects must be 'countered' (Chesney and Citron 2019).

Critics have also raised concerns about the impact of deepfakes on memory practices. It is suggested that the sense of immersion and immediacy (Bolter and Grusin 2000) that viewers get from videos, especially hyper-realistic deepfakes, could contribute to the creation of false memories (Liv and Greenbaum 2020; Murphy and Flynn 2022). Individuals exposed to deepfakes might later recall those fabricated events as genuine experiences, impacting their understanding of the past and their perception of reality.

Given these concerns, scholars have been keen to stress the importance of critical media literacy in response to the proliferation of deepfakes (McCosker 2024), and the development of technical countermeasures and detection strategies to identify and flag them. AI algorithms can be trained to detect subtle inconsistencies in videos, helping to expose deepfakes where that might be deemed necessary (Rini 2019). Such technical solutions are fraught with difficulty however, as are legal and regulatory fixes. Literature has explored the challenge of regulating deepfakes, considering legal frameworks related to defamation, fraud and the misappropriation of likeness (Westerlund 2019). However, scholars also caution against overly broad regulations that could stifle what might be considered legitimate uses of the technology or infringe on free speech rights. 'Legitimate' use of deepfakes (Westling 2019) has been defended within the contexts of entertainment (Lees et al. 2021; Lees 2023), education (Anderson 2019) and artistic expression (Rees 2019; Cuseum 2019). As we explore in Chapter 6 for example, deepfakes have been used to enhance museum experiences by allowing visitors to interact with historical figures or engage in conversations with artists from the past (Maras and Alexandrou 2019; Kidd and Rees 2021). In such a context it is worth considering whether demarcating deepfakes as somehow less legitimate, less authentic or more troublesome than other forms of historical representation runs the risk of flattening debates about the extent to which those other forms also present 'intractable conundrums' around authenticity (Lowenthal 1990), not least given their performative and constructed qualities. Ross Parry has examined what he calls the 'fictive tradition' in museums, concluding that an over-emphasis on questions raised by 'artifice' can turn us towards naive or misleading conceptualizations of the 'real' elsewhere in an institution (Parry 2013a). Marcus Boon has suggested that making copies is now 'pervasive' and 'part of how the universe functions and manifests' (2010: 8) but asserts that we still have an instinct to contain or restrict these practices. Such instincts overlook the fact that the quality of authenticity itself should be understood as unsettled, emergent and performed, to the extent that it needs 'constant negotiation, examination, re-evaluation, and upkeep' (Rossi 2010: 338). Debates about deepfakes – and about their ambivalence – will be a recurring theme in the chapters that follow.

Digital memory

Digital memory studies is an interdisciplinary field concerned with how digital technologies transform – or on occasion perhaps sediment – how we create, store, access and understand memory. It draws from fields such as media studies, cultural studies, archival science, history and the digital humanities to investigate both the technical aspects of digital memory (such as data storage and retrieval systems) as well as cultural, social and ethical implications. Scholarship highlights the dynamic and multifaceted nature of digital memory, exploring how it is shaped by both human and non-human actors.

Work on digital memory moves us away from more linear – and perhaps passive – understandings of the past. According to Garde-Hansen et al. (2009: 7) digital memory is an 'active, subjective, organic, emotional, virtual and uncertain production of the past and present at the same time'. Digital memory works at the interstices and blurs boundaries between the past, present and future, the real and the virtual, the living and the dead, and between public and private spaces and practices. Scholars have highlighted the materiality of digital memory, paying attention to the physical infrastructure required to store and process data, as well as the situated and embodied aspects of remembering (Reading and Notley 2015). Indeed, recognizing the materiality of digital memory is crucial given the ethical and environmental implications of our reliance on digital technologies for memory work. More broadly, scholars have stressed the importance of considering the social, cultural and political contexts in which digital memory is produced and consumed (van Dijck 2007; Liew et al. 2015; Bond et al. 2016; Fawns 2022). This includes understanding the role of power dynamics, commercial interests and platform governance in shaping digital memory (Kitchin 2023). Marc Esteve Del Valle and Rik Smit (2021) remind us that memory work is always embedded in a specific context, and this context must be taken into account when analysing how digital technologies shape our understanding of the past. There is some suggestion in the literature that an erosion of the boundary between what we might call organic and inorganic memory could be a consequence of these developments (Garde-Hansen et al. 2009), with potentials for the 'contamination' and manipulation of memory (Schincariol et al. 2024). Any convergence of human memory and silicon memory raises questions about the ontological status of digital memories and their relationship to embodied and lived experiences.

Andrew Hoskins has extensively explored the effects of what he calls 'the connective turn' (2011) on memory, focusing on how the immediacy, volume and ubiquity of digital media and archival resources shape our perception of the past and influence its role in the present. Hoskins has argued that in an era marked by media abundance and post-scarcity, we can find ourselves overwhelmed by persistent forms of past-ness to an extent that is as unsettling as it is comforting. More recently, he has made the case that (generative) AI blends the human and the machinic to usher in a 'third way of memory' (Hoskins 2024). He proposes:

> Generative AI changes what memory is and what memory does, pushing it beyond the realm of individual, human influence and control, yet at the same time offering new modes of expression, conversation, creativity, and ways of overcoming forgetting. This is part of a battleground between humans and computers in the shaping of reality. (Hoskins 2024)

The significance of this third way of memory is difficult to overstate then, influencing the ways past-ness is visibilized, deciphered, felt and distorted in the present, as we explore in this book.

There has been significant emphasis on studying memory within the context of social networks, some of which has touched on the role of algorithms; in ordering our timelines, for example, or filtering our photos (Robards and Lincoln 2017; Prey et al. 2018; Liebermann 2021; Jacobsen and Beer 2021a; Jelin 2021; Manca et al. 2022; McCammon 2022; Henriksen 2024). Algorithms do not neutrally archive and remediate human memories, but 'select what to remember as well as suggest how to remember' (Lee 2020: 2). In a study of Facebook as collective memory (2017), José van Dijck reminds us that social media are underscored by algorithms that construct and take advantage of users, rather than simply enabling connections (as is their conceit). Social networks are ambivalent at best, and exploitative by design. In the context of memory work, these are not simply technical observations, but ethical ones too (see also, Rumsey 2016). Smit et al. argue that 'highly dynamic' memory practices within social media sites (in their case Facebook) are underpinned by operational logics which help to popularize and stabilize particular narratives, representations and mnemonic discourses, 'driven by a commercial strategy revolving around visibility and "the new"' (2018: 3122). Over time it is entirely possible that, as Benjamin Jacobsen and David Beer argue, platforms and their logics of selection and prioritization ('On This Day' or 'Memory' features, for example) begin to distort our relationship with and understanding of our own biography (2021b), impacting how we feel about our memories (2021a). To

Jacobsen and Beer it is becoming increasingly clear that quantification impacts memory. So, for example, knowing that an image we post has received many likes might impact how we feel about a memory that the image connects us to. How platforms use algorithms to curate and present memories to users raises questions about the automation of memory too and about the potential for algorithmic bias. Recent work on griefbots has pushed these observations further (Voinea 2023), raising ethical questions about the commodification of grief and the potential for these technologies to alter our grieving processes. This work highlights the potential for manipulation and the creation of false memories, blurring the lines between what we might understand as an actual past and an imagined one. As this discussion reveals, the sociotechnical infrastructures of digital media play a crucial role in shaping memory, and in moulding our sense of self. Robert Prey and Rik Smit capture this complexity well, noting that while Facebook serves as a platform through which 'we compose ourselves', it simultaneously 'composes us' – largely through its proprietary algorithms (2018: 218).

Literature also highlights the tension between technological affordances that seem to insist on remembering and preservation, and the potential consequences of a culture that loses its ability or drive to forget (Hoskins and Halstead 2021; Hoskins 2024). As we go on to explore, technology, particularly AI and social media, contributes to a culture of 'foreverism' that prioritizes the constant preservation and resurfacing of information, potentially hindering our ability to intentionally and selectively forget. Elena Esposito (2022: 69) argues that the internet's vast storage capacity and the proliferation of digital memory tools have shifted our relationship with forgetting, noting that 'whereas in the past the problem of memory was the inability to remember, now the problem of social memory is increasingly connected to the inability to forget'. The ease and affordability of digital storage encourage a 'habitual' preservation of everything, making forgetting a deliberate, and often challenging, exception rather than the norm (Esposito 2022: 70). This perpetual present, where everything is constantly accessible and potentially revivable, undermines the natural process of forgetting and its emotional significance. Forgetting is not simply about erasing the past; it is a crucial cognitive process that allows us to make sense of our experiences, manage our emotional well-being and shape our individual and collective identities (Smith 2020; Jelin 2021). Reclaiming forgetting as an essential cognitive process by making more deliberate choices about what we share, save and delete, and developing data and digital literacy skills, might allow space for new experiences and perspectives to emerge. The 'right to be forgotten' in European law, which allows individuals to request the removal of certain information from search engines (although under very limited conditions), is increasingly challenged by the logics of algorithmic culture and data retention.

As mentioned in Chapter 1, the idea of perpetual preservation relies on the assumption that digital methods and digitization secure information intact to be accessible through time. However, in reality the fate of our digital assets is far from certain. While some digital files endure, others are vulnerable to being lost forever or becoming otherwise inaccessible. Unlike physical objects or traditional forms of memory that might be transmitted through generations, digital assets are susceptible to rapid obsolescence. The fragility of our data lives raises questions about the fulsomeness and longevity of digital memory and challenges the foundational principles of archival work and cultural preservation in the twenty-first century. As we have noted however, the idea of digital data's persistence is seductive, not least in the context of discussions about death.

Death and digital memory

As we shift from a notion of self-grounded in atoms to one 'made of data' (Cheney-Lippold 2017), it can be argued that identities continue to evolve, even after death. Digital remains[2] evidently challenge traditional notions of death and closure (Beaunoyer and Guitton 2021; Kneese 2023), creating a sense of a deceased person's ongoing presence through a digital realm which is 'teeming with ghosts' (Sisto 2020: 27). As Sam Hjorth and Larissa Hinton note: 'The Western idea that the funeral marks the end of the death and

2 Across a number of fields of practice – including archaeology, conservation, museum studies and anthropology – there has been extensive debate about the conditions under which human remains should be handled, represented and disposed of (Cassman 2008; Jenkins 2010; Giesen 2013; Dreyfus and Anstett 2016; Clegg 2020; Biers and Stringer Clary 2023). While these discussions remain unresolved and often ethnocentric, they have contributed to the development of ethical codes and professional guidelines for such work. However, how these frameworks might need to adapt to address the handling of *digital* human remains is a question we are only beginning to explore.

grieving process needs to be more fully interrogated in a world where images and the deceased haunt our devices, and may even speak to us through archived posts and automated reminders' (2019: 179). The emergence of Death Studies as a discipline demonstrates that this interrogation is now well underway (Davies 2005; Holmberg et al. 2019; MacCormack 2025), with the role of mediation a key part of that inquiry (Sumiala 2013, 2022). As Tonia Sutherland notes, 'The use of technology to reanimate the dead comes with a complex set of social, cultural, technical, and ethical concerns – including questions of race, representation, embodiment, commodification, memorialisation, and spectacle' (Sutherland 2023: 12). These concerns are pressing in literature about death and digital memory, and are all themes we explore in this book.

Digital environments provide numerous ways for users to engage with and remember the deceased. As Elaine Kasket observes, the deceased are 'everywhere you go online, their images on your screens, their voices in your ears – accessible anytime, in the palms of our hands' (2019: 33; see also, Hjorth and Hinton 2019, Walter 2015). The digital landscape calls for a reassessment of how we understand loss and connection, an issue that became more pressing during the COVID-19 pandemic, when death and grief so comprehensively moved online (Beaunoyer and Guitton 2021; Harrington 2020). Lambert et al. note that 'as death becomes increasingly mediated by digital technologies, the relationship between the dead and the living becomes more complex and dynamic' (Lambert et al. 2018: 158). Davide Sisto (2020) explores the omnipresence of death in online spaces and the implications of digital 'ghosts', analysing the gap between the active online presence of the living and the static, repetitive presence of the deceased and questioning the implications of what might be termed 'digital immortality'. A number of studies have explored what digital immortality might mean, for example, in social networks (Stokes 2021; Savin-Baden and Mason-Robbie 2020; Öhman and Watson 2019; Kania-Lundholm 2019, Kasket 2019; Harrington 2020; Sisto 2020, 2021; Bassett 2022), through AI systems (Meese at al. 2015; Savin-Baden and Burden 2018; Rodríguez Reséndiz and Rodríguez Reséndiz 2024) and in the context of death-tech more generally (Sofka et al. 2012; Arnold et al. 2018; Beaunoyer and Guitton 2021; Biçer and Yıldırım 2022; Nansen et al. 2023). We introduce and develop these discussions at various points in the book.

It has been suggested that digital remains can contribute to the construction of 'posthumous personhood', allowing the deceased to retain a kind of social presence and agency even after death (Lambert et al. 2018: 158). This raises ontological questions about the nature of selfhood in the age of algorithms (Boyle 2024), and the extent to which our digital identities can survive our physical demise (Meese et al. 2015). Concepts like 'digital zombies' (Bassett 2015) attempt to capture the ways in which the deceased continue to interact with the living through their digital remains. Timothy Recuber rejects this characterization however: 'A zombie is a body without a self. The digital dead are almost precisely the opposite – selves without bodies' (Recuber 2023: 9). The notion of 'distributed personhood' (Meese et al. 2015: 415) is perhaps more helpful as a way of describing how digital remains 'materialise new forms of persona that persist beyond death and establish relations with the living'. According to Meese et al., 'these interactions are ontological, rather than representative', and 'implicated into a wider commercial start-up economy' (2015: 416), what has been called the 'digital afterlife industry' (Öhman and Floridi 2017: 640). This suggests there are both ethical and social implications, for example, relating to privacy, ownership, commercialization, authenticity and dignity. Technology companies play a significant role in shaping how we interact with digital remains, influencing the accessibility, management and presentation of digital legacies. Much of the literature on digital remains calls for greater transparency and accountability from these companies, urging them to consider the ethical implications of their practices and to design technologies that support healthy grieving processes (Morse 2023).

It stands to reason that digital remains impact how we grieve and mourn, providing new avenues for 'continuing bonds' with the deceased (Hjorth and Hinton 2019: 44), and allowing us to revisit their words and images. This inevitably raises questions about which ways of engaging with the deceased online are the most (and least) useful, and about how to manage digital legacies (Kasket 2019). In their exploration of the standardized, automated videos created from our photo and video content by online platforms like Facebook, Lambert et al. (2018) introduce the concept of the 'algorithmic afterlife'. These platforms leverage algorithms to 'filter, merge, rearrange, reshape and render visual data to produce novel digital artefacts' – such as Facebook Look Back videos – and these outputs are 'explicitly mnemonic' (2018: 157; see also,

Jacobsen and Beer 2021b). Operating at the intersection of everyday memory, biography, social and public memory, as well as documentation and archival practices, these algorithmic processes highlight the ethical complexities of remembering and forgetting. Lambert et al. (2018) consider the potential harms of these outputs, particularly for individuals who are grieving. They argue that the inability of these systems to engage in 'personalised emotional labour' often results in the videos doing a poor job of performing 'death work' (see also, Sisto 2021; Kneese 2023). This notion of 'algorithmic afterlife' is of course intriguing given the focus of our own analysis, and one we will return to.

Of course, these are not new developments given 'media's status as technologies for bridging the ultimate frontier of human mortality' (Kopelman and Frosh 2023). Alexandra Sherlock (2013) traces the evolution of 'symbolic immortality' through media, from photography and film to the internet, examining how digital technologies offer new possibilities for remembering and connecting with the deceased. Relatedly the term 'necromancy' – and now digital necromancy (Hutson and Ratican 2023) – is persistent; a way of describing how people seek (digitally) to represent and commune with the dead (Sherlock 2013). The intersection of death and technology is thus ethically and psychologically charged, challenging our understanding of memory, self and identity, including how we experience them corporeally.

The business of nostalgia and the lure of 'foreverism'

Turning aspects of the past into products or services to be bought and sold raises ethical and social concerns, as we will demonstrate in this book. As Katharina Niemeyer and Emily Keightley (2020) note, it is critical that we 'recognise the various economies in which memory and remembering activities and practices are situated', and this is all the more urgent in the context of AI which 'cannot be divorced' from its capitalist conditions (Pilkington 2024). This case has been robustly made in literature on deathbots (our focus in Chapter 4) and on the virtual 'resurrection' of celebrities (our focus in Chapter 5).

Services such as deathbots might offer comfort to some users, but are understood by many scholars to be exploitative, not least of users' emotional vulnerability (Fabry and Alfano 2024). As these companies become gatekeepers to the digital afterlife, commercial considerations may begin to shape how the deceased are represented and remembered. Carl Öhman and Luciano Floridi (2017) argue for robust ethical frameworks and regulations to ensure that the dignity and autonomy of the deceased are respected, and that their digital remains are not exploited for profit. In relation to virtual performers, Jenna Pei-Suin Ng and Nick Bax (2023) have extensively analysed the ABBA Voyage show as a case study of the past's commodification. Through their analysis they suggest that the exploitation of digital apparitions extends the reach of capitalism beyond digital objects to encompass time itself, turning 'pastness' into a marketable commodity.

These developments can be seen as part of a thriving 'nostalgia culture' (Sayers 2020: 2) which critics have argued reduces the complexity of the past, simplifying and distorting our perspective of the world and idealizing a distorted view of reality (Chrostowska 2010, Sisto 2020).[3] Ryan Lizardi argues that nostalgia constructs pasts that lack any 'critical or radical difference' (2014) and there is concern that it is being 'weaponized' by political figures or movements to rally support (Smith 2020). Through appeals to nostalgia leaders may tap into people's longing for a perceived better time in order to promote regressive policies or ideologies. For example, persistently referencing nationalistic or exclusionary visions of history can support the reinforcement of outdated power structures and the marginalization of certain groups. There are also concerns about how nostalgia interacts with our emotions within today's marketing-driven society (Routledge 2016). Jacobsen and Beer introduce the concept of 'quantified nostalgia' as a way of describing how social media platforms use metrics and algorithms to resurface past content and evoke nostalgic feelings in users, driving engagement and profit (2021a: 2). By resurfacing past content that is likely to trigger positive emotional responses, these platforms aim to increase user engagement and, ultimately, their profits. This commodification of nostalgia raises concerns about the manipulation of users' emotions and the creation of a sanitized, commercially driven version of the past (Lizardi 2014).

Grafton Tanner (2023) elaborates the concept of 'foreverism' to describe the cultural trend towards perpetually revitalizing and reanimating the past

3 We might note, however, that such concerns have been expressed throughout history, particularly since the invention and growth of photography in the nineteenth century (Raun 2018).

through digital technologies: 'It is the rejuvenation or rebooting of things lost, the breathing of new life into moldering corpses.' (Tanner 2023: 18). This is reminiscent of the 'expansionist logic' that underpins the 'never-ending' population of AI systems (Crawford 2021: 121). For Tanner, the compulsion of foreverism – driven by commercial imperatives – leads to an oversaturation of the past in the present, potentially hindering our ability to move forward and engage with the future. This begs the question: 'What happens when nothing ever ends?' (Tanner 2023: 23). This is a profound question in relation to the accumulation of digital memory given that 'endings are needed not as cessation, but as a way of thinking to open up meaning' (Ng and Bax 2023: 13).

Other scholars offer more mixed – and even positive – assessments of nostalgia's potentials however (Smith and Campbell 2017). According to Nicola Sayers, nostalgia often acts as a 'container of conflicted desires' (Sayers 2020: 196), and Katharina Niemeyer advocates for discussing 'nostalgias' in plural, emphasizing their varied interactions (2014: 6). Janelle Wilson (2005) argues that nostalgia can be progressive and productive, with the capacity to inspire action or provide individuals with a strong, coherent sense of identity. In a study of nostalgia on TikTok, Viki Askounis Conner (2023) identifies nostalgia's restorative and reflective dimensions, suggesting that 'creative and mnemonic practices are entangled in algorithmically structured aesthetic social formations of nostalgia' on the platform. This is a possibility we embrace in Chapter 3, exploring interactions between differing readings and uses of nostalgia, and embracing its complexity and ambivalence.

Algorithmic culture and the shaping of reality

The term 'algorithmic culture' captures the now pervasive influence of algorithms on our social, cultural and personal lives (Striphas 2015), as well as on our practices of memory, as we noted in the previous section. It encompasses the ways in which algorithms – 'sets of defined steps structured to process instructions/data to produce an output' (Kitchin 2017: 14) – increasingly shape behaviours, influence decisions and structure experiences within society. This influence can be found in all facets of our everyday existence in digital societies, for example in our media consumption, social interactions and even identity formation, but often in ways that are invisible or taken for granted (Ruckenstein 2023). Of course, we don't all experience or interact with technology in the same ways, and so the extent to which algorithms shape our reality will differ depending on such things as who we are, the work we do, where we live and the regulatory and policy frameworks which govern our uses of them.

There are numerous well-established critiques of algorithms and algorithmic culture (Noble 2018, Kennedy 2018; Hristova et al. 2021; Azar et al. 2021; Hepp et al. 2022; Lindgren 2023; Browne et al. 2023; Bonini and Trere 2024) and these will be cornerstones in discussions throughout this book. For example, we will highlight concerns about surveillance and datafication especially where they lack transparency, about personalization where this shapes (and limits) behaviours and norms, about the automation of tasks and work where it alters economic structures, and about the systematization and amplification of bias through algorithmic processes. Algorithms are clearly not neutral and are deeply embedded in social and cultural contexts, reflecting and reinforcing existing power dynamics and values (Bucher 2018; Crawford 2021). As we increasingly delegate cultural tasks to algorithms – tasks like sorting, classifying and hierachizing information, as well as making recommendations and predictions on those bases – there is a profound risk that social biases and inequalities will be exacerbated.[4] The real-world implications of such biases are felt by, for example, 'black individuals who fall victim to errors in facial recognition systems, women whose professional resumes are overlooked by sexist algorithms on job search platforms, [and] employees of large corporations whose performance is assessed by systems that monitor their real-time movements' (de Almeida and Rafael 2024).

These challenges are heightened by the opacity of algorithmic systems, and the informational asymmetry that characterizes them; users typically have limited understanding of how such systems work and how their data is being used, while technology companies hold significant power and control over these processes. This lack of transparency raises concerns about accountability,

4 See debates about uses of facial recognition technology, for example (Andrejevic and Selwyn 2022), and about search engines (Noble 2018; Graham 2023).

fairness and the potential for manipulation. Alongside these critiques, studies have examined the emotional dimensions of algorithmic culture; the 'structures of feeling' that emerge from our interactions with algorithms (Nguyen et al. 2023; see also, Ruckenstein 2023). While some users might feel the benefits of algorithms in terms of convenience and pleasure, others express anxieties related to dataveillance, algorithmic bias and the erosion of human agency (Nguyen et al. 2023). These more pernicious impacts of algorithmic culture are not experienced equally of course.

As we have suggested, the extraction and exploitation of data is a key concern here, which brings debates about AI and data colonialism to the fore. As Helen Kennedy notes, the 'colonizing impulse' of AI (Kennedy 2018: 11) centralizes power by controlling how the world is measured and defined, while obscuring the political nature of this process. As such, AI operates as 'politics by other means' (Kennedy 2018: 19); driven by a few dominant companies and individuals who exert influence, extract resources and shape the social and cultural landscape. Data has been viewed as a resource to be consumed and capital to be extracted, leading to a 'pillage of public space' (Crawford 2021) by a few privately owned companies with enormous power, and limited explicit consent. Ulises A. Mejias and Nick Couldry (2024) characterize this as a 'data grab'. AI systems have also created a supply chain which presents huge social concerns related to data workers' job security and dismal working conditions (Muldoon et al. 2023). The ways algorithms are instrumentalized can embed and amplify existing power and knowledge structures, a characteristic often associated with colonial practices, with the result that culture and identity become subject to the control and impositions of algorithmic logics (Striphas 2015). The colonizing predisposition of AI should be of concern to institutions – not least cultural, public and educational ones – that have placed such emphasis on decolonizing their practices in recent years. Decolonizing AI will mean first and foremost recognizing what Stephen Cave and Kanta Dihal (2020) call the 'whiteness of AI', including how representations of AI – humanoid robots, chatbots or images of AI, for example – 'are refracted through the White racial frame; their Whiteness a proxy for how we perceive their status and potential' (Cave and Dihal 2020). We are only beginning to explore how the decolonization of AI might intersect with memory work (Nieto McAvoy and Kidd 2026).

In an algorithmic culture, as we will demonstrate in this book, memory is increasingly encoded within what Massimo Airoldi has called a 'machine habitus' (2022: 28); where machine learning systems as 'socialised agents' trained on imperfect data 'recursively' interact with users with a host of consequences, not least ethical ones. Airoldi observes how cultural values and assumptions are embedded in the design and development of systems ('culture in the code'), but also how algorithms, once deployed, begin to shape and influence cultural practices and beliefs ('code in the culture') (Airoldi 2022: 1). Systems develop what has been called an 'algorithmic gaze', that is, a particular way of 'seeing' the world, which can normalize and standardize representations, marginalizing those that do not conform to dominant patterns in training data and producing stereotypes as a result (Rettberg 2023: 118). Jill Walker Rettberg (2023) uses the concept of 'machine vision' to explain how AI systems perceive and interpret, highlighting the situated, embodied and inherently biased nature of algorithms and their impacts on our perception of reality.

In recent years, AI has been somewhat mainstreamed in our interactions with media through (for example) SnapChat and Instagram filters, which Cristian Vaccari and Andrew Chadwick refer to as 'common, banal forms of this technology' (2020: 7). Such uses are not inconsequential, however, as they 'pull users in' and seed new norms when it comes to the adoption of these technologies and behaviours around them (Natale 2021). These technologies (as other technologies) are in and of themselves materially ambiguous and ambivalent, although of course not neutral. It is critically important then that we 'consider the attendant ethical and policy questions' that our uses of such techniques suggest (Paris 2021: 1; see also, Hepp et al. 2022). To Anette Grønning it is imperative that studies of mediated memory are grounded critically and remain mindful of 'socio-technical developments and the affordances of the digital modes of communication' (2021: 744). In our study, we have responded to this prompt.

Methodological considerations for studying AI afterlives

One of our ambitions in studying AI afterlives has been to experiment with an expanded suite of methods, and to reflect on their application (see Chapter 8, our Data Coda). In this section we introduce some of the methodological considerations that have shaped previous work in these fields.

Memory studies is a broad field which emerges from a range of disciplines including psychology, neuroscience, philosophy and anthropology. The complexity of (unobservable) memory processes, resultant difficulties in 'measuring' them and the subjective nature of personal memory accounts has led to a range of methodological challenges and limitations. The heterogeneity of memory, influenced by factors such as age, culture and cognitive capacity, means memory is an unstable and capricious thing, and it stands to reason that one-size-fits-all approaches to its study are of limited value. There have been criticisms of the cultural biases in memory research too, in that it has been conducted largely in industrialized and democratic societies, which are unlikely to be representative of how memory functions in all populations. Memory is influenced by cultural norms, social contexts and processes, as well as language, yet many studies have overlooked these factors, as well as the temporal dynamics of memory; it changes over time, and is retrieved and reconstructed in and through a 'present'.

Studies of social and cultural memory are more proximate to the concerns of this book, in that they examine how societies remember, forget and interpret their pasts (Le Goff 1992; Ricœur 2004; Roediger and Wertsch 2008). These studies work across disciplines such as history, sociology, literary studies and media studies, but they also face methodological challenges given that the social construction, transmission and institutionalization of memory is also dynamic, multifaceted and contested. Cultural memory studies have tended to differentiate between collective, cultural and individual sites of memory as a way of emphasizing memory's distinct dimensions (Halbwachs 1925; Wang 2008; Weedon and Jordan 2012; Pennebaker et al. 2013). These categories are of course not always clear and influence each other in myriad ways, but their separation can be helpful as a way of holding memory – and memories – up for analysis. The distinction between public and private memory has also been a helpful one, allowing scholars to examine how memories are presented in public discourse as compared to, say, those held in private or familial contexts (Keightley and Pickering 2013). In methodological terms we find it is informative to identify how a study is situated in relation to these categories of memory, and this is something we pay attention to across the chapters in this book. We also articulate how we understand interactions between memory, time and place, as well as the spatial dimensions of memory, here including digital spaces, given that these impact the ways memories are narrativized, understood and transmitted.

As we noted earlier, digital memory studies takes as its focus how individuals and societies store, retrieve and interact with memory specifically through digital technologies. Studying digital memory also presents some key methodological challenges which are variously highlighted in the literature. Accessing digital data, for example, can be fraught with complexity, given the (shifting) structures of data ownership that typify networked infrastructures, and the fragility of many online platforms and services. Digital memory can be lost due to technical failures (server crashes, hardware malfunctions, data corruption), deletions, account bans or terminations and the discontinuation of digital services (such as the shutdown of a website or app), and it can become inaccessible due to changes in platform policies or APIs (for example). As we noted previously, this adds a layer of instability to digital memory that researchers need to be mindful of. There are of course ethical issues too when it comes to collecting and analysing digital data such as personal communications or social media posts, raising significant privacy and ethical issues. These ethical issues are compounded in the study of digital memory given the data is often also that of deceased persons, as it is in a number of case studies used in this book. Notions of public and private when it comes to digital spaces are also not fixed, and need to be thoughtfully navigated. Obtaining informed consent can be difficult, especially in large-scale studies involving personal data, and safeguarding sensitive information is another challenge. Establishing a dataset can be tricky then, and we run the risk that analyses of digital memory are led not by the questions we think are the most pertinent or interesting, but by the availability of data.

Studies of digital memory need also to reckon with its fragmentation across multiple platforms and formats (social media, email, photos and online documents, for example), as well as how it interacts with other 'offline' data points that might be impossible to factor into an analysis. This dispersal of data complicates studies, and is itself underexplored in the literature. How these fragments are 'curated', and how and where they emerge more spontaneously is also not well understood. Studying the affordances (Prey and Smit 2018;

Grønning 2021; Jacobsen and Beer 2021b; Recuber 2023) and vernacular (Gibbs et al. 2015) of different digital platforms is clearly a significant task for researchers, as each will have its own way of structuring and presenting memory. On Instagram, for example, memories will likely emphasize visual components (Hu and Kidd 2024), whereas on Discord they might be more text-based. Digital assets that circulate in platforms are often removed from their original context, and this can often be significant, and crucial to understand. Flows of visual content – including memes and GIFs which have become important affective, cultural and social lexica – become proxies for how memories function in real-world contexts, and the need to understand their significance is pressing. As we have noted in this chapter, digital tools and platforms often use algorithms to curate what is remembered (through recommendations or auto-suggestions, for example), and these algorithms are themselves difficult to hold up for analysis as objects of scrutiny for a host of reasons, not least the fact that they are black boxed, and change regularly (Kitchin 2017).

Studying digital memory also needs to be underpinned by a keen understanding of access issues and the role of digital – and data – literacy (Yates and Carmi 2024). Clearly not everyone has equal access to digital devices or the internet and so studies of digital memory are likely to be skewed towards certain socioeconomic, geographic or demographic groups who have greater access to digital technologies. This creates a bias in research, and is an important reminder that we should not assume that digital memory practices will be universal across all populations.

These challenges are not insurmountable, but they do suggest the importance of transparency in terms of methodological and philosophical approach. The interdisciplinary nature of this field means that scholars should remain mindful of disciplinary boundaries and biases, and may wish to be conversant in multiple methods and approaches. Quantitative studies clearly have their place, and large datasets can tell us something about (for example) the preponderance of certain activities, key trends or the sharing practices that shape digital memories, but it is unlikely to capture their emotional significance or the complex ways memories are being negotiated, performed, reshuffled and put to work in and across digital environments. Lev Manovich (2020) makes the case for studying the 'long tail' of digital culture, that is, going beyond large samples capturing snapshots of what is happening in conspicuous places, to adopting more maximalist strategies in smaller research sites. This is an approach we have woven into some of our own studies.

Analysing digital traces of personal experiences is inherently complicated, and as the digital landscape continues to evolve, researchers must adapt their methods to account for these limitations and take into consideration the rapidly changing nature of digital memory practices. How we have done this is set out briefly in each chapter, and more substantively in our Data Coda (Chapter 8).

This chapter has introduced literature to support our examination of AI afterlives in this book. We have examined three key areas: synthetic media (deepfakes and virtual performers, for example), digital memory (how digital technologies shape memory creation, storage and access) and algorithmic culture (the pervasive influence of algorithms on our lives and memories). Finally, we have introduced a series of methodological considerations for studying these complex phenomena, acknowledging the challenges of researching digital data and the evolving nature of digital memory. In the chapters that follow, we turn our attention to the ethical, cultural and mnemonic implications of AI afterlives in a range of contexts, starting with (in Chapter 3) genealogy sites.

3

Genealogy platforms and AI afterlives

Services offered by genealogy companies are increasingly underpinned by computational remediation and algorithmic power.[1] Users are encouraged to create progressively more sophisticated forms of synthetic media featuring their (often deceased) ancestors. Machine learning processes are inserted into the very fabric of personal archival assets such as photographs, 'remediating' (Bolter and Grusin 2000) memories through recursive and mechanized algorithmic logics (Kidd and Nieto McAvoy 2023). As the promotion of deepfake and voice-synthesizing technologies intensifies within genealogical contexts – aggrandized as mechanisms for bringing people 'back to life' – it is critically important to examine these processes and the sociotechnical infrastructures that underpin them, as well as their mnemonic impacts.

To respond to this challenge, in this chapter we present a mixed-methods analysis of *MyHeritage*'s deep learning feature, *Deep Nostalgia*. *MyHeritage* was founded in 2003 and is one of several crowd-sourced genealogy platforms providing users with the ability to research their family histories. Platforms like *MyHeritage*, FamilySearch, Ancestry and Findmypast, are underpinned by billions of historical records and other data points that allow users to create family trees, find records of their ancestors and identify new and previously unknown relatives, past and present. The sharing of information and experiences is a fundamental component of these data platforms, both because of the connective impulse of genealogy and also their dependency on the data submitted by users to expand their databases. As of 2023, *MyHeritage* had 88 million users, 5.4 billion profiles (including those of ancestors, deceased and alive) and 78 million family trees (MyHeritage 2023a).

1 Here, we borrow the term 'algorithmic power' from Taina Bucher (2018).

Most online genealogy platforms use automated processes for a range of tasks, but primarily to match data across users and profiles – what Ancestry calls 'hints' and *MyHeritage* 'discoveries'. *MyHeritage*'s Record Matches, for example, finds relevant historical records for users' family trees, while Smart Matches compares information across family trees to match people with unknown ancestors. DNA Matching allows users to find relatives based on their shared genetic sequences and to contact them to further collaborate on researching a possible shared family history. Users are responsible for verifying the source of every piece of information before they accept the match and add it to their family tree.

Since 2021, *MyHeritage* has launched a series of AI tools to augment users' family photos; *Deep Nostalgia*, *DeepStory*, *AI Time Machine* and *LiveMemory*. In this chapter we take *Deep Nostalgia* as a case study to illustrate how AI intensifies the genealogical impetus. Understanding *Deep Nostalgia* within the framework of genealogical services is important here, as it has significant implications for how it is used and perceptions of its credibility. We present a critical study of *Deep Nostalgia* creations and discourses circulating around them shared on Twitter[2] during the two-week period following the feature's launch in 2021 (n. 6,935 tweets). To support that analysis we have also scrutinized the company's policies and Terms and Conditions, as well as those of the D-ID studio that created the underlying technology. Further information about these approaches, and the data they produced, can be found in Chapter 8 (our Data Coda). Across these social media and platform analyses we have been able to interrogate *Deep Nostalgia* creations as examples of remediated and algorithmic memory which are ultimately shaped by corporate interests.[3]

We begin with an introduction to the *Deep Nostalgia* tool. We follow this with an overview of digital memory scholars' work on genealogy platforms, before turning to our data to explore five themes. In our analysis we firstly unpack *Deep Nostalgia* as a mechanism for what we call 'remediated memory', before moving on to a critique of the 'algorithmic nostalgia' it produces. We then explore how the logics of sociotechnical infrastructures shape *Deep Nostalgia*

2 It was at this time Twitter not X, and so we refer to the platform as Twitter and posts as tweets.
3 Some of this analysis has been published elsewhere (in Kidd and Nieto McAvoy 2023 and Nieto McAvoy and Kidd 2024) and is reproduced here with permission.

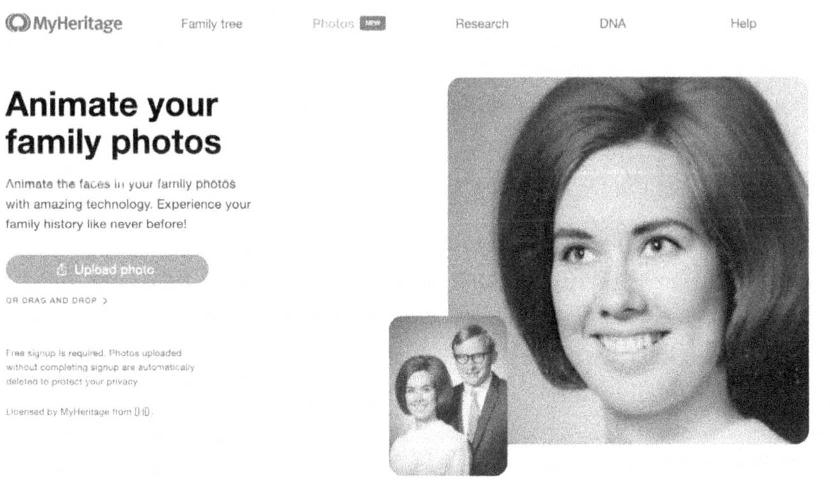

Figure 3.1 *MyHeritage* website introduces *Deep Nostalgia* (screenshot).

and its outputs, before highlighting the ethical and data entanglements it suggests. We present some thoughts on the likelihood of 'deceptive genealogies' emerging in and through these practices, before offering some final reflections.

Introducing *Deep Nostalgia*

On 25 February 2021 the *MyHeritage* genealogy service posted a tweet introducing its new *Deep Nostalgia* feature to nearly 80,000 Twitter followers. *Deep Nostalgia* uses deep learning technology to animate faces from historical photos, creating a short, looped video of the result which can be easily and freely shared in social networks.[4] According to *MyHeritage*, more than 114 million animations have now been made (Figure 3.1).

Deep Nostalgia enhances old photographs by increasing their resolution, before animating them so that the subject can be seen smiling, blinking and turning their head. These gestures are modelled from blueprint ('driver') videos sourced from recordings of real humans, mostly employees at *MyHeritage*. Each of these drivers is a video with a fixed looped sequence of movements and gestures. The driver is applied to the face in the photo to make them

4 Screenshot created 13 September 2024.

appear to move.[5] The technology underpinning *Deep Nostalgia* is licensed by *MyHeritage* from D-ID, a private company specializing in generative AI technology, including the production of synthetic media outputs such as live portraits.[6]

At the time of the *Deep Nostalgia* launch, *MyHeritage* said the following:

> Some people love the Deep Nostalgia™ feature and consider it magical, while others find it creepy and dislike it. Indeed, the results can be controversial and it's hard to stay indifferent to this technology. We invite you to create videos using this feature and share them on social media to see what your friends and family think.[7]

No doubt a marketing ploy to attract new users to its site, a technology like *Deep Nostalgia* provokes searching questions of relevance to the themes of this book; about our interactions with our own and others' pasts, and the uses we make of our increasingly complex personal archival apparatuses, not least within social networks. What are the affective dimensions and resonances of these algorithmic creations, and just how deep is any nostalgia elicited? And how might we begin to understand and explain the intense virality of *Deep Nostalgia*? In this chapter we explore these questions, unpacking what *Deep Nostalgia* tells us about how personal memory practices are already being impacted by algorithms and automation. In doing so, we understand *Deep Nostalgia* as a form of 'mnemotechnology', one which showcases quite remarkably how memory emerges or is situated at the interstices of the social and (techno-)material world (Prey and Smit 2018, following Bernard Stiegler).

Genealogy platforms and digital memory

Our analysis in this chapter draws on studies of digital memory which emphasize the manifold ways mediated memories now have a generative function in our everyday personal lives; 'creating and re-creating a sense of

5 The process is demonstrated in this video: https://www.youtube.com/watch?v=d9NF3VbElZM&t=11s (accessed 13 February 2025).
6 More information can be found at https://www.d-id.com/liveportrait/.
7 https://www.myheritage.com/deep-nostalgia

past, present, and future of ourselves in relation to others' (van Dijck 2007: 21).[8] As we proposed in Chapter 2, mediated memories 'stretch' the very idea of the past (Worcman and Garde-Hansen 2016), such that it becomes 'continually emergent', not least within the sociotechnical parameters of platforms (Esteve Del Valle and Smit 2021: 1816). Within these contexts algorithms, automation and commercial imperatives 'intervene' in the ways the past is packaged and recalled (Lee 2020: 1). A number of studies have explored the ways platforms sort and label our past (Lambert et al. 2018; Jacobsen and Beer 2021a, 2021b; Henriksen 2024), participating in what Helen Kennedy and Rosemary Lucy Hill call the 'quantification of things previously qualitative' such as friendship and likes (Kennedy and Hill 2018). Within genealogy platforms these processes and interactions extend posthumously also, impacting the ways we are constructed, remembered and datafied after we die (Cheney-Lippold 2017; Sisto 2020, 2021; Harrington 2020). This has profound ethical implications, as we explore in this chapter, and the next.

Online genealogy platforms remain under-researched, which is a significant oversight given that genealogy 'was part of the early Internet and is fundamentally embedded within its current manifestation' (de Groot 2015: 114). Platforms such as *MyHeritage* are not 'simply' genealogy companies however given how fully their business models rely on the connection and circulation of digital information (de Groot 2020: 25). As we demonstrate in this chapter, it is becoming imperative that we interrogate their broader sociotechnical impacts (Willever-Farr and Forte 2014); impacts on the very definition and construction of history and of family, for example, or on how – and what – we remember. As algorithmic systems are sedimented into genealogy platforms, these impacts will become more urgent, but perhaps also more difficult, to discern.

'Relations of descent' (Moore et al. 2020), or genealogies, are a key mechanism for organizing our world and helping us understand our place within it (see also, Knauft 2017). As Thomas Laqueur notes, genealogy 'is a form of communion with those we take to be ancestors' (2023) such that we might imagine and articulate bonds with them, even after death. Genealogy

8 See also, van Dijck (2017), Garde-Hansen et al. (2009), Hoskins (2011, 2018), Smit et al. (2018), Smit (2020).

offers narratives that shape us, but that are evidently not static. Instead, they are open for 'renegotiation and reknowing', providing opportunities to 'grapple with past and present, self and other, personal and collective memory, and individual and group identity' (Barclay and Koefoed 2021). Online genealogy platforms clearly provide a rich context for such grappling. Since the 1970s there has been an upsurge of public interest in and exploration of how relations of descent are 'strung together' (Kretsedemas 2017). This has often been in tension with professional accounts of history, not least because in asking 'Who am I?' genealogists segue into inquiries about 'Who are we?' which are profoundly political (Morgan 2021). This begins to suggest the myriad ethical considerations that work with family memory produces, especially when it relies on ephemeral traces, deals in 'secrets and silences' and (maybe distinctly in the context of online platforms) is negotiated, recast and legitimized 'from below' (Barclay and Koefoed 2021). It follows that genealogy has been celebrated for its democratizing potentials (Evans 2011; de Groot 2015) where it challenges the nation-focused and state-driven patriarchal histories that tend to constitute academic scholarship (Evans 2020).

Accuracy and authenticity are key concerns for genealogists, and family historians are expected to work to guidelines and agreed standards of proof (Moore et al. 2020). However, the surging popularity of online genealogy has raised concerns within the family history community about the adequacy of users' skills in archival intelligence and artefactual literacy (Friday 2014; Willever-Farr and Forte 2014). In a study by Heather L. Willever-Farr and Andrea Forte (2014: 481) the presence of 'clickologists' and 'half researchers' was lamented by family history researchers; those who they perceived as careless, or as prioritizing increasing the size of a family tree at the expense of accuracy in their work. They also noted the 'insidious role' of automation in the mix, suggesting that inexperienced researchers mindlessly accept automated suggestions from platforms without verification, 'leading to family trees full of erroneous information or "genealojunk"'. (Willever-Farr and Forte 2014: 481).

Such concerns about accuracy and authenticity are intriguing in light of this book's concern with synthetic media, and the emergent (techno-)material and mnemonic possibilities which flow from those media. In this chapter, we use *Deep Nostalgia* as a case study to interrogate how genealogy research is being enlivened through those possibilities. In the following section we introduce our findings.

Five themes from our analysis

Here we turn to an exploration of our data to expand on five themes identified in the analysis. First, we explore *Deep Nostalgia* creations as what we term 'remediated memory', before questioning the value of the 'algorithmic nostalgia' those creations produce. We then explore how the logics of varied sociotechnical infrastructures shape the *Deep Nostalgia* tool and its outputs, and zoom in on the ethical and data entanglements the analysis suggests. Finally, we question whether *Deep Nostalgia* creations can be understood as deceptive genealogy, and if so, what implications might follow.

Deep Nostalgia's remediated memory

The language used by the *MyHeritage* platform – including in the immediate framing of *Deep Nostalgia* – is explicitly mnemonic: *MyHeritage*'s re-enactment technology is 'intended for nostalgic use, that is, to bring beloved ancestors back to life', taking users 'on a meaningful discovery journey that unites [their] past, present, and future' (MyHeritage 2023c). While family history is often conceived as a way of uncovering, verifying or correcting family memories, its practice is itself considered memory-work whereby affective connection to the past helps genealogists establish 'links between the historical, the personal, and political' to understand the present, and for future and younger generations also (Evans 2020).

As we have outlined *Deep Nostalgia* is powered by a deep learning algorithm created by D-ID to match each uploaded photo with a compatible 'driver' video to support that photo's animation most convincingly. It does so by analysing key features in the photo such as head orientation, and matching those features to a suitable blueprint video. We can understand this as a process of 'platform seeing' (MacKenzie and Munster 2019). This means that, like other algorithmic systems, *Deep Nostalgia* operates best at a degree of abstraction; in the design of such a system, a programmer will exclude more atypical or 'chaotic' data inputs in a bid to secure more predictable and persuasive outputs (Markham 2020: 10). This underpinning logic leads to a degree of uniformity and conformity during *Deep Nostalgia*'s process of remediation (Kopelman and Frosh 2023). These are not the subject's own movements; they have, to all intents and purposes, been directed by a programmer.

This shift, from photograph to animated image (now with driver video sedimented within it), is clearly significant in its attempt to maximize immediacy. As the subject in the photograph is set in motion, so too is the user's line of vision, a potentially more involved and intimate engagement. This is what we conceptualize as a 'remediated memory' of that person. The short, looped video refashions other media (the photograph, the blueprint video), and any memory attached to the photo comes to be represented, echoed or distorted, within a new medium. Stretching this idea further, the process could even be said to put those memories into conversation with other(s') memories in that it relies on movements and expressions that are borrowed from another; the coming together of two datafied 'bodies'.

This process of mnenomic remediation was an important theme in the tweets in our sample. As is shown in Table 3.1, we found evidence in comments on the technology, on the movement of bodies and on the authenticity of the resulting animations:

Deep Nostalgia's remediated memory is intriguing to consider in light of broader scholarship about the ambiguity of digital memory practices which, according to Garde-Hansen et al. (2009), destabilize the boundaries between life and non-life, and organic and inorganic things. *Deep Nostalgia* creations can be considered a vivid example of AI afterlife given the qualities of 'synthetic resurrection' (Ajder 2019) that are evident in these embodied animations. These qualities were a recurring theme commented upon in 61 per cent of tweets in our sample.[9] For example:

> *Thank You to @MyHeritage for animating this photo of my Grandfather. He tragically died at the hands of another in 1966, years before I was born. This is the first time I've seen him smile. #DeepNostalgia #RootsTechConnect.*[10]

9 Of these tweets, 62 per cent used a positive tone and 9 per cent negative, while 29 per cent were coded as neutral – that is, referring to bodies and movement, animation or 'coming to life' without qualitative judgement.

10 All social media content is italicized.

Table 3.1 Breakdown of Themes Related to Remediation in Our Twitter Analysis (Data Subset n. 316)

References related to remediation	No. of tweets	Percentage
References to BODIES ('seeing them move', 'come to life')	192	61
Commenting on the TECHNOLOGY (The AI-powered output is 'amazing')	116	37
Finding the animations UNCANNY/CREEPY/ WEIRD	35	11
Commenting on AUTHENTICITY ('My face does NOT move that way')	25	8

In our sample we identified two key mnemonic responses to *Deep Nostalgia*'s practices of remediation, sometimes in isolation, and in other instances, in combination, in keeping with the ambivalence we record in this book.

In the first response, remediation solidifies or even amplifies an image's mnemonic significance; the animation is understood to restore the person in the image and further solidifies any extant attachments of memory. Here the emphasis is on the ways artificial intelligence underscores a kind of fixity or eternalization, resurrecting people (however incompletely) through animation, and even supporting the creation of new posthumous memories. We see this demonstrated well in the quote mentioned earlier; the user now has a memory in motion of their grandfather's smile, something they never actually witnessed during his lifetime, although we can't know from the tweet how 'sticky' the memory and the feelings now attached to it are (Ahmed 2004).

In the second response, the process of remediation seems somehow to undermine an image's memorative clout. The meaning of the image, and perhaps its associated mnemonic qualities, become(s) less certain or fixed through remediation. Bolter and Grusin (2000: 28) suggest that in a still photograph it is the light reflecting off a person which provides the invaluable contact point between that person and their representation in the resultant image.[11] In *Deep Nostalgia* creations such contact points are obscured by, or perhaps find themselves in antagonism with, the algorithmic process; they

11 Wolfgang Ernst (2013) has written about the technologization of light, and how its manipulation in different ways has been a 'central tool' in 'representing the historical imagination'.

begin to bend and flex in a way that is not wholly convincing or comforting. In such moments, the 'operational' quality of these (moving) images is visibilized in a disconcerting way (Parikka 2023). Perhaps for this reason *Deep Nostalgia* outputs amount to forms of 'virtual creepiness' for many users (Anderson 2019: unpaged); in 11 per cent of tweets our sample users referred to these outputs as '*uncanny*', '*creepy*', '*weird*', '*freaky*' or in similar terms:

> *Ok so some of the #DeepNostalgia stuff is so uncanny it's terrifying, but I took a photo of my grandad from the archive of family photos I made a while ago and ran it through and honestly – the result is quite neat!*

Nehal El-Hadi captures this sense of uncanniness well when she calls *Deep Nostalgia* outputs 'digital frankensteins' (2021); creations of people with gestures that they perhaps never intended or meant. The notion of the uncanny is interesting, referencing debates within robotics and artificial intelligence about feelings of unsettlement provoked by representations that are human, but not quite human enough. The uncanny, according to Silke Arnold-de-Simine, can be enabling where it allows people to 'hold potentially conflicting reactions (disturbing/comforting) in suspension' (2019: 92) and we saw this in the ambivalence expressed by many in our sample who displayed conflicting responses simultaneously: '*I'm both in awe and creeped out. Still super cool*'. This demonstrates well the unsettled and ambivalent quality of our responses to these technologies, and of the technologies themselves (Davis 2012).

As we have seen in the examples mentioned earlier, users interpret remediated memories as still having the familiarity and singularity of the image uploaded, yet through processes of abstraction, animation and recursion, their reliability is also undermined. This jarring coexistence has implications for memory work both individually and collectively where it unsettles or recasts our connections with our past(s). There are profound ethical considerations here related to broader debates about memory modification and enhancement, as well as the externalization of memory, through new and emerging technologies (Michaelian and Sutton, 2013). We might note how cautious *MyHeritage* is in its wording about the authenticity of *Deep Nostalgia* creations: 'The end result is not authentic, but rather, a technological simulation of how the person in your photos would have moved and looked if they were captured on video.'[12] Notwithstanding these efforts, debates about authenticity do circulate around these recreations (see Table 3.1), and 8 per cent of tweets in our sample referred to these. These concerns are not new, however, having been a feature of debates about deepfakes (Maras and Alexandrou 2019; Kidd and Rees 2021), but also in relation to other forms of historical recreation such as theatre or copying (Jones 1990; Parry 2013a). In relation to representations of the past, David Lowenthal has argued that 'all "olden times" are potentially fraudulent' (1990:17). Within the context of developments in technology, however, we should expect these debates to re-surface, as we see here amongst a small percentage of users.

Algorithmic nostalgia

Here we explore *MyHeritage*'s claim that *Deep Nostalgia* 'bring[s] beloved ancestors back to life' for nostalgic purposes. We begin with a short overview from the perspective of our data sample, before explicating the concept of algorithmic nostalgia.

In our study, we were attentive to 'the emotional landscape' (Powell 2018: 13) produced by *Deep Nostalgia*'s creations. *MyHeritage* noted proudly in a tweet on March 3 that '*#DeepNostalgia is bringing MyHeritage users to tears!*' and this emotional resonance was in evidence in 60 per cent of our sample. People were willing to overtly perform their (largely positive) emotional responses to these moving images within social networks:[13]

> *Animei a foto do meu avô no #DeepNostalgia e mandei pra minha mãe no whatsapp. A véia ficou tão emocionada que chorou: 'Como vc conseguiu isso? Chegou me da nervoso, parecia ele com sorriso mesmo'. [I animated my grandfather's photo on #DeepNostalgia and sent it to my mom on whatsapp. The old woman was so moved that she cried: 'How did you do that? It made me nervous, he looked like he was smiling']*

12 https://blog.myheritage.com/2021/02/new-animate-the-faces-in-your-family-photos/. All animations feature a number of icons in the bottom left corner to indicate the processes that have been applied to them. Once they are enhanced, they feature a magic wand icon, once animated they feature a motion icon and if they have also been colourized, they will feature an icon of an artist's palette. Authenticity is also an important concept for genealogists that seek reliable information about their family trees, and DNA testing has become a crucial part of that process, facilitated by companies like *MyHeritage*.

13 88 per cent of comments featuring emotions were positive and 8 per cent negative.

This can be understood as ethically jarring; the calculations made as *Deep Nostalgia* processes an image are computational and abstract, but the impacts they produce are emotional and psychological.

Interest in our digitally mediated emotional lives has been increasing in recent years, not least for commercial reasons (McStay 2018: 1). The imperative to make people feel – and to encourage expression or performance of feeling – is now strong, whether it be excitement, pride, anger or despair that we are experiencing. Advertisers and brands, as well as political and cultural actors, have paid increased attention to expressed or implied 'sentiment' (Puschmann and Powell 2018), and emoji and animated GIFs have become part of the day-to-day vernacular of digital communications (Miltner and Highfield 2017). This is worthy of note in relation to *Deep Nostalgia* given the ambitions of the corporate actors here: *MyHeritage* aims to promote and increase users for its genealogy services through exposure, and social media companies (including Twitter) create economic value through connectivity and the collection of data. The likelihood of both these ambitions being met is significantly increased where users' emotions can be mobilized.

In our sample, *Deep Nostalgia*'s affective dimensions could in large part be attributed to a kind of 'biomediation' (Garde-Hansen et al. 2009: 12); where technology interfaced with the human and communicated in ways that were more than semiotic and cognitive (Angel and Gibbs 2006). We saw that it was often movement in the images that triggered emotional resonances. This was unsurprising given that most of the animated images featured deceased relatives, many of whom would not (or could not) have been captured through moving imagery in their lifetime. In its framing *Deep Nostalgia* encourages users to animate faces of ancestors, family and historical figures, not 'photos featuring living people without their permission'. This was predominantly the case in our sample,[14] where the majority of images were, as far as we could discern, of deceased family members or people from history (65 per cent of images). This begins to indicate certain ethical considerations that are thrown into sharp relief by D-ID, *MyHeritage*, *Deep Nostalgia* and its creations. Of particular concern is the question of how a deceased person might be

14 Our sample included: 195 reanimated photographs, 30 paintings, 9 sculptures and 12 other types of image including comic characters, bank notes or children's drawings (70 tweets were n/a).

considered to have consented to the uploading of their image. Although it may be true that the dead cannot object, and there are no legal obstructions that prevent a relative from animating an image, there are clearly ethical and moral considerations here where a person's right to be forgotten meets another person's sense of a duty to remember, and the agency that they might feel comes with that.

Deep Nostalgia recreations are about more than their deceased subjects, however, to which they have more than an indexical relationship. They become symbolic mnemonic objects that mediate users' own identities and not just those of their deceased relatives. The chance *Deep Nostalgia* gives to users to reanimate photographs from their personal archives can be read as filling in gaps in familial histories (although clearly not straightforwardly), and another aspect of self-construction. The use of imagery more broadly within social media has become an important aspect of identity construction and self-representation, and how a person's photos intermingle with the photos of others is an important aspect of those processes. *Deep Nostalgia* might contribute to the co-creation of networked identities as 'users contribute to the stories of each other' (Leaver 2018), in this case including those already dead. Photos – especially portraits (including selfies) – shared in social networks also come with the 'expectation of engagement' targeted at a 'semi-private audience' (Trillò et al. 2023).

Susan Sontag understands photographs as 'incitements to reverie' (2008:16, see also, Walter 2015), and we understand our dataset to be nostalgic in that it constitutes a psychosocial mobilization of emotion (as we saw earlier) more often than not galvanized around past-ness; pasts that are constructed as silent and smiling in the *Deep Nostalgia* outputs. We questioned whether this amounted to an excess of 'historical musing' which is 'myopic, perpetual and ultimately destructive', or whether it could instead be understood as a 'reflexive, collective or adaptive view of history' (Lizardi 2016). Our research suggests that the history on offer in *Deep Nostalgia* is more persistent than adaptive, and quite literally perpetual in that it plays on a loop. These mechanisms are coded by programmers in ways which are no doubt context and culturally dependent, and the nostalgia assembled is (over)determined and situated as a result. This was evidenced in our sample in the way that the *Deep Nostalgia* interface made it possible for users to easily on-board, upload and animate their photographs and, crucially, share the resulting output on social media, effectively nostalgia-ficating what is otherwise a marketing tool. Affective remediated memories underscored a pervasive 'algorithmic nostalgia' in our dataset then; outputs which tended towards uniformity and conformity fed a generalized nostalgia which was generated and organized through automated and recursive mechanisms.

It is too easy however to dismiss *Deep Nostalgia* creations and the algorithmic nostalgia they elicit as sentiment and myopia. As Sayers notes, 'nostalgia is not always, or only, a sign of stuck-ness' (2020: 190). In some moments we saw uses of *Deep Nostalgia* that accorded well with the general sense we can have in social networks, and in society more generally (according to Lipovetsky 2005), of living in a perpetual present; distanced from the past and feeling insecure about the future. But in other moments, there was interest in the past which might be understood as productive or generative. Significantly, we found uses of the technology aimed at revindicating a collective memory of people that experience racism in ways that seemed more productive than myopic, for example, in the frequent animation of the Black abolitionist Frederick Douglass.[15] There was curiosity evident in our sample also – about what future for remembering these outputs might anticipate or set in motion, and what possibilities might flow from that. *Deep Nostalgia* creations are then about the past, the present and the future, a paradox symptomatic of the ambivalence of this technology, and of responses to it in our dataset. This is unsurprising given that, as Clay Routledge contends, nostalgia is a 'complex emotional experience' (Routledge 2016: 44) that can be both past and future-oriented in its adaptive qualities and which can itself be felt as ambivalent.

Algorithmic nostalgia is clearly of interest in relation to the technology's memorative effects and affects, as well as how these are achieved through processes of automation and remediation. It is also intriguing to examine in the context of social networks' algorithmic and datafication practices, where monetizing connectivity and user data emerge as considerations. A crucial part of the mnemonic language used by platforms – the mobilization of nostalgia – is of course not neutral, becoming more profitable as it becomes more visceral

15 An example of which can be seen here: https://twitter.com/amplify285/status/1366039719499415554?s=11&t=jYk7_A6xiPb5ohSG4Gfldw.

(Routledge 2016). In the next section we explore these considerations in more detail.

The logics of sociotechnical infrastructures

In our study we saw how social media's connective and attention logics shaped how users interacted with *Deep Nostalgia*, resulting in dialogic practices that were communicative, performative and extractive as well as mnemonic.

Sharing via social media is clearly an integral part of the logic of *Deep Nostalgia*, blurring the boundaries between private and public memory. In our sample, 70 per cent of tweets shared animated images, a figure which increased in the members of the public category, where 88 per cent of people had shared them. Some used (and shared) *Deep Nostalgia* more than once, posting threads of multiple outputs: '*I'm still obsessed with #DeepNostalgia*'.

An intriguing affordance of these platforms and their 'vernacular' (Gibbs et al. 2015) is evidently their sharing and connective logic. Nearly a quarter of tweets featured the default suggested text when sharing directly from the *MyHeritage* app or website: '*I love the way MyHeritage brought the people in my photo to life! Try it too and be amazed. #DeepNostalgia*'. These users therefore acted as inadvertent champions for the company, given that sharing an animated photograph was inextricably linked with promoting it. When looking at the comments, the success of this strategy can be seen, as we found many comments in response asking how to use the feature and where to find it. Animated images contained backlinks to the *MyHeritage* website in most cases, where to use *Deep Nostalgia* new users were asked to sign up and relinquish, at the very least, a name and email address, and to agree to the *MyHeritage* Terms and Conditions (MyHeritage 2022a, 2022b, 2023b, 2023c).

For *MyHeritage*, the sharing of animated images thus performed as an invaluable social advertising function where promotional messages were blended with users' sense of identity and belonging (van Dijck 2017). In terms of public endorsement and brand image, such an approach is invaluable for a company like *MyHeritage*; their product (genealogical services) was turned into a story that could be excitedly shared. According to José van Dijck (2017), such practices do not constitute social or collective memory however so much as mere 'connectivity' in service of the social media platforms and their business models. Echoing Paolo Bory's observations, elements of the spectacle were in evidence here, employed by a company as a way of advocating for its products (Bory 2019). This was noted by some users who criticized or ridiculed the technology for these very reasons: '*Deepfake technology is used to bring dead relatives back to life. I'm sure marketers are already strategizing this for marketing plans down the road.* 🙄 *#deepnostalgia #deepfake*'.

We found in the tweets, as one would expect, many of the vernacular elements of Twitter as a platform. The playfulness of social media interactions appeared in 13 per cent of tweets in our sample. Such posts frequently featured GIFs as a framing device. Several tweets also made connections to other popular representations of posthumous animation, for example, in the Harry Potter storyworld, offering a critical reading of the purportedly innovative nature of the technology. Here we were reminded that the adoption or 'domestication' of these technologies is not always linear; users found alternative ways of employing them, including those that were subversive or whimsical (Kitchin 2017: 19). Such responses were present although not prevalent in our sample, but were nevertheless a helpful reminder of how images make meaning in social media cultures (e.g. Leaver et al. 2019) and the extent to which the entire *Deep Nostalgia* campaign was enmeshed within and shaped by the 'internet's visual turn' (Vaccari and Chadwick 2020).

Social media companies are navigating the emergence of deep learning technologies in real time and are clearly disinclined to restrict activities that are gaining traction and attention, not least given the importance of 'compulsive connectivity' (van Dijck 2017) to their business models. Perhaps for this reason, the response of social media companies to developments like deepfakes has been slow and, so far, mixed; TikTok has now issued detailed 'Integrity and Authenticity' guidelines,[16] Facebook has issued guidelines for 'manipulated media', although with exceptions for parody and satire,[17] and X's policy does not allow 'inauthentic' or 'misleading' media.[18] Our data suggests that most users were not overly troubled by concerns about synthetic media's

16 https://www.tiktok.com/community-guidelines/en/integrity-authenticity (Released August 2025, accessed 16 September 2025).

17 https://about.fb.com/news/2020/01/enforcing-against-manipulated-media/ (Guidelines dated January 2020, accessed 16 September 2025).

18 https://help.x.com/en/rules-and-policies/authenticity (Rules dated April 2025, accessed 16 September 2025).

deceptive or manipulative potentials, however, or were at least able to put them to one side in order to participate in what had become a shared mnemonic experience within peoples' social media feeds.

The viral nature of this case study is worth reflecting on here, alongside a broader look at the ways AI is discussed in society. According to Nguyen et al. (2023) developments in AI are typically framed within discourses about technological trends, economic potentials, data risks and questions of governance, but *Deep Nostalgia* also has cultural and historical dimensions which are less common, and a strong personal and familial aspect too. This unusual emphasis may explain *Deep Nostalgia*'s rapid (albeit fleeting) popularity within social networks; a chance to partake in an activity that was somehow dissonant or not normative, yet also familiar given its characteristics. The easy-to-use capability for sharing creations on Twitter and Facebook[19] coupled with the novelty of the technology and the combination of emotional resonance and playful elements, no doubt contributed to the viral success of *Deep Nostalgia* in the weeks following its launch. The connective nature of genealogy communities online might also bear on its popularity, given that 'genealogists use technology to research their family, but they also use technology like social media to connect with other family researchers and to share ideas and information' (Kennedy-Eden and Gretzel, 2021). *Deep Nostalgia* did not trend for long however and was ultimately unable to sustain itself as a phenomenon at that level. Following Simone Natale, we might note this as the point when *Deep Nostalgia*'s deceptions became 'banal' and disappeared into the fabric of social media and our daily lives (2021); the fact that it so quickly became predictable and ordinary contributed to its recuperation. Nevertheless, its work for *MyHeritage* was done.

Garde-Hansen et al. (2009) suggest that the ability and encouragement to 'share' have become powerful factors in how we think about memory and its uses. Elena Esposito agrees, arguing that image production increasingly happens for the purpose of sharing rather than storing memories, and as such, its aims shift from 'temporal preservation' to 'social multiplication' (Esposito

19 Despite the visual nature of Instagram, sharing on the platform is less straightforward and likely explains it not featuring as one of the options offered by *MyHeritage* for users to share animated films.

2022: 83). In the case of *Deep Nostalgia* the frenetic social media sharing which occurred around its launch demonstrated that shift extraordinarily well, with what might have started as 'intimate' remembering (Hjorth and Hinton 2019: 172) transferring quite comprehensively into the public domain. This was significant because it required that memories and remembering were shaped to fit the sociotechnical parameters of the social networks being utilized (Esteve del Valle and Smit 2021), and demonstrated how – through what might be termed 'posthumous performances' – the dead continued to be made productive, 'generat[ing] capital' for those companies 'in collaboration with the living' (Stanyek and Piekut 2010: 14). This is an idea we pick up again in the following chapters.

Social media sites are of course implicated in the success of online genealogy platforms more generally. Reliant on data extraction and accumulation, the business model of *MyHeritage* and other genealogy companies is optimized for operation adjacent to social networks and must increasingly consider and conform to those networks' logics in their design as we noted earlier. Within online genealogy communities dissemination of findings is widespread (Evans 2011), but connections to social networks extend these possibilities further. As Jerome de Groot notes (2015: 117): 'The purpose of the network is the growth of the network. It tends towards openness and through that, revelation.' The practices explored in this chapter further encourage the unhindered sharing and movement of information (data), and the promotion of tools to those who might not otherwise consider themselves family historians. We explore these data entanglements further in the following section.

Ethical and data entanglements

As noted earlier, *Deep Nostalgia*'s significance for *MyHeritage* is principally as a function of marketing; outputs are destined within this context to be shared, ideally to attract fresh audiences to the platform. As such, each creation becomes a 'transaction in a data network' (Dewdney 2022: 24), both within an exchange relationship between a user and the company, but beyond that to other *MyHeritage* users and social networks too.

Sharing and connecting is not just an ethos then, but crucial to the company's business model in order to accumulate data, and attract new (potentially paying) users. The ethics of 'socio-economic systems heavily dependent on the massive extraction and predictive analysis of data' (Airoldi 2022) needs to be considered here, particularly in its exploitation of our individual and collective pasts for commercial benefit. Reliant on crowdsourcing, accessibility is an important feature of online genealogy and most platforms offer a first tier of services that are free at point of use, although you do first need to register for a user account. For example, performing a search might be free but to see most records you need a paid subscription. *Deep Nostalgia* is available on a freemium plan (with a limited number of free uses before having to buy a subscription), but it is worth considering what happens to users' data after the event (i.e. what happens to the data they have volunteered as 'payment'). According to the *MyHeritage* Terms and Conditions (2022b), photos uploaded to Deep Nostalgia belong to users and not the platform and can be deleted at any time; they are stored and manipulated on the *MyHeritage* servers and never shared with third parties (MyHeritage 2022a). According to the Terms and Conditions (2022b), none of the AI-based features used by *MyHeritage* collect or retain any biometric information or biometric identifiers from photos that are uploaded.

There are, however, caveats to these claims that raise ethical concerns about data extractivism. Several features use third-party technologies, which complicate *MyHeritage*'s data footprint. For example, the Photo Tagger feature uses a facial recognition technology model (i.e. biometric information) that is powered by Amazon to help users tag people in their photos quickly and easily. The disclaimer notes that this feature is not enabled by default and requires the user's explicit consent (MyHeritage 2022a). Similarly, as has been noted, *MyHeritage*'s business model is predicated on sharing on social networks, mainly Twitter and Facebook, which each has their own set of Terms and Conditions. Both companies claim that the content posted on their platforms belongs to the user who retains copyright; however, in order for Facebook to provide their services (for example), they claim to need 'a non-exclusive, transferable, sub-licensable, royalty-free, and worldwide license to host, use, distribute, modify, run, copy, publicly perform or display, translate, and create derivative works of your content', which is automatically accepted by the user every time content that is covered by intellectual property rights is shared, posted or uploaded (Meta 2023).

Copying and using content and data that might belong to others without their permission is at the heart of concerns raised by synthetic media more generally, as well as generative AI. D-ID, the company that developed the technology underpinning *Deep Nostalgia*, claims on their website that they will 'work hard to ensure' that their customers (in this case *MyHeritage*) use their technology 'in ethical, responsible ways' (D-ID 2021a). Alongside technology and media companies such as TikTok, OpenAI, BBC R&D and Witness, D-ID belongs to the Partnership on AI, which published 'Responsible Practices for Synthetic Media' in 2023, a framework for developing, creating and sharing synthetic media that avoids online harms such as spreading misinformation, committing fraud or bullying and harassment (PAI 2023).[20] There are concerns arising from the widespread use of deepfakes in the media that span harms to the self (such as faking memories) to the social implications of 'epistemic contention' such as 'doubt in scientific experts, fake news, deep disagreement, [and] "post-truth"' (Rini and Cohen 2022). But they also raise more specific concerns for users engaging in the practice of creating synthetic media, such as unknowingly contributing labour or data. On whether *Deep Nostalgia* uses uploaded images to train algorithms, *MyHeritage* specifically says that this is not the case when uploading photos to AI *Time Machine*,[21] but does not specify for any of the other AI-based technology licensed by them (MyHeritage 2023c). Even if not using the images for training AI systems, the underlying technology (*Time Machine*, for example, uses text-to-image technology licensed from Astria and based on Stable Diffusion) has most likely been trained on data collected from others without their consent, which, in some cases, might contravene the EUs General Data Protection Regulation or copyright law (Vincent 2023). Moreover, there are also questions to be asked about how *Deep Nostalgia* creations (or similar) might in time be collected and used to train other algorithmic models (Jacobsen 2023).

Regardless of how aware of these data practices *MyHeritage* users are (and despite agreeing to the Terms and Conditions), the ethics of data transactions and legacies on the platform become knottier once one considers that most

20 PAI is a non-profit that brings academic, civil society, industry and media organizations together to create 'solutions so that AI advances positive outcomes for people and society'. https://partnershiponai.org/about/.

21 Another service offered by the company.

images animated by *Deep Nostalgia* are of users' deceased relatives. This raises the question of what ethical considerations should inform work with digital human remains, and whether a deceased person can be considered to have consented to a (remediated) AI afterlife, created posthumously on their behalf. This is heightened by the fact that this new 'immortal' identity on the internet will not only be managed by others, but potentially persist indefinitely; their re-enactment having an impact on a collective family history and, because of their inscription into an extensive and often public database, potentially on a world-wide kinship graph (Willever-Farr and Forte 2014).

For all of *MyHeritage*'s emphasis on digitally reviving the dead, it is important to remember that, like other online genealogy platforms, *MyHeritage* is currently a biotechnology company that processes and accumulates genetic information, also with many ethical ramifications. It has been argued that by sharing DNA with genealogy sites, users – or their relatives – might become 'genetic informants', with still unknown consequences (Ford 2018). Furthermore, *MyHeritage* uses aggregated and anonymized genetic data for research – with users' prior and explicit consent as an opt in (MyHeritage 2022a). In creating these huge biobanks and databases, corporations have replaced the academy as gatekeepers and controllers of access to this knowledge, as well as conferring users a 'dual status as customers and research participants' that is fraught with ethical issues in terms of informed consent at the very least (de Groot 2020). The many ethical ramifications of using DNA to biologize 'ethnicity' have also been highlighted, whereby these processes of value extraction and the capitalization on affective attachments are characterized as biopolitical techniques of surveying and surveilling (Cachoian-Schanz and Schwerzmann 2021). Understanding the materiality of the practice of genealogy is crucial as the externalization of memory on servers in the cloud 'involves a commodity chain of extracted and mobilized material resources' with environmental implications also (Reading and Notley 2015).

As Jerome de Groot (2020: 9) has argued, these companies present themselves as organizations enabling and empowering ordinary people. Users feel that they can 'conquer time and space to get our dead loved ones back' (Tackett 2021), but they also become accountable for using the technology appropriately. The responsibility for abiding by the principles and values of family history, including provenance, credibility and authenticity are ultimately placed on the user (see also, Scharlach et al. 2023; Carmi 2021).

First, *MyHeritage* asks its users to only upload their 'own historical photos' and never photos featuring living people without their permission, or that of their parents or guardians if minors (MyHeritage 2022a). Second, *MyHeritage* also outsources to the user the responsibility to be respectful and truthful, asking users to never upload content that is obscene, false or offensive (MyHeritage 2023c).[22] These responsibilities are somewhat opaque, however, given the insidiousness of the virality that has surrounded these outputs. Once creations have been shared via Facebook or Twitter, questions about permissions, reproduction and respectability have their parameters changed. The sociotechnical infrastructures of the internet intermediaries, and the logics underpinning specific platforms – their unique 'vernacular' (Gibbs et al. 2015) – influence in profound ways the patterns and practices of their use, and these extensions are worthy of much closer scrutiny.

We have considered here the agency of the programmers and developers of these platforms and AI systems, acknowledging, as Simone Natale (2021) points out, that users have agency also. The democratizing claims of genealogy companies and the distribution of agency can be seen in the way users are not just asked to verify what an algorithm identifies as a potential link to a family member or historical record, but to engage in specific practices of (re)creation of mnemonic digital objects and the remediation of memories. This agency is shared however and ultimately outsourced. The homogenizing tendencies of the algorithm highlight tensions between the search for authenticity that underpins genealogy, and the creative deceptions brought about by generative AI. In the next and final analysis section, we explore further what this might mean for genealogy services.

Deceptive genealogy?

In the context of its use by *MyHeritage*, D-ID notes that this 'technology offers today's generation a tangible link to their ancestors and proves that artificial intelligence can be leveraged to deepen one's connection to their family

22 To use their latest technology, *Time Machine*, *MyHeritage* asks users not to 'upload photos of children, photos with nudity or photos that are offensive. No photos of Nazis. Do not use AI Time Machine™ to make fun of politicians – keep Putin, Biden, Trump and other politicians out of this. Do not share results that may humiliate or offend anyone' (MyHeritage 2023d).

history' (D-ID 2021b). We have demonstrated that *MyHeritage*'s promotion of *Deep Nostalgia* as a way to establish a unique and personalized mnemonic experience – 'Discover and treasure your unique family history' (MyHeritage 2023a) – is profoundly unsettling given the algorithm's propensity to homogenize during the remediation process; abstracting, blending and building from pre-scripted prompts, and producing a 'synthetic' output as a result. Remediation leaves little room for what Quadflieg et al. (2022) term 'disobedience' in the face of algorithmic power, resulting in a high degree of conformity in outputs.

Given their illusory qualities, and current limitations in the remediation process, it is tempting to conclude that these outputs represent simply a new kind of 'genealojunk' (Willever-Farr and Forte 2014). Instead, however, we prefer to understand them as examples of what we call 'deceptive genealogy', echoing Simone Natale's recognition of deception as increasingly 'banal' (Natale 2021: 128), especially in the context of artificial intelligence where trickery has become domesticated, subtler and more pervasive. Natale proposes that rather than assessing only whether deception is occurring, we should instead seek to understand what specific outcomes and implications flow from those deceptive effects; what feelings, thoughts, beguilements or diversions (for example) do they produce? It could be argued that the deception of these digital re-enactments is no different from the speculative nature of genealogists' interpretations of their ancestor's personality or other attributes. Storytelling is at the heart of family history; relatedness and kinship not 'a biological given but a social construct' whereby genealogies are the narratives we construct to actually 'make' people our ancestors (Zerubavel 2011). By selectively remembering and forgetting, users 'accommodate personal as well as collective strategic agendas of inclusion and exclusion' (Zerubavel 2011). Not only genealogy, but digital immortality is designed 'from the perspective of those who remain, not of those who have died' (Sisto 2020: 64). In relation to *Deep Nostalgia* specifically, accepting that the representations they produce are similarly specious, we should ask why – or in what ways – their deceptions really matter within genealogy contexts and for individual and collective memory more broadly.

Synthetic media can raise psychosocial and philosophical questions about the provenance of memories which become difficult to resolve, particularly when considering the mix of sources and agents at play. Yet the idea that memory might be open to manipulation and falsity is not new (Loftus and Pickrell 1995; Loftus 2005). 'False memories' can be said to occur when 'mental images of a fictional event are mistakenly recognized as the product of lived experience' (Murphy and Flynn 2022: 480–1) and are particularly likely where a mental experience has the qualities of a real memory; rich details, imagery (including moving imagery) and sensory information such as sound (Nightingale and Wade 2022). Deepfakes – and, we contend, outputs such as *Deep Nostalgia* – have the potential then to be particularly rich stimuli for false memories, 'engaging neural networks and controlling mental, perceptual, emotional, and cognitive states' (Liv and Greenbaum 2020).[23] In response to such stimuli, researchers suggest that our brains tend to 'auto-fill' false details, and to do so with high levels of confidence (Liv and Greenbaum 2020). 'Digital trickery' coupled with our imaginations, can lead to 'remarkably high levels of belief and memory distortion' according to Nash et al. (2009: 421), to the extent that 'false evidence can, in effect, change the past'. Such implications would be intriguing, and of course troubling, and further research will be needed as algorithmic procedures are used to more comprehensively underscore interactions with our individual and collective pasts.

Conclusion

Given their resultant uncanniness (often referred to by users as 'creepiness' as we noted earlier) we might ask why users wish to reanimate 'their' dead in this way at all. Introducing new technologies to our ancestors demonstrates our deep human need to 'live with them in more or less proximity' (Laqueur 2015: 4); giving us a (techno-)material sense of their intimate and continuing presence in our day to day. According to Davide Sisto (2020: 24), through the invention of photography, radio and television 'the dead now have their voices and even their ability to move restored', giving them 'a unique opportunity to "survive" death through sounds, images, and movement: repeating the

23 Although Murphy and Flynn propose that fears about drastically increased memory distortion in response to deepfakes may be overblown (2021).

same scenes for eternity'. *Deep Nostalgia* extends those opportunities quite explicitly and remarkably, but produces ethical considerations as we have noted. The algorithmically generated outputs result from semi-automated data collaborations and mashups (behind the scenes and less explicitly), which – in the insertion of drivers and other information – become ever more dissociated and detached from their source materials, while giving the impression of immediacy.

Ethical entanglements relate to the extent to which creations can be considered exploitative of those who have died, or a breach of (often unspoken) social and cultural norms around death. Although there are no legal barriers preventing a user from creating an output with one of these tools, there are of course moral considerations here in relation to (for example) a person's right to be forgotten, or their wish perhaps to be remembered in particular ways. Claiming the dead as our own, and for our own purposes, is of course what has driven genealogical research since its earliest days (Laqueur, 2023), but it takes on new significance within these emergent formats where 'algorithmic afterlife' (Lambert et al. 2018) or 'synthetic resurrection' (Ajder 2019) work across the technological and the material in ways which can be particularly affective, but unsettling also. The animated human bodies produced by *Deep Nostalgia* are recognizable but flimsy, seeming to channel the past, present and (lost) future simultaneously. Such material and temporal disjunctions might best be described as 'hauntological' (Fisher 2012: 16).

But despite these concerns about memory, and about representation, we have observed a knowingness in the ways these tools are used too. Whereas traditionally we might have understood photographs to represent an 'uncorrupt' representation of the past (Stone and Zwolinski 2022), most people are now familiar with the manipulation of digital images. Indeed, *MyHeritage* users are actively encouraged to engage in what we have termed 'deceptive genealogy' by initiating a remediated memory without any pretence of its being authentic or truthful (MyHeritage 2023b). All synthetic media produced in *MyHeritage* has watermarks and symbols to signal that they have been generated or augmented by AI, and *MyHeritage* asks users not to remove these. In the wake of that knowingness comes playfulness too, with many users pushing at the boundaries of (or ignoring) that guidance, creating animated versions of their own image, artworks, celebrities or historical figures. The uncanniness, the creepiness and the deception, become a part of the 'magic' in user engagement terms, underscoring the intense virality of these outputs beyond *MyHeritage* as they stray into other platforms (notably Twitter and Facebook) wherein the company's networked ambitions can be realized.

In reanimating the dead, users of *Deep Nostalgia* are – whether for playful or mnemonic purposes (or both) – effectively hijacking their ancestors' free will, making them move in predictable ways but with movements they never intended (Tackett 2021). Sara Kopelman and Paul Frosh refer to *Deep Nostalgia*'s creations as the 'restless' dead; 'neither dead nor alive but perpetually in motion' (Kopelman and Frosh 2023). Technology is also about power, and in this particular instance, it is not just the uncanniness of the moving image, but issues of control that we must pay attention to. The *MyHeritage* platform emerges here as a particularly potent form of mnemotechnology: crafting new kinds of algorithmic afterlife and posthumous performance; suggesting new possibilities and connections for our own and others' datafied bodies; facilitating the (re-)scaffolding – and even creation – of memory; building tools which reach into other platforms, operate seamlessly in relation to them and consequently expand the company's user-base. *Deep Nostalgia* reminds us that digital memory work 'moves back and forth, on a relational level, between self and others, the private and the public, the individual and collective, and the human and nonhuman' (Esteve Del Valle and Smit 2021: 1814). Our concept of deceptive genealogies highlights the ambivalence of the machine habitus which makes these practices possible. That they are deceptive is never in doubt – their uncanniness is a part of their appeal – but their ambiguity is ethically consequential, as we have begun to demonstrate.

In Chapter 4 we push these observations further with an analysis of how a suite of more personalized and bidirectional mnemonic resources are experienced by users.

4

'Deathbots' and the platformization of remembering

In this chapter we turn our attention to the ways AI systems are supporting more personalized and inter- or re-active mnemonic recreations. We take a focused look at platforms purporting to story and archive memories, including through the creation of what have been termed 'deathbots'. This focus allows us to further explore how platforms intervene in individual memory practices, extending our discussion to consider the ethics of using avatars trained on data from a person's digital footprint as a mnemonic resource or even proxy.

Through an analysis of four platforms we explore a range of practices in depth, elucidating what is at stake as (some of) our means for life story reflection and recollection move to platforms, interacting evermore with algorithms and automation. Given the nature of these platforms and how they are packaged, consideration of processes, rituals and norms around death and grief also become a part of the picture. Key questions we explore include: How do platforms encourage users to 'story' and archive a person's past, or to use extant digital data to do this? What kind of mnemonic resources do these platforms *actually* produce, and how is their use experienced and felt? And how is care and responsibility understood and exercised by corporate entities in relation to these practices, especially given the emphasis of these tools on remembrance and grief?

The platforms we explore in this chapter operate as part of what has been termed the 'Digital Afterlife Industry', that is, they are all 'commercial goods or services that involve online usage of digital remains' (Öhman and Floridi 2017). In the next section we present an overview of this 'industry', introducing a raft of debates that have arisen around these goods and services. Following that we present findings from our analysis of the four platforms. These are: *Almaya*, *HereAfter*, *Seance AI* and *You, Only Virtual*. As has been noted elsewhere (Nansen et al. 2023; Brescó de Luna and Jiménez-Alonso 2024) digital afterlife services are often precarious and can be short-lived, but these four platforms together comprise a neat gateway into the digital afterlife industry at the time of writing this book.[1] The services offered through these platforms – from forms of purposive life story archiving, to 'deathbots' targeted at grieving relatives – are all designed to be accessed (posthumously) through conversational AI, where natural language processing and machine learning compute and respond to human language, whether it's spoken or written. The conceit across these approaches is that connections built in life might be extended beyond death, and that AI is a powerful mechanism for supporting such continuance.

To better understand the four platforms we have used a branched approach to data gathering which is fully explained in our Data Coda (Chapter 8). This has included a series of sociotechnical walkthroughs of each platform as user-researchers (following Light et al. 2016; Ritter 2022; Troeger and Bock 2022; Duguay and Gold-Apel 2023), alongside a detailed quantitative and qualitative analysis of official public documents relating to each platform, including Terms and Conditions, Privacy Policies and Frequently Asked Questions (a total of ten documents, 34,967 words). As a result, we have been able to produce empirical knowledge and understanding systematically in order to underpin the discussions that follow. After introducing our findings we conclude with reflections on the platformization of remembering. Extending our discussions in Chapter 3 we draw on Thomas Poell, David Nieborg and José van Dijck's (2019) definition of 'platformization' to highlight the combination of infrastructural, economic and governmental dimensions which 'reorganize' cultural practices – including mnemonic ones – around platforms.

1 In addition, we have experimented with many other similar services while researching these themes – such as Project December, Replika, StoryFile Life and LifeNaut.

Dialoguing with the dead

As we have noted elsewhere in this book 'necro-technologies' (Nansen et al. 2023) are not new. They have taken many forms, from gravestones, to funeral books, memorial pages and now 'deathbots'. What distinguishes our focus in this chapter from elsewhere in the book is the potential for what might be considered (not unproblematically) bidirectional forms of 'imaginal' dialogue between the living and those who have died (Brescó de Luna and Jiménez-Alonso 2024).[2] As this bidirectionality is increasingly experienced multimodally – in terms of data inputs and presentation techniques – these approaches are suggestive of 'new kinds of social links and symbolic rituals' around death (Sisto 2020: 20), and potentially potent new forms of 'conversational pasts' (Hoskins 2024) produced through human-machine collaboration.

In the opening section of this chapter we have used the term 'deathbot' a number of times, and it is important to clarify what we mean by this. A deathbot is a conversational bot or avatar that has been programmed from the digital data of a deceased person – often their social media or voice data – so that it can simulate their conversational style, speech patterns, demeanour and intellectual inclinations (Bao and Zeng 2024). A deathbot might be created by a person while still alive or crafted posthumously by a bereaved relative as a means of securing continuance for a relationship through 'new' interactions after death. There has been interest in what the impacts might be on processes of grieving and mourning now the dead can reinsert themselves into the lives of the living in this way, and in what it might mean for memory when 'new' posthumous exchanges become possible (Recuber 2023).

While it used to be considered that grief was a thing to be purged, curtailed and moved on from, we now talk more about learning to live in and with our grief (Elder 2020); continuing bonds not severing them. Relationships carry on (albeit changed and changing), even as life ends (Kasket 2019: 62) and we now have fewer 'grief norms' (O'Connor and Kasket 2022: 118), recognizing

2 Thus differentiating it from one-way immortality where data from the deceased is more straightforwardly preserved and presented for future generations, such as in a digital memorial (Galvão et al. 2021: 2).

that the grieving experience is fluid, culturally situated and socially embedded (O'Connor and Kasket 2022: 124). This change has coincided with a shift in societal attitudes to death heralded in part by the growth of the internet where 'symbolic representations' of the dead now circulate pervasively amongst the online activities of the living (Morse 2023: 242). The creation and use of deathbots is symptomatic then of these shifts. Despite these developments however, popular misconceptions about grief endure. For example, that there is a normal way to grieve which can be 'hindered' by technology, necessitating that we find ways to manage how technology impacts bereaved persons (O'Connor and Kasket 2022: 124). This attitude is no doubt underscored by more generalized concerns about technology's impacts on individuals and society, meaning that public debates about these developments are characterized by oversimplification and normative statements. Indeed, we demonstrate as much in Chapter 5.

Given that the platforms introduced in this chapter are driven by computer systems reliant on probabilistic responses rather than the needs of mourners specifically (Bao and Zeng 2024), there have been many concerns expressed about their emergence (Brescó de Luna and Jiménez-Alonso 2024). As noted in Chapter 3, companies which rely on the collection and processing of digital information raise questions about privacy and data rights and these arise perhaps more acutely here in the context of death and bereavement (Elder 2020; Harbinja et al. 2024) where the 'ethical and legislative conundrum' in relation to consent, and the ongoing data custodianship responsibilities of companies, remain to be worked through (Savin-Baden and Burden 2018: 100). Harbinja et al. 2023 remind us how limited post-mortem rights are, and go as far as championing a 'do not bot me' clause as an express wish that could be inserted into digital wills, although they acknowledge this would be hard to enforce. Meese et al. (2015) express concern that memorializing and remembering are being 'implicated into a wider commercial start-up economy' (2015: 416, see also, Kneese 2023) and there is uneasiness that digital afterlife services will ultimately aim to display only the most profitable or 'consumable' version of a dead person rather than other versions a user might wish to remember, or that might feel more 'accurate' (Öhman and Floridi 2017: 649). Relatedly, Cristina Voinea (2023) raises concerns that griefbots might in time be used for advertising, or for other forms of manipulation.

In response to these concerns, Carl Öhman and Luciano Floridi have proposed that a constructive ethical approach, including the development of a robust regulatory framework for digital afterlife industries,[3] should reckon with the dominance of commercial data management services and that it should challenge what they perceive to be perverse values and incentives (e.g. monetization of data and connectivity, technocentricity and limited stakeholders). Failure to do so, they say, may mean that the historical value of digital remains, as well as any cultural or scientific value they might produce, could well be lost. These commercial imperatives, they argue, have previously been neglected in research on digital afterlife (Öhman and Floridi 2017).

A set of broader ethical issues have however been more extensively covered in scholarship on these systems. Some authors have focused on the importance of maintaining the integrity and dignity of deceased persons' memories (Buben 2015; Brescó de Luna and Jiménez-Alonso 2024; Fabry and Alfano 2024) as well as being mindful of the dignity of users (Lindemann 2022). There has been concern too about: the psychological well-being of users when it comes to the possibility of developing dependent behaviours (Bao and Zeng 2024), the delineation between simulation and reality (Brescó de Luna and Jiménez-Alonso 2024), the possibility of self-deception or self-delusion (Fabry and Alfano 2024) and how to regulate emotions in the orbit of these creations. As noted earlier, this is an especially important matter given that the logics of these systems are not based on therapeutic criteria but on commercial considerations (Brescó de Luna and Jiménez-Alonso 2024: 107). Aorigele Bao and Yi Zeng (2024: 6) remind us that 'despite their advanced programming, deathbots operate within the realm of AI algorithms and data processing'. They are an 'ethereal instrument of utility' (2024: 5), and as such, do not 'shoulder' emotional responsibilities in any human sense. Regina E. Fabry and Mark Alfano have made the related case that 'a better understanding of the affective roles of so-called deathbots is needed' (2024: 757).

Philosophers too have raised concerns about developments within the digital afterlife industry as they pertain to our understandings of personhood and of mortality, our processes of mourning and our patterns of remembering

3 Archaeology provides some ideas for how this might be achieved according to Öhman and Floridi (2018).

(Sisto 2020, 2021; Stokes 2021). These are neatly summarized as a series of questions by Timothy Recuber:

> But what is at stake when people purposefully use digital platforms and online technologies to craft messages that will outlast their physical bodies? What does the ability to digitally continue a relationship six months or six years after one's death say about the nature of the self? What happens to the processes of grieving and morning when we can re-insert ourselves into the lives of our loved ones for years after our bodies have grown cold? What is the nature of one's responsibility to one's families and friends in an age where such posthumous social interaction is relatively easy to achieve? Is it really possible to maintain agency over one's own legacy after one's death? How does the memory of a departed loved one change when new interactions are potentially just around the corner? What sorts of inequalities or biases are liable to emerge in a future where digital technology promises to extend our interactions beyond this mortal coil, and what role do the various platforms and technologies themselves play in encouraging or discouraging postmortem forms of sociality? (Recuber 2023: 4–5)

Given these expansive concerns and questions, some scholars have concluded that the use of deathbots should be more tightly regulated, for example, so that it is time-limited (Bao and Zeng 2024) or only available within therapeutic contexts (Lindemann 2022). Others have argued that developers would benefit from more robust ethical frameworks and guidelines (Savin-Baden and Burden 2018).

Mórna O'Connor and Elaine Kasket remind us that these technologies are not neutral; rather, they are 'framed by developers who incorporate their own beliefs about grieving into platforms and services' (2022: 117). As we argue throughout this book, algorithmic systems are coded by programmers in ways that are context and culturally dependent, which suggests further ethical considerations that might emerge from their training data, and about what broader cultural assumptions might be embedded within them, including in relation to how the deceased are represented, and how, why and for whom we remember. Tomasz Hollanek and Katarzyna Nowaczyk-Basińska argue for increased 'thanatosensitivity' in interaction design (following Massimi and Charise 2009), noting that improved attention to matters of death in system design is both desirable and do-able (2024: 63). They make a series of recommendations for mitigating risk in deathbot design which are worth reviewing here at the outset. These include sensitivity around the 'retirement' of deathbots, providing clear disclaimers about their capabilities, restricting access to adults and obtaining mutual consent from data donors and recipients (Hollaneck and Nowaczyk-Basińska 2024). Voinea (2023) suggests that designers should embed transparency thoughtfully within systems, as well as repeated reminders that any outputs produced 'lack intention and consciousness'. Galvão et al. (2021), reflecting on their own focus group research with potential users of these systems, concluded that the consideration of 'human values' will be 'a must' as developers push beyond the technological challenges of building these systems (see also, Leaver 2019). Scholars agree then that there are serious ethical issues to consider which have, to date, not been adequately addressed in system design or articulation.

As this section demonstrates, there has been quite some dialogue about the use of deathbots, much of which has remained in the realm of ethics and the philosophy of technology. Limited studies have carried out research into the perspectives of potential users of deathbots (see, e.g. Morse 2023; Galvão et al. 2021) but there is less by way of platform analysis or detailed study of user experiences. This is where our own work in this chapter intervenes.

Before we introduce our study further it is worth noting as an important part of the context for these practices that these technologies and their claims to eternalization have received significant media attention in recent years. The *Black Mirror* episode 'Be Right Back' (2013) is a regular touchpoint in writing about deathbots, and more extended treatments such as *Marjorie Prime* (2017), *Love Machina* (2024) and *Eternal You* (2024) have explored varied dystopian visions of these technologies. Stories about deathbots appear regularly in the news media too, where the captivating – but unsettling – potentials of 'digital resurrection' are repeatedly referenced. There is thus a broader public discourse emerging about these practices which is an important contextual consideration; a discourse which is likely to accelerate and become more cacophonous in the short to medium term. Nancy Baym has noted how 'new media often stir up fears of moral decline' which take the form of 'dystopian rhetorics', and these are consequential as they inform policy decisions and, ultimately, shape the uses and effects of those media (Baym 2015: 41). These cultural touchpoints provide an important backdrop to the platformization of remembering, our focus in the next section.

How, what and for whom does a platform 'remember'?

Storified and imaginal memories: Four approaches to digital legacies

In this section we explore the first of our questions as set out at the start of this chapter: How do platforms encourage users to 'story' and archive a person's past, or to use extant digital data to do this? We briefly introduce the four case studies used in this chapter, offering a high-level summary of the user experience for each. As will be seen, the framing of these platforms in promotional materials and on websites is very explicitly mnemonic. This is exemplified across the screenshots reproduced in this section, where references to memory, legacy and acts of remembrance are centred, and where death, grieving and the posthumous are conjured in terms like 'hereafter', 'seance' and repeated references to 'loss'. The platforms produce these storified and imaginal memories in different ways however, as we outline here in turn.

Case study 1: Almaya

Almaya encourages users to record their memories as an 'interactive digital biography' which can be 'preserved' as an 'eternal treasure' or 'Legacy' within the system and accessed by 'loved ones' over time. Those loved ones then interact with Alma smart chat – an AI guide – to navigate through the content (Figure 4.1). *Almaya* claims that thousands of people have already used the system to 'create their life essence'. It is available in Spanish and English.

The user first downloads the *Almaya* mobile app and signs up for a package.[4] On opening the app they are encouraged to start leaving recordings of memories to create a 'Legacy'. The categories the system uses for prompting memories are quite standardized; 'food', 'my parents', 'family anecdotes' and the like. The user's reflections are then organized into 'chapters' and 'books' within a 'library', which highlights and familiarizes the storied quality of this

4 *Almaya* PRO is $6.99 a month, or $39.99 a year (as of January 2025).

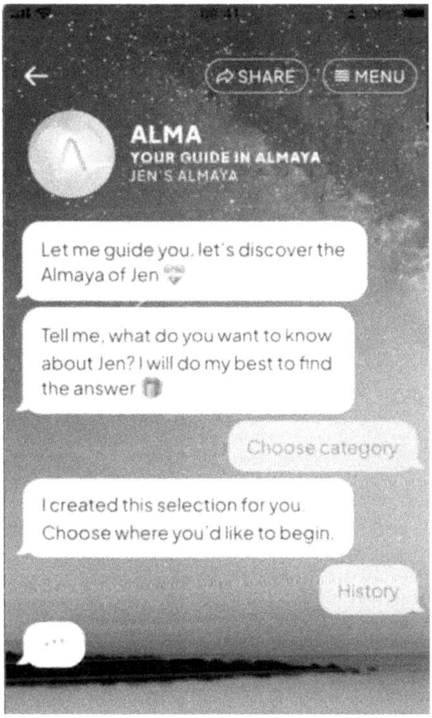

Figure 4.1 *Almaya* app screenshot, October 2024. Text reads: 'ALMA has accessed the chat 👋 All set for us to tour Jen's Legacy. Let's begin!'

endeavour. This library can then be shared with family or friends, who can interact with it as an archive or via the Alma chat. Using text or speech-to-text they can choose a category of interest or suggest that Alma surprises them with a memory. Once they have chosen a category the system then finds a relevant video from the Legacy and opens it. After playing the video, it brings the loved one back to the chat so they can pick another. When they end the conversation, the system prompts them to come back again at any time as Alma, and the Legacy, 'will be here' for them.

Case study 2: HereAfter

Much like with *Almaya*, the *HereAfter* platform features an interface within which users can easily audio record stories about their life in response to a range of audio and text prompts. They can also add photos. *HereAfter* then saves and organizes content so that it can be accessed by loved ones either in

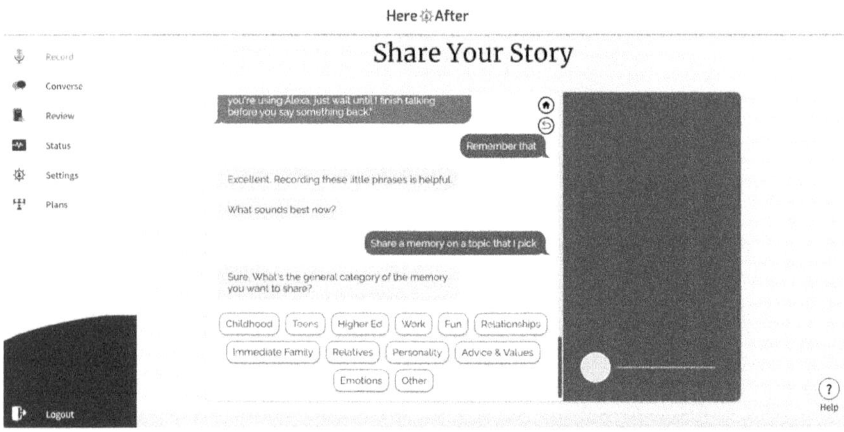

Figure 4.2 *HereAfter* screenshot, October 2024. The 'Share Your Story' interface where memories can be recorded and archived, featuring text (on the left) from the automated interviewer, and (on the right) the user making their selections.

the here and now, or posthumously. A basic demo service can be accessed for free, but paid packages allow for more interactivity, including the creation of 'life story avatars' which family members can then 'converse' with.[5] *Hereafter* purports to enable 'all of your memories' to 'live forever': 'Say hello to the virtual you. To learn about your life and personality, loved ones simply speak questions to the app. They'll see your photos and hear your memories in your actual voice.'

HereAfter uses an automated interviewer to elicit stories from users (Figure 4.2). This can be personalized to some degree by changing the sex and accent of the interviewer, and through the removal of prompts that might not be relevant. After each audio recording the user is prompted to ask the system to 'remember that', an explicitly mnemonic cue despite the fact the system is not 'remembering' in a way we might recognize cognitively. Following this prompt the system adds the memory to the archive. While recording memories (again in rather regimented categories like 'childhood', 'higher education', 'work' and 'relatives') the interviewer also asks the user to record a series of instructions to guide loved ones so that their interactions are more seamless and personalized. For example, users record a welcome and introduction: 'Hello. I'm looking forward to sharing my memories with you.'

5 After a free trial, packages range from $3.99 a month to $7.99 a month (as of February 2025).

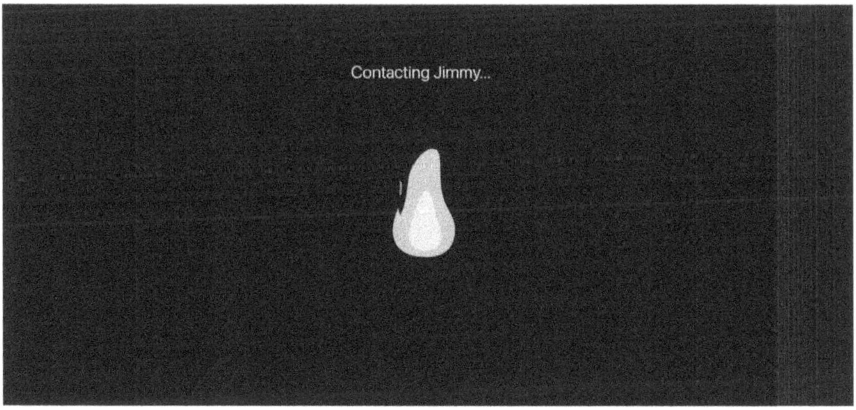

Figure 4.3 *Seance AI* is 'Contacting Jimmy' in the spirit world, screen grab September 2024.

Once shared with a loved one, that person can then interact with an 'avatar' created by the system, which gives them access to the audio recordings via a chat function. There are also instructions that enable *HereAfter* to be linked to an Amazon Alexa whereupon users can 'open Hereafter' and converse with the avatar via voice commands.

Whereas *HereAfter* and *Almaya's* algorithmic and automated capabilities are structured around fidelity to a user's original testimony, our remaining examples are more generative in their uses of AI.

Case study 3: Seance AI

Using AI and storytelling, *Seance AI* provides an interface through which users can 'connect' with 'those who have passed beyond'. The platform is very clear about the fact that this is a fictional tool through which users can explore 'the spirit world' and that it does not 'possess the ability to connect with real spirits or deceased loved ones', however the company's use of the term 'séance' is powerfully evocative.

Seance AI features a straightforward interface, where users can create an account but do not have to sign up to a package.[6] When creating a new 'séance' a user is prompted to enter details about the deceased person they want to

6 Premium access is $10 and there is an option to create a custom package.

(fictionally) interact with, including their date of birth, date of death, cause of death and religion. The system asks for some prompts about their character also – the extent to which they are agreeable, eccentric and extrovert, for example – as well as details about their close relatives and friends including names which it can then use in conversation. The programme also asks the user what mood they are in: 'nostalgic, angry, lonely, melancholic, depressed, sad, frustrated, confused, anxious, content, hopeful, grateful, excited or happy.' Finally, it asks for some sample text from the person the user wishes to connect with so that the system can 'find their voice' as if in the afterlife; understanding how they wrote so that it can 'recreate their style more accurately'. *Seance AI* then sets about 'contacting' them (Figure 4.3) for the séance to begin. During that process, and as can be seen in the image, a visual of a flickering flame indicates to the user that the AI is processing the request, focusing the user on the forthcoming moment of 'connection' with anticipation. During a séance of course, a flickering flame is understood to signal the presence of the deceased; their spirit or presence is near. Once the system has processed this request, a chat box opens so that the séance can take place (Figure 4.4). Figure 4.4 shows – on the right – the user's contributions to the chat, alongside – on the left – responses generated by the system based on the data that has been uploaded.

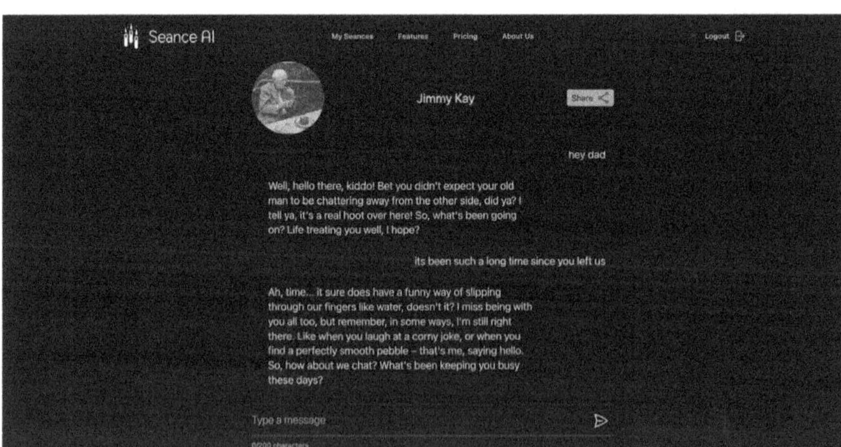

Figure 4.4 Screenshot from *Seance AI* demonstrating the chat function, October 2024.

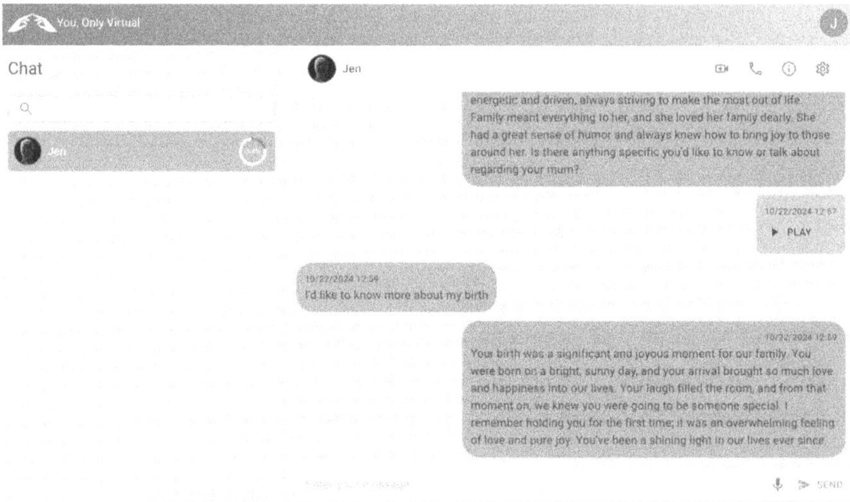

Figure 4.5 *You, Only Virtual* Versona chat. Here a user can interact with the Versona of 'Jen' using text and audio prompts, and producing text and audio outputs. Screenshot, October 2024.

Case study 4: You, Only Virtual

You, Only Virtual provides several services, including the creation of 'virtual personas' or 'Versonas'; 'designed to offer the most authentic experience possible when staying connected with those you've lost.' These take the form of multimodal text or voice deathbots, created from voice data or text extracted from social networks. The company proposes that 'as technology evolves … Versonas will reshape how we experience grief and loss, offering new ways to stay connected to those who matter most', creating 'a virtual connection beyond your imagination'. The notions of connectivity and continuance are lent on strongly here.

Creating a Versona involves firstly opening the *You, Only Virtual* portal and creating an account.[7] The user is then prompted to give their Versona a name, and to give the name of a person for whom the Versona is being created. They are asked to give the Versona a series of characteristics in a one to three sentence overview starting with 'You are …'. The more challenging part of the process then involves uploading data to 'build' the Versona. The

7 If paying monthly the service costs $39.99 (as of February 2025).

system includes instructions for the extraction of social media and SMS data for upload, as well as for uploading voice data to underpin a 'voice profile'. Once enough data has been uploaded, the Versona can be accessed and shared with the loved one for whom it has been created so that they can interact with it (as in Figure 4.5). The user can enter text or voice prompts to interact with the Versona, which responds with text and an audio file, where the Versona's 'voice profile' speaks the text.

These four services – all commercial enterprises and mostly based in Silicon Valley[8] – demonstrate a range of practices currently being developed within the digital afterlife industry. In the next section we explore their mnemo-social implications in more detail.

Deathbots and avatars as mnemonic interactants

In this section we turn our attention to the second research question: What kind of mnemonic resources do these platforms *actually* produce, and how is their use experienced and felt? Here our analysis of personal mnemo-technological practices stretches that provided in Chapter 3 given that – as we have seen – these platforms power more (or differently) complex AI afterlives, where stories and memories are primed for bidirectional interaction. We examine how the platforms introduced in the previous section utilize text, voice, video and image resources to create personalized deathbots and avatars, emphasizing the complex relationship between digital representation, embodiment and affect that they produce.

Personalization, bidirectionality and agency

As noted previously, the *You, Only Virtual* system aims for a high degree of personalization, requiring a unique dataset for each Versona a user creates, and encouraging the identification of specific characteristics in response to the prompt 'You are …'. However, we found the system's (over-)reliance on pre-set phrases such as this problematic as it tended to render the Versona's

8 We tried to diversify our range of examples here in terms of geography and business model, but this was nigh on impossible. The *Seance AI* service is provided by AE Studio in California, YOV Inc. and HereAfter Inc. are also registered in California, and *Almaya* is registered in Delaware.

communication style repetitive and clunky, as noted in the following extract from the walkthrough notes:

> *I'm instructed to give myself (as the Versona) some characteristics in 1–3 sentences and prompted to start with 'You are …' so I enter: 'You are a funny and kind person. Energetic and driven. You love your family dearly.' This refrain then appears quite relentlessly in the Versona's communications, and it is somewhat jarring.*

Hereafter enables personalization by allowing the user to adjust voice preferences and select prompts relevant to their life experiences as they record their memories into the system. There is – notionally at least – a high degree of agency over content given that users can refine and edit as they go, but the platform's categorization of memories under predetermined headings suggests a level of structure that could limit personalized expression and, by extension, curb purposeful 'mnemonic freedom' (Recuber 2023: 22). *Almaya* works in a similar way, offering personalization by allowing users to organize their recorded memories into chapters and books within a 'library', creating a structured narrative of their life. The platform's AI chatbot, Alma, then guides users through this library, retrieving content based on selected categories. This approach emphasizes discovery rather than direct conversation with the deceased; the user can choose categories or allow Alma to suggest content, making the interaction more akin to an interactive archival exploration than a dialogue. There is a tension here then where personalization and agency rub up against the homogenizing tendencies of the system (as we saw also in Chapter 3).

Rather uniquely in our sample, *Seance AI* personalizes each 'séance' by incorporating data like the deceased's date of death and cause of death. Despite having requested these details however, the system was reluctant to foreground these aspects in conversation. This was noted in our reflections as a tussle for control in the exchange: '*It does not want to talk about death: "It's not something I'd wish for anyone to dwell on. It's all a bit foggy now, to be honest … Let's chat about something a bit cheerier, yeah?"*' The platform's focus on maintaining an upbeat tone – even when discussing sensitive subjects – suggests a pre-determination which feels less than genuine. This likely demonstrates an attempt at sensitivity to matters of death and grief that was designed into the system as avoidance of those subjects ('thanatosensitivity' perhaps, Massimi and Charise 2009). Although how realistic this is in an exchange explicitly framed – however fictionally – as a postmortem 'séance' with the 'spirit realm' is questionable.

It became very apparent when using *Seance AI* just how sensitive these systems can be to different kinds of data input. For example, a séance between two people where the only variable was the source dataset changed dramatically in tone as a result. When 'trained' on text from emails the system used a fairly formal conversational style: '*Hello, it's your old friend. It's rather peculiar communicating in this manner isn't it? But rest assured, I'm here. What's on your mind?*' When trained on WhatsApp data it used an entirely different idiom however; peppered with emoji, short sentences and exclamation marks. The system was of course unable to move between these differing communicative vernaculars on the basis of conversation topics in a way that would have felt more human, and ultimately more sensitive in the context of grief.

As can be seen then, one element of personalization we consistently emphasized in our notes as important was instinctive communications, with both resonances of the deceased person's personality and a kind of interior consistency being desirable. Such consistency ensures that the 'delusions' being crafted 'sustain our motivation' to interact with the system (to borrow from Bortolotti 2023), but this is clearly something these systems struggle with at present. A Versona created by *You, Only Virtual*, for example (trained on social media data and voice notes from a mobile phone), was incongruous given the intended user of the bot, a teenager. The voice and text did not convincingly resonate as that of a parent in interaction with a (their own) young person. This highlights the need for highly specific and personalized data to create convincing representations, but it is clearly a challenge to find voice data that accurately reflects how a person communicates across varied contexts, and potentially with different users through time. As Regina E. Fabry and Mark Alfano suggest: 'Time also matters here: a chatbot fine-tuned only on the last six months of someone's correspondence will behave differently from one fine-tuned on the last ten years of their correspondence' (2024: 761).

When it came to evaluating the promise of bidirectional conversations then, practical experience with these platforms highlights the challenge of replicating genuine or authentic human connection in the digital legacy environment.

Although *You, Only Virtual* showed more bidirectional promise, there were glitches in the avatar's speech patterns, and it was often inconsistent, switching between first and third person which was unnerving, and not very human-like.

If the promise of such interactivity is that it can help support an 'imaginal dialogue' (Brescó de Luna and Jiménez-Alonso 2024: 107) with a loved one over time, we would suggest that – at least at present – there is too much friction in these systems. This is also compounded by the lack of social cues which Nancy Baym contends are key to trust in communications (Baym 2015). It is not enough for two persons or personas to 'be together' in this way, 'their interiorities must resonate' too (Bosch et al. 2022). Merely exchanging information does not bring us close enough to the affective and substantive realities of everyday conversation to narrow the ontological gap between humans and artificial companions (Bosch et al. 2022). This brings us to the notion of personhood, and reminds us of its materiality.

Personhood in the absence of bodies

The premise of digital legacy services hinges on the eventual absence of the physical body, and we were able to explore how these four platforms reckon with the extraordinary challenge of capturing human personhood digitally. That is not to say that the mediated (digital) representations produced were fully abstracted or incorporeal. On the contrary, they were often grounded in bodily traces, whether voice data, audio-visual recordings or images. The use of voice data to underpin a sound profile (in *You, Only Virtual*) highlighted the profound significance of voice as a unique marker of individual identity. While disembodied in its digital form, a voice still carries traces of the physical body, its inflections, tone and timbre hinting at the speaker's physicality (a point we return to in Chapter 5). That the synthesized voice profile created in *Life, Only Virtual* was in one case – according to the person for whom it had been made – both *too posh* and *the wrong accent* suggests that even subtle vocal cues and distortions can evoke strong responses, including emotional ones. Such reactions highlight the complex interplay between the body, voice and emotional perception, demonstrating how even seemingly disembodied traces of the body can significantly impact a user's experience, and shape their response to a digital representation. This is true both for loved ones, but also for those creating digital legacies, who will in all likelihood – due to complexities in audio perception – already be inclined to dislike hearing their own voice back, let alone a full voice profile speaking words that they have not uttered:

> *I then listen to the voice it has created for me which is disconcerting. There is something recognisable in there, but it is uncanny. It tells me a terrible joke and then starts getting a bit glitchy (the voice that is – the text is much better). It also slips between the third and first person in a rather peculiar way.*

Some platforms include photographs – for example, in *Seance AI* and *HereAfter*, suggesting a desire to preserve visual representations alongside narratives and voice recordings. Such visual elements add another layer to the construction of a digital persona, further complicating the interaction between digital representations and the absent body.

Whether the affordances of digital technologies might be able to underpin a kind of personhood in death is a point of ongoing discussion in literature about digital death. Patrick Stokes (2021) makes the case that being a person is a kind of narrative social construction and that as such, a person can live on in systems of representation and meaning – such as those we are concerned with in this chapter – after bodily death. According to Meese et al. these systems of digital representation can even 'materialise new forms of persona that persist' ontologically beyond death (Meese et al. 2015: 415).[9] Lambert et al. (2018) go as far as to propose that the persistence of 'posthumous personhood' in this way means we can begin to acknowledge a 'seeming agency of the dead, to socialise with them, and expect they deserve moral rights' (Lambert et al. 2018: 158). Jason Stanyek and Benjamin Piekut raise the question of ethics given these observations (2010), a point we return to later in this chapter.

There is an assumption that over time, and as these systems improve, they will offer increasingly sophisticated forms of multimodal communication; combining text, audio, images and video to craft more fulsome and intricate personas. If that is the case, the potentials for 'remediated memory' would seem to be amplified and diversified in these platforms, perhaps way beyond those we saw in relation to *Deep Nostalgia* (Chapter 3). Multimodal composition of these mnemonic recreations would ideally mean both seamless integration

9 To Stanyek and Piekut, this project cuts 'across clear distinctions of materiality/ discourse, technology/organicity, and bounded lifetimes/eternal deaths' (2010: 18).

of different modes into the system as data inputs, as well as the ability for loved ones to interact with digital representations built from those data in diverse ways, and across formats. Such functionality may help to secure more convincingly vivid and embodied interactions, and begin to gesture at new potentials for posthumous personhood, but this is as yet unproven. Using these platforms in their current manifestations prompted us to reflect on what aspects of a person might be considered indispensable when preserving their 'essence' in digital form, and highlighted the huge gulf between the promise of these platforms and their actual outputs. Rather than 'symbolic immortality' (Morse 2023: 241), or even 'posthumous persistence' (Savin-Baden and Burden 2018: 101), these platforms stutter towards the creation of an 'idyllic specter' (Bao and Zeng 2024: 5) that remains far out of reach.

Emotional and mnemonic resonances

Our walkthroughs did allow us to understand and experience something of these systems' emotional resonances, which we noted took a number of forms in and around these practices. Firstly, and perhaps most obviously, the underlying motivation for engaging with these platforms is to preserve memories and maintain an emotional connection with loved ones beyond life. The act of curating and sharing personal stories, even through a digital medium, can be seen as an emotionally driven effort to extend and shape a legacy. Secondly, reflecting on the points above about the *disconcerting* and *uncanny* nature of some of these representations, the potential for emotional discomfort or at least complex emotional responses, is apparent. *You, Only Virtual* could be particularly prescient here given users are encountering a digital representation that is attempting to mimic a deceased person which might evoke a particularly strong and complex mix of emotions, perhaps exacerbating feelings of loss or creating an otherwise unsettling experience. Thirdly, we noted that as users we modified the tone of our contributions (for example, in *HereAfter*, or in *Almaya*) on the basis of who we imagined might interact with them. This process of emotional editing emphasizes the user's agency in shaping the emotional tenor of a digital legacy, and in considering the potential emotional responses of future interactants. It also raises questions about whether the avatar created is really intended as a faithful and interactive reflection of an individual, or is instead a carefully curated version of self that prioritizes – and preserves in aspic – specific aspects of a personality or stories and ways of telling them. Lastly, as noted above, we found times where the tone of a deathbot or conversational avatar seemed out of step with some of the subjects being discussed (death, for example), evidencing the potential for an emotional disconnect between a system's design and a user's expectations. Such disjunctures might be jarring at best, and emotionally deleterious at worst. This highlights the need for developers of these platforms to consider the diverse emotional states of potential users and incorporate greater sensitivity in their design and functionality. In the next section we will return to this point.

We found the idea of memory to be both directly and implicitly referenced throughout these platforms, and experienced in different ways. Platforms like *Almaya* and *HereAfter* operate on the premise that memories – as distinct units of testimony that can be contained – are valuable, worth preserving through archival and narrative structures and capable of being shared digitally. This echoes Wendy Hui Kyong Chun's observation that digital media developments often rely on a conflation of memory with storage, and thus as something static. Chun argues that a memory really must be 'held' in order 'to keep it from moving or fading' (2008: 164). The everyday usage of the term 'storage' in relation to memory does interesting work Chun suggests; it glosses over the 'impermanence and volatility of computer memory', which are in fact the very aspects that *do* make it like human memory (2008: 164). *Almaya* positions this storage capability as a way to create a 'Legacy', suggesting that memories are not merely fleeting experiences but building blocks for a lasting personal narrative that can persist through time. The platform then offers two ways to engage with stored content: through a structured directory or via 'Alma', an interactive AI that guides users through the recordings. This AI interaction suggests an attempt to create a more dynamic and personalized experience of accessing memories, potentially mimicking how memories are recalled and shared in real-life contexts. *HereAfter* focuses more explicitly on an interactive conversation that allows authorized family members and friends to ask questions and receive answers in the recorded voice of the deceased. This functionality emphasizes the dialogical aspect of memory, suggesting that memories are not simply static records but can be dynamically accessed and explored bidirectionally. However, we have discussed the challenges of delivering on this promise in an authentic way.

Platforms like *Seance AI* and *You, Only Virtual* cannot faithfully re-visit memories as testimonies in this way, seeking instead to generatively evoke – playfully and fleetingly – fragments or glimpses of persons past by echoing their communicative tone and cadence. However, as mnemonic resources, we found the outputs produced by these platforms largely fell short of their functional and imaginal promise. Interacting with these mnemonic resources was an emotionally unpredictable and complex process; very occasionally because a system would seem to find the perfect story to share or tone to use, more often because the output produced would be jarring or unsettling, and sometimes because it would entirely fabricate a 'memory' that we would find problematic or vexatious.

These platforms demonstrate a tension between archival and generative memory modes then. *Almaya* and *HereAfter* lean towards the archival: they structure content for future retrieval, preserving fidelity to the original user's narrative. In contrast, *Seance AI* and *You, Only Virtual* represent memory as generative and affective, using algorithms to produce plausible, emotionally resonant responses, designed to encourage engagement (McStay 2018).

All platforms though normalize certain ways of remembering, privileging legacy and continuance, linear narratives and emotionally responsive interfaces. They also enact not just remembrance and legacy, but new forms of personhood – classified, inferred and composed by algorithms, where the agency of users is limited and distributed, and the agency of the deathbot is fabricated and ultimately deceptive. As we increasingly interact with algorithmic versions of the self and others, the lines between simulation and authenticity, manipulation and empathy, become ever more fragile.

In the next section we turn our attention to an analysis of the language and messaging used by these companies in more formal interactions with users, as well as the adequacy of the protections they grant. In doing so, our attention turns from the more infrastructural dimensions of platformization to encompass economic and governmental concerns also.

Platform governance, digital legacies and care

In this section we introduce key findings from our document analysis in response to the third research question: How is care and responsibility understood and exercised by corporate entities in relation to these practices, particularly with reference to remembering and grief? We examine how these platforms understand and manage user responsibility for the content they create, the ethical implications of data privacy and security, and the potential for misuse of these services. As noted in the introduction to this chapter, this section is supported by a quantitative and qualitative analysis of ten public facing documents across the four platforms. These include Terms of Service, Privacy Policies and Frequently Asked Questions, and are fully detailed in the Data Coda (Chapter 8). Across these documents, the platforms cover key operational areas: account management, intellectual property, data practices, user conduct, fees and payments and dispute resolution.

The tone and depth of engagement with these issues depends on the type of document. Legal documents tend to be formal and transactional, primarily concerned with compliance and risk management. FAQ documents, by contrast, more often foreground the connective, emotional aspects of platform use; that is, the attributes that actually bring users to these platforms. For example, *HereAfter's* FAQs highlight 'memories', 'stories' and 'family', while *Seance AI*'s FAQs frequently reference 'spirits' and 'storytelling'. Table 4.1 illustrates these variations in vocabulary. The FAQs use accessible everyday language and are more user-focused, aiming to address common queries in a legible and straightforward way. Due to their concise nature, these resources tend to focus on addressing immediate user concerns relating to practicality and usability without fully exploring the broader implications of the technology however, including ethical entanglements. *Seance AI*'s FAQs, for instance, clarify that the app is fictional and doesn't offer genuine spirit communication, but it doesn't address the potential emotional impact of simulated interactions, or of recreating a deceased person's personality through AI.

Table 4.2 introduces key themes from our qualitative analysis. Notably absent are references to user wellbeing and dignity, and minimal attention is paid to death and memory. Instead, the documents are more thorough on consent, copyright and data rights, as we go on to explore.

The terms of use documents focus on legalities and user obligations, a focus which clearly limits in-depth ethical discussions, often reducing complex issues like data privacy, content ownership and impersonation to clauses outlining permissible and prohibited actions. *Almaya's* Terms of Use, for example, state

Table 4.1 Distinctive Words Across the Sample (Compared to the Rest of the Corpus), According to Voyant Tools Analysis

Distinctive words (n. references)					
FAQs_Almaya	Almaya	Legacy	Alma	Answer	Videos
FAQs_Hereafter	Memories	Hereafter.ai	Story	Family	Recorded
FAQs_Seance	Spirits	AI	Seance	You're	Storytelling
Privacy_Almaya	Processing	Collected	CCPA	Opt	Owner
Privacy_Seance	Seance	AI	Policy	Collect	Personal
Privacy_ You,OnlyVirtual	Media	Social	Process	Short	Request
Terms_Almaya	Owner	Application	Shall	Service	Coupon
Terms_Hereafter	Owner	Application	Withdrawal	Shall	Service
Terms_Seance	Studio	AE [AE Studio]	Seance	Platform	AI
Terms_You,OnlyVirtual	Services	Contributions	Dispute	Legal	Arbitration

Table 4.2 Themes in the Documents

	Almaya			HereAfter		Seance			You, Only Virtual	
	FAQ	T&C	PP	FAQ	T&C	FAQ	T&C	PP	T&C	PP
Account suspension/deletion										
Age limits										
Connection/communication										
Consent										
Copyright										
Data/privacy rights										
[Mention of] Death/passing										
Dignity										
Memory										
Wellbeing of users										

that the platform does not moderate content but retains the right to remove material it deems inappropriate. *Seance AI*'s terms emphasize the fictional nature of the service and include disclaimers about simulated personalities. Users are consistently held responsible for the content they share and agree to indemnify the platforms against any claims arising from such content. These approaches prioritize legal defensibility over ethical reflection, particularly around death, grief and memory.

Privacy policies typically go deeper into data practices, reflecting a more robust response to regulatory requirements. For instance, *You, Only Virtual*'s privacy policy details data categories, legal processing bases, retention timelines, user rights and third-party sharing practices. *HereAfter* states it will not sell user information and highlights its data protection measures, but acknowledges that user data may flow through and be retained by third-party services, raising questions about the extent of user control once data leaves the original platform (we noted this in Chapter 3 also). While these documents touch on ethical questions of transparency and informed consent, broader emotional or moral considerations are left unaddressed. While users retain ownership of the content they create, platforms are often granted broad rights to reuse it. The platforms' ability to remove and reuse content at their discretion, without user recourse, reveals a power imbalance that becomes especially stark when considering deceased users and their digital legacies.

In our work we understand consent and ownership as broader issues related to dignity however, and it was telling how little this came up as a theme in the documents, either in relation to the dead or to those they leave behind. Memory – the conceptual cornerstone of these platforms – is rarely mentioned explicitly in any document outside of a few FAQ sections. Given the promotion of these platforms as part of a digital afterlife industry, users need to feel prepared and equipped to engage in these services in a meaningful way, and an absence of guidance and assurances across and between the themes of death, remembering and dignity might exacerbate the risk of a loved one misinterpreting or misusing a digital legacy or of them having unrealistic expectations in relation to meaningful connection and closure.

Though documents acknowledge potential misuse, there is a lack of detail about what those misuses might look like or to whose detriment they might lead. Issues such as manipulation, reputational damage or exploitation of sensitive information are rarely addressed. *You, Only Virtual* prohibits impersonation, but this primarily applies to living users; whether recreating a deceased person through AI constitutes impersonation remains unaddressed. *Seance AI*'s disclaimer that the app is fictional sidesteps the ethical questions raised by its emotionally evocative simulations. The ability to recreate the voice, likeness and personality of deceased individuals clearly raises complex questions about authenticity, misuse and deception, but these are an ethical grey area, and largely absent from the documents. Could a Versona, for example, be used to manipulate or deceive others, particularly if those interacting with it are not aware of its artificial nature? At present, these documents only offer a glimpse into these complexities.

As we saw in the platform overviews, companies do acknowledge the potentially sensitive nature of the services they provide in their framing and promotions, but in their formal documentation they generally avoid explicitly addressing ethical considerations related to death, grief and posthumous communication or connection. On occasion their language does more implicitly acknowledge they are in the business of digital afterlives however. *Almaya* speaks of creating a 'Legacy' and uses terms like 'Namesake' and 'Loved Ones'. These concepts suggest an awareness of mortality and the intergenerational work that might take place around a Legacy. *Seance AI* allows users to 'commune with lost friends and family via AI', also suggesting a focus on connecting with deceased loved ones, and *HereAfter* explicitly states its purpose is to allow authorized family members and friends to learn about a loved one's life by listening to their recorded memories, even after the person is no longer alive. The *HereAfter* FAQs address what happens if an account holder dies or is unable to pay the subscription fee, implying that the service is designed to outlive the person who created the recordings. *You, Only Virtual* is described as a 'patented communications system that digitally maps and recreates the relationship dynamics between you and your loved one through conversation – enabling authentic communication upon one's passing'. Despite this language, the documents focus heavily on technical and legal aspects of digital legacy creation, avoiding questions about the emotional and psychological effects on grieving users, or the nature of the authenticity on offer. Ethical concerns only surface where they intersect with data privacy or content ownership.

We noted at the start of this chapter that designers typically overlook matters of death in the development of new technologies and systems (Hollanek and Nowaczyk-Basińska 2024). Death generally comes to light as a 'glitch' in systems which reveals needs that have not been anticipated by designers (Kneese 2023). We might expect that in the design of deathbots and other services intended to outlive their users, there would be more consideration of these issues. Our research suggests this is not the case. The lack of comprehensive guidelines on responsible usage (beyond age limits in three cases), coupled with the absence of integrated grief support resources within the platforms (with only *You, Only Virtual* offering minimal resources from its website), highlights a gap in addressing the emotional and ethical complexities surrounding death and digital legacies. This lack of a robust ethical framework is a likely consequence of the relatively nascent character of these technologies and the need to shore up the legal and technical bases of these platforms to satisfy regulatory requirements. As disturbing as this might be, it should not come as a surprise given the persistent focus of technology companies on survivability over ethics (Munn 2023).

In most legal systems as it stands our obligations to the deceased are minimal at most (Harbinja 2022; Harbinja et al. 2024) given that 'death begins nonexistence' (Buben 2015: 29). But as Adam Buben (2015: 21–2) notes, this does not fit well with most peoples' 'everyday intuitions and practices related to the dead'. Elaine Kasket has highlighted the difference between a culture that remembers the dead and a culture that cares for the dead, and this distinction is both material and meaningful in light of the digital practices we have explored in this chapter (2019: 44).

Conclusion

Our analysis in this chapter suggests that the platformization of memory in digital afterlife services operates with a critically over-simplified understanding of memory, and of connection. We argue that this significantly de-emphasizes the extensive suite of ethical considerations associated with these digital practices, and the role of emotion and social context in memory formation and recall. These AI systems are framed as extensions or remediations of previous cultural practices of communication and remembrance, a framing which no doubt mitigates anxieties about their use and encourages adoption, at the same time as it obscures the ethical implications of 'chatting with the dead'. This is typical of our 'platform society' where differing value systems, as well as private and public interests, find themselves in conflict (van Dijck 2017).

Voinea (2023) suggests that deathbots can help us not only to remember a person, but to 'recreate what we were in connection with them'; not preserving their existence, but rather keeping alive 'that part of yourself that was molded by your relationship with them'. This is perhaps a more prescient take on the potentials of digital afterlife services. For the living they propose novel modes of commemoration (Bao and Zeng 2024: 4) supported by a novel repertoire in remediation. In practice however the platforms in our analysis – owned by private companies and largely emerging from Silicon Valley – do a pretty poor job of what Lambert et al. call 'death work' (2018); the personalized emotional labour associated with bereavement. The AI afterlives they create are commercial products, functioning as 'serviceable others' rather than 'equivalent' ones (Bosch et al. 2022). These services are being developed with an emphasis on legal and technical requirements, rather than human values. Given these companies are in the business of producing and archiving 'data bodies (a term we introduced in Chapter 3) this observation is ethically consequential; data becomes proxy flesh, offering a facsimile of presence.

Platforms like *Almaya* and *HereAfter* archive and structure memories, facilitating access via AI as an end in itself. This undervalues the emotional and relational aspects of memory. The memories produced are too flat, too rigid, too tame somehow. But the more generative outputs of *Seance AI* and *You, Only Virtual* don't fare much better. They cannot faithfully re-visit 'memories' of events or people, seeking instead to generatively evoke fragments or glimpses of deceased persons. We found the 'conversational pasts' (Hoskins 2024) they facilitated to be wholly insincere and very weird. At best, in their current manifestations, these platforms structure only 'pseudo-bonds' with those who have passed (Lindemann 2022); contrived apparatus and laboured continuance.

As commemoration becomes more and more an interaction between human and non-human actors, including AI (Smit et al. 2024), the digital afterlife industry will need to better understand the situated and emotional complexities of grief, and of memory. Indeed, there is a strong commercial imperative for doing so; more human systems will likely fare better in the market (Galvão et al. 2021). As Tama Leaver (2019) has argued, recognizing the precarity of these services, 'contemporary start-ups need, at the very least, to come up with ethical, not just technical, approaches for dealing with the unlikely event of their own success.'

5

Datafied bodies on stage and screen

Whereas in previous chapters we highlighted personal interactions with AI afterlives, in this chapter we explore these developments in relation to more mainstream media output and the processes of cultural memory-making they are associated with. We start from the observation that working with AI afterlives is becoming increasingly commonplace within the creative industries, and that the 'revival' of cultural figures – including singers, actors and celebrities, for example – is likely to accelerate. Through an in-depth exploration of nine case studies we examine how public narratives about these developments are evolving over time, as these practices become both more familiar, and more (or differently) contested.

As we will demonstrate, these narratives expose deep ethical questions about legacy, ownership and custodianship: How should we work with digital (or digitized) human remains of public figures and cultural 'icons' and when shouldn't we? In what ways do AI afterlives on stage and screen shape cultural memory work? Who has legal rights and duties for datafied bodies within these contexts? And what are the implications of these practices for the future of labour in the stage and screen industries? Our analysis in this chapter is deeply informed by emerging work on virtual performers, idols and influencers (Stanyek and Piekut 2010; Harris 2013; McLeod 2015; Jørgensen et al. 2017; Ng and Box 2023; Matthews and Nairn 2023), but pushes this scholarship in a new direction by exploring more specifically the mnemonic and historical concerns of this book. Before presenting our analysis, we offer some context on debates about synthetic media within the creative economy.

Synthetic media in the creative economy

Synthetic media present a series of challenges for the creative industries which are intensifying as AI (and in particular now generative AI) becomes more embedded. These challenges are multifaceted and have epistemological, ethical, social, legal and policy dimensions. Some of these challenges connect with debates in earlier chapters – about deepfakes, for example – as they relate to the trustworthiness of audio-visual content and synthetic media's potentials for impersonation and manipulation. Other challenges we have not yet considered at length in the book – such as synthetic media's impacts on employment, on notions of creativity and on legal principles such as copyright. In this section we briefly review these debates.

One of the most contentious issues is AI's potential to impact on employment within the creative industries (De Cremer et al. 2023; Epstein and Hertzmann 2023; Jiang et al. 2023). While some scholars express concern that it may lead to widespread job losses (Bender 2023), others argue that it will prompt a transformation – rather than a disappearance – of creative work. Ziv Epstein and Aaron Hertzmann (2023), for instance, reject the idea that AI spells the 'end of art', suggesting instead that it represents a new medium that will redefine creative roles and practices. They acknowledge short-term threats but ultimately foresee AI enabling new forms of creativity. Similarly, Vinchon et al. (2023) predict that AI will serve as a valuable tool in the creative process, while humans retain high-level conceptual and strategic roles. Mark Fenwick and Paulius Jurcys (2023) call for a departure from the Romantic ideal of solitary, human creativity, advocating instead for a view of creativity as a multi-staged process involving networks of human, corporate and machine actors. Stuart Marshall Bender (2023) likewise encourages a rethinking of the divide between 'creative skillsets' and 'creative mindsets', emphasizing the continued importance of transferable conceptual abilities. Together, these perspectives suggest that the future of creative labour will likely depend on how effectively practitioners can integrate AI into their workflows and reorient their skillsets accordingly.

Copyright presents another complex terrain. Concerns include the legality of data scraping – particularly of copyrighted material – for training AI models (Fenwick and Jurcys 2023), as well as the question of whether AI-generated outputs qualify for copyright protection (Zibner 2019; Hugenholtz and Quintais 2021). Scholars have debated whether such works meet the originality threshold and, if so, who should own the rights to them (Abbott and Rothman 2023). This legal uncertainty complicates the commercialization of AI-generated content, with many companies hesitant to proceed without clearer guidance on potential infringement risks. Questions of authorship also arise, including whether a work can ever be wholly AI-generated. Fenwick and Jurcys (2023) argue that a 'human in the loop' remains essential – either during input or output stages – but acknowledge that this may not always be the case in future developments. The 'human in the loop' as a solution to AI's ethical shortcomings is well-articulated across numerous contexts, but is not without its critics who argue that human judgment may not be enough to correct the underlying flaws and biases in AI models, that it will provide only superficial oversight, and will be too difficult to scale in practice (Cranor 2008; Calo 2015; O'Neil 2016; Angwin et al. 2016).

Despite concerns about creative labour and the disruptive potentials of AI, several studies foresee benefits of synthetic media for the creative industries, especially if underpinned by robust ethical and regulatory structures. These include applications in creative education (Bender 2023), entertainment and personalized user experiences, particularly in advertising (Westerlund 2019; Millière 2022). Optimistically, scholars like Gelayol Safavi and Sepehr Ghazinoory (2024) argue that AI will be part of a suite of technological solutions that will result in increased interconnectedness, efficiency and adaptability for businesses, including creative ones. However, unlike traditional manufacturing, creative endeavours often rely on subjective judgment, artistic expression and human-driven innovation, and as such, creatives may face unique obstacles in integrating these technologies. Several studies have explored how AI reconfigures the very notion of creativity, suggesting that definitions may need to evolve to better capture practices of co-creativity and human–AI collaboration (Magni et al. 2024; Wingström et al. 2022; Bender 2023; Vinchon et al. 2023).

Any turn to synthetic media thus points to significant regulatory challenges for the creative industries, which are clearly difficult for policymakers to respond to in a fast-changing landscape. Existing frameworks are rooted in human authorship and reflect long-established values around artistic, musical and narrative production. Adapting these to account for AI-driven or hybrid creative processes may demand far-reaching reforms.

In this chapter, we explore public narratives about uses of synthetic media in the creative economy with a specific focus on 'afterlives'. We have carried out an analysis of 793 news reports from international English language publications covering a series of mainstream synthetic media 'revivals'. This was followed by a systematic thematic analysis of a subset of 150 of those articles (full details of this work package can be found in Chapter 8, the Data Coda). This longitudinal study captures debates spanning more than a decade (2012–23), and charts how – across a range of technologies, including now AI – synthetic afterlives have become part of our more collective cultural horizon. The analysis reveals who is speaking and shaping debates about these approaches in the context of the challenges we have identified, which themes, values and related discourses are activated, and how discussions about ethics play out in relation to these high-profile cases. It also allows us to examine both how debates about each case, and about the issues in more general terms, have been evolving over time.

Tupac, Hepburn, Kardashian and more

The mainstreaming of AI afterlives on stage and screen suggests an unabashed and unprecedented commodification of the past which we explore further in this chapter. This 'puppeteering of pastness' (Ng and Bax 2023: 2) becomes a way to sell, to craft 'experiences', and of course to entertain, and it does so on the basis of these stars' perceived status and ongoing resonance with the public. This suggests there are mnemonic dimensions also; these 'icons' are understood to have value as shared cultural resources, value that can be materialized and then commercialized.

The nine case studies we discuss in this chapter are as follows:

Tupac Shakur

More than fifteen years after his death in 1996, Tupac Shakur became the star turn at the 2012 Coachella music festival in California, when he appeared on stage in front of more than 100,000 festivalgoers alongside Dr Dre and Snoop Dogg as a 'hologram'. The effect was created by the Digital Domain Media Group using a version of what has been called 'Pepper's ghost', an illusion created when images are projected onto an angled surface. Permissions had been provided by Shakur's family.

Audrey Hepburn

In 2013, Audrey Hepburn – who had died in 1993 – was featured in an advert for Galaxy chocolate. Using a body double, visual effects techniques and computer graphics to model the actress, Framestore were able to create a replica of nineteen-year-old Hepburn with permissions in place from the Hepburn estate. Hepburn is seen riding a bus along the Amalfi Coast to a soundtrack of Moon River (famously sung by the star), before disembarking and enjoying some chocolate in the back of a classic Mercedes-Benz driven by a handsome stranger.

Bruce Lee

Bruce Lee, who died in 1973, was 'revived' (following family approval) by advertising agency BBH for a Johnny Walker whiskey advert in 2013. In the ninety-second spot Lee – created by The Mill using a similar technique as in the Hepburn case – can be seen on a balcony in Hong Kong, as the voiceover quotes his philosophy in Mandarin (with subtitles): 'Empty your mind, be formless, like water'

Robin Williams

When Robin Williams died in 2014 it emerged that he had placed tight restrictions on the 'exploitation' of his likeness for a period of twenty-five years after his death, meaning there could not be any authorized outputs until 2039 at the earliest. After his death there was considerable interest in these restrictions as, at the time, this kind of estate planning was extremely innovative.

Carrie Fisher

Carrie Fisher's infamous depictions of Leia (first Princess, then Master) in the Star Wars franchise continued even after her death in 2016. Following much debate amongst the team about how best to recreate Leia for the 2019 release of *The Rise of Starwalker*, the decision was made to avoid CGI techniques, instead creating her presence by splicing shots from old, deleted scenes into the film.

Whitney Houston

In 2020, nine years after her death, a 'hologram' of Whitney Houston went on tour so fans could enjoy 'An Evening with Whitney Houston'. The show, which was put on by Base Entertainment, featured a four-piece band, four dancers and 'Whitney'. Here, a computer-generated face was grafted onto a body double creating footage that was projected onto a theatre drop or scrim. Houston's family had approved the show.

Robert Kardashian

In 2020, for Kim Kardashian's fortieth birthday, her (then) husband Kanye West worked with production company Kaleida to create a 'hologram' of her father, the late Robert Kardashian. Later that day Kardashian shared a video of the hologram on social media alongside her reaction: 'It is so lifelike and we watched it over and over, filled with emotion … Thank you so much Kanye for this memory that will last a lifetime.'

Elis Regina

In 2022, Volkswagen released an advert featuring popular Brazilian singer Maria Rita duetting with her deceased mother Elis Regina. Regina, who died in 1982, was depicted using a body double with digitally recreated face grafted on top using AI. The company stated that it had the blessing of the family to produce the advert.

Miłogost Reczek

Polish actor Miłogost Reczek was well known for his voice work on video games. After his death in 2021 at the age of sixty, he went on to voice the character of Viktor Vektor in Cyberpunk 2077. CD Projekt Red hired another actor to voice the new lines, before processing the recordings with an AI-powered voice synthesizer to fit the voice of Reczek. This was done with the permission of Reczek's family.

As can be seen, these cases span a range of technical initiatives in order to 'revive' cultural icons from archival materials (voice, image or video data). They allow us to explore the discourses associated with these varied practices – from the emergence of what have been termed 'holograms' of cultural figures (Shakur, Houston and Kardashian in our sample) to debates about 'voice clones' and 'digital twins' (Regina and Reczek). Some of our cases (Hepburn and Lee) detail the use of body doubles and face 'swapping', emphasizing the fusion of datafied bodies which we introduced in Chapter 3.

Our other two cases come at these issues from rather different perspectives. One (Williams) demonstrates an actor going to considerable lengths to resist these approaches being used posthumously. The other (Fisher) centres a decision *not* to use such approaches and instead to use previously shot and discarded footage, but resultant confusion amongst viewers (of *Star Wars: The Rise of Skywalker*) about what it was they were actually seeing on screen.

We can see how talk about these techniques unfolds by exploring the presence of key terms across the full sample (n. 793), an example of which can be seen in Figure 5.1. The graphic, which organizes cases by date, shows the relative frequency of talk about techniques in our dataset, with 'hologram' ordering talk about particular cases, and 'artificial intelligence' becoming a theme in the later reports. Other key technical terms such as 'projection', 'CGI', 'twin', 'clone' or 'deepfake' crop up infrequently, and are correlated very closely with particular cases:

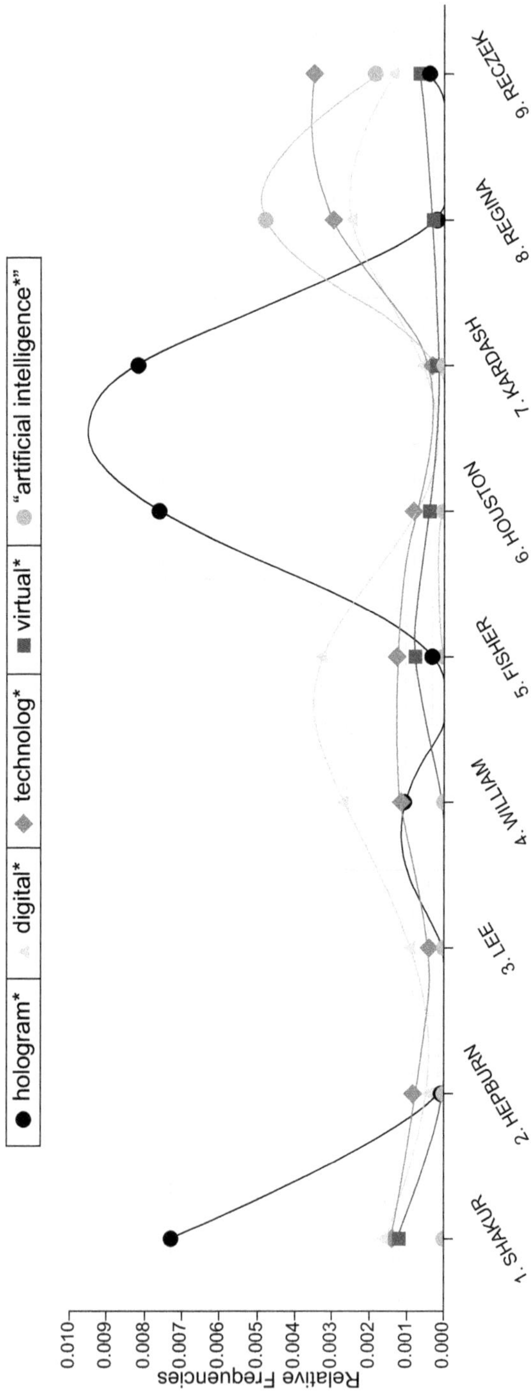

Figure 5.1 Key terms ordered across the different cases.

Table 5.1 Overarching Themes in the Sample and the Percentage of Articles that Feature Each

Theme	Percentage of articles
Ethical Issues	73
Bodies or Revival	64
Emotional Resonance	59
Technology	56
Fidelity	53

In the next section, we introduce a series of themes from the analysis which explore the framing of these practices, and of debates about them.

Findings from the analysis

> *It's the kind of sentence you have to read twice: 'Kanye West surprised wife Kim Kardashian with a hologram of her late father, Robert Kardashian, for her 40th birthday.' Blink. Blink. What? Then: of course he did; this is not a couple that gives one another bath salts.* [RK12]

In our thematic analysis of the subset of reports (n. 150), a number of macro-level themes were identified across the cases. Themes reflected in each article were recorded, and as can be seen in Table 5.1, there was some substantial overlap, with most articles recording multiple themes. As the table shows some 73 per cent of articles referenced ethical issues at some point (these are sub-categorized in Table 5.2), 64 per cent of articles talked about bodies and their revival – whether in terms that were positive, negative or mixed – and 59 per cent referred to the emotional resonances of these synthetic afterlives. 56 per cent of articles discussed the technology underpinning these practices,[1] and 53 per cent debated accuracy or realism in representation, what we call here the fidelity of these recreations.[2]

1 49.5 per cent positive, 11 per cent negative and 39 per cent mixed across all instances.

2 The overarching figures in Table 5.1 mask some nuance in the data however, such as the fact that all articles for cases 4, 8 and 9 referenced ethical issues, whereas fewer did for the others.

Table 5.2 Detailed Breakdown of the Ethical Issues Theme and the Percentage of Total Articles that Feature Each

Ethical issues referenced	Percentage of articles
Consent or Permissions	45
Memory or Legacy	36
Potential for Profiteering	29
Future of Creative Work or Labour	21
(In)humanity	9
Deception	8
Datafication	1

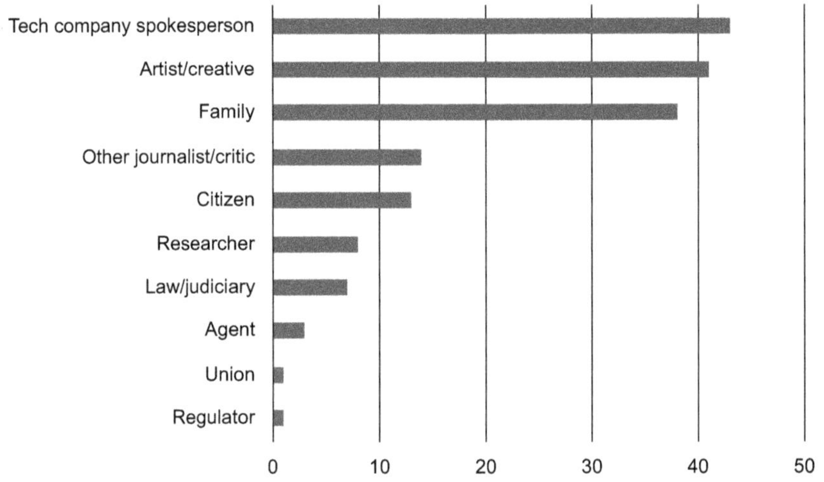

Figure 5.2 Breakdown of sources cited across the subset of reports (n. 150 reports).

One unique contribution of this study has been the assessment of who gets to speak about these issues within reporting, and our findings on this question can be seen in Figure 5.2 a breakdown of 171 spokespersons across the ninety-two articles in our subset that cited sources:

The data show that it was largely technology company spokespeople, creative practitioners and family members who are given space within reporting to comment on the synthetic afterlives of cultural icons. This is good news in a context where (as we will demonstrate) there are widespread concerns about consent and the future of creative work. But the frequency of technology company spokespersons (25 per cent of all sources) should give us pause for thought given how deeply and consequentially enmeshed (and invested) those companies are in these developments. Unsurprisingly, those spokespersons gave largely positive assessments of these technologies, their future potentials and trajectories. The prominence (even dominance, according to McKelvey et al. 2024) of technology firms and investors within discourses about AI has been noted in other studies, with the result that algorithmic systems begin to seem inevitable rather than the product of 'human choices and power arrangements' (Walker 2022).

Conversely, we found there is an almost complete lack of voices from unions, agents, regulators or the law. This is concerning given the ethical issues we go on to highlight in this chapter. As Jenna Ng and Nick Bax have noted, 'the questionable ethics of "resurrecting" dead artists to generate profits … require[s] specialist literacies beyond lay people, and currently rest unchecked in the power of media and technology companies' (Ng and Bax 2023: 15). Our data support this assessment.

The remainder of this chapter will examine themes from our dataset in further detail, introducing insights from the subset of articles (n. 150) and putting them into conversation with the literature. This is done in two sections. Firstly, we explore how bodies and their 'revival' are discussed in the articles, including assessments of the ghostly, creepy and weird qualities of these synthetic afterlives, and the recurring trope of digital 'magic'. Secondly, we introduce key ethical issues with respect to memory and legacy, and the future of creative work. We then close with some concluding remarks.

Bodies, revival and digital 'magic'

Tupac is alive. I know he is because I saw him. [T6]

In this section we explore how news reports in our sample reference the corporeal and temporal logics of personhood, and how they make sense of technology's capacity to unsettle these through synthetic (including AI) afterlives.

As noted earlier, 64 per cent of articles in the data subset reflected on seeing a person 'come back to life' through these approaches. The majority of articles referencing this theme presented a mixed account of these practices (58 per cent of articles where this theme was present) demonstrating some ambivalence in relation to reanimation in this way and whether it might be considered a good thing. The remaining 42 per cent of articles were equally split between those that were wholly positive, and those that were wholly negative in their assessment.

In the case of the Tupac Shakur revival these discussions often unfolded quite playfully, as if Tupac's holographic form was in some way '*inevitable*' [TS1]. The star's mythic and venerated status – which has endured since his death through rumoured sightings of the star and an extensive series of posthumous artistic endeavours – is a feature of these articles, with frequent reference to the persistent legacy of Tupac and the circumstances of his death. '*What could be more fitting than to resurrect a man who many still believe never died in the first place?*' [TS1] says one commentator, and another concludes that '*He has had one of the most remarkable afterlives of any probably dead celebrity*' [TS19]. According to Ken McLeod, Tupac's simultaneous 'ethereality' and sense of 'presence' have been highlighted in innumerable ways since his death in 1996 (McLeod 2015; see also, Sutherland 2023), yet his 'appearance' at Coachella proved particularly influential. For Harris (2013), this is because it coupled narratives about Tupac somehow surviving his own death with the 'sheer novelty' of this technology; the resultant performance produced 'maximum impact' both at Coachella and on social media in the moments that followed. The above mentioned quotes begin to reflect commentators' assessments that this kind of resurrection '*illustrates a less rigid interface between technology, life and death*' [TS14]. In some reports however this plasticity is seen as a far from positive development. One critic suggests that the Whitney Houston hologram is akin to '*grave robbing*' [WH7] and another proposes that the Robert Kardashian hologram amounts to a '*posthumous molestation by death tech*' [RK11]; a form of '*interference*' [RK11] with his humanity or personhood which is unwelcome.

In other reports concerns about a '*missing human element*' [WH1] came across strongly:

> '*The reanimated dead are never the people they were before. Oh, they sing the same, and rap the same, and have the same distinctive tattoos and hand gestures. But they don't have the complexity, or the humanity, to really compel our interest … the Tupac who walked on stage last week was a thing of digital shreds and patches.*' [TS19]

> '*And as oddly captivating as it was, it proved something that should give hope for humanity: the robots haven't won yet. A hologram is no substitute for the real thing.*' [WH6]
>
> '*These recreations are, at their very best, a poor facsimile … but at their worst, a horrendous Frankensteinian monster.*' [MR10]

Some commentators were keen to assert that humanity '*can't be reproduced*' [WH1] through these approaches, and references to Frankenstein and zombies were not uncommon (as we saw in Chapter 3). Darren Ellis and Ian Tucker make the case that the 'human' is often used 'as a category to critique digitality' and set it up as in some way threatening (2021: 1), and we see this in evidence here.

Recent scholarship on virtual idols can help us to understand the material complexities of these synthetic revivals, and the profound forms of human-machine hybridization that references to Frankenstein seem to imply. Daniel Black notes that 'the virtual idol is a literalization of the idea that the body can be reduced to a set of information' (Black 2008), yet Nick Prior argues that such idols are not 'non-material' (Prior 2017). Rather, their materiality is 'composed of diffuse digital bits spread exponentially' through the circuits of corporate media (Prior 2017). The embodiment of virtual idols – much like the embodiment of Shakur, Hepburn or Regina – 'emerges in multi-scalar processes that fold together innumerably relayed materials' (Prior 2017), some simulated, and others not. Prior concludes that the notion of 'assemblages' perhaps more fittingly captures how a virtual idol's form converges as a result of varied human and non-human inputs or 'forces': 'silicon and carbon, corporate and grassroots, algorithmical and fleshy, local and infrastructural' (Prior 2017). As Sy Taffel (2021: 38) notes, thinking in terms of assemblages underscores entities as 'a series of nested systems' rather than 'holistic totalities', which is in keeping with the notion of remediation introduced in earlier chapters (Bolter and Grusin 2000). Jenna Ng and Nick Bax push this observation further with reference to the Abba-tars of ABBA Voyage, suggesting that in the context of 'posthumous performances' formed of data, 'the real and the virtual become actually the same with different degrees of information density or resolution' (2023: 6). As a result, they conclude, 'the digital apparition beckons a new epistemology of the real' (2023: 6) which must reckon with the impact of technology companies, infrastructures and devices on the materiality, temporality and spatiality of personhood. It must also reckon with how normative assumptions inform design decisions about bodies and how they move within these nested systems; assumptions that are often based on the generic body measurements of 'those who are male, white, 'able-bodied', and of unremarkable weight' (Harvey 2024: 2).

The persistence of terms like '*revival*', '*resurrection*' and '*alive*' in our sample suggest that such a reckoning may be underway, although there were a handful of commentators who actively resisted this framing, making the case that technology infrastructures (and perhaps corporatization also) are irrevocably in tension with being 'animate':

> *It is clearly no coincidence that this bizarre Frankensteinian experiment took place in California, home to the world's most advanced computer engineers. It is also no surprise that in a culture infected by digital utopianism it was reported using words like 'resurrected' and 'returned from the dead' when in reality the new Tupac is a digital zombie manipulated by its creator, not an animate being, not 'resurrected' at all.* [TS29]

However such an assessment underplays how comprehensively digital practices – including their manipulation by those who code – already shape our understanding of what it means to experience personhood and (a)liveness in the twenty-first century. Frew et al. note that binary distinctions between the real and authentic on the one hand, and the virtual, fake and inauthentic on the other, are increasingly 'obsolete and distractive' (2023: 203; see also, Cull 2015) given how our physical and digital lives are bridged in ways ever more ingrained, embodied and networked (Cleland 2009; Kneese 2023). As N. Katherine Hayles observes, 'our bodies are no less actively involved in the construction of virtuality than in the construction of real life' (1996: 1).

The varied approaches to synthetic revival in our case studies participate in a long history of media use designed for purposes that might be understood as 'intermundane' (Stanyek and Piekut 2010: 14; see also, Leaver 2019; Sisto 2020; Kopelman and Frosh 2023), that is, they extend across or through human life and death. As one of the commentators in our sample noted, human beings '*find it hard to part with their dead*' [RK11] and this is evidently also true when it comes to parting with 'our' cultural icons. There is persistent reference to '*immortality*' [TS29] across our sample, where death becomes '*in many respects … temporary*' [CF10], as these technologies undermine '*the finiteness of life*' [ER3] and enable artists to '*live forever*' [AH20]. These observations are not new of course, as a commentator on the Tupac case study noted: technology '*has always helped humans to refashion the deceased into what we want them to be. From the phonogram to the videocam to the hologram, advances in audio-visual media have altered the mechanics of mourning as well as those of entertainment. At Coachella, they did both*' [TS14]. Echoing what we have seen in previous chapters, these approaches grant cultural icons a kind of 'symbolic immortality' (Sherlock 2013) through 'ad hoc forms of transcendence' that are available to us in the online age, and which can 'salve' fears about our mortality, particularly in secular populations (Recuber 2023: 21; see also, Nowaczyk-Basińska and Kiel 2024).[3] The issue of ethics begins to emerge then as a profound point of consideration given the potential for exploitation that emerges in the context of entertainment, as artists continue to 'live' not only through time, but across any medium: '*From the world of the deceased, these citizens are dredged up to serve roles for the living*' [RK11]. We consider these consequences further in the next section.

The 'revival' of dead cultural figures is, according to F. Cull, increasingly being sought by audiences so that they can 'invoke' (2015: 111) or 'connect to' the past (119), but also so they might experience an artist's work 'in a new setting, time and place' (Matthews and Nairn 2023: 286). At the heart of these approaches' appeal then is the production of '*spatial and circumstantial displacement*' [ER3]. One of the striking things we might note about these 'revivals' is the decision in many cases to create a likeness of the artist or performer as a younger person. 'Posthumous performativity' (Hjorth and Hinton 2019) clearly opens up avenues for the 'puppeteering' of past selves (Ng and Bax 2023: 2):

> '*This technology trend would have serious implications in the image and aging obsessed world of Hollywood, where it is increasingly common for actors to have their faces and bodies scanned while they are still young.*' [RW7]

3 As compared to more theological accounts of immortality as an eternal afterlife granted by a deity.

> '*The basic limit – one human, the voice they own, the languages they know, and the age they are – that's now something we can change*.' [MR10]

Such 'temporal discombobulation' is not new, and is in some senses a characteristic of all recorded, and now digital, media (Ng and Bax 2023; Kitchin 2023), but Ng and Bax make the case that the subversion of conventional chronology evident with virtual performers (in their case the ABBA-tars of ABBA Voyage) discombobulates differently, and is thus consequential. These 'de-aged digital apparitions' seem to exist both in and outside of time simultaneously (Ng and Bax 2023: 12). The body is freed from the biology of aging and can be refashioned through the latest technology, but this can be done in a way that matches consumer tastes ad infinitum, again suggesting lines of ethical tension which we pick up in the next section.

Despite the ambitions of producers to revisit what might be understood as a quintessential – even iconic – look or era for a cultural figure, commentators in our sample were wary of 'perfection', especially if it meant a synthetic recreation was in danger of falling into the uncanny valley. Lou et al. (2022) note that synthetic recreations are more convincing and more acceptable to viewers where they possess human-like flaws and don't look too 'doll-like'. This reflects Daniel Black's assessment of how crucial it is to the success of virtual idols that they 'appear like a human body, rather than a piece of technology' (Black 2008). Where there is 'pure exteriority' and smooth unbroken surfaces, audiences may struggle to get past their fabricated or uncanny qualities (Black 2008). We saw this critique reflected in a number of our case studies, with the synthetic Hepburn referred to as '*more of a creepy Stepford Wife than adorable onscreen coquette*' [AH7] and Houston as a '*plasticised dolly*' [WH10]. Critics noted the eerie '*impressiveness*' [WH5] of the Houston hologram in particular, but found it wanting when it came to authenticity in performance because it was deemed to be somehow *too* flawless. Whitney Houston was of course a huge singing talent, but one who often struggled to perform towards the end of her career. In hologrammatic form the way this humanity and vulnerability was obscured made her digital likeness too one-dimensional for many commentators in our study. Here, the producers' decision to disrupt the chronology of Houston's life made her less convincing and accessible to fans who were acutely aware of the singer's complex emotional life:

> *We pay to see pop stars not just for the music, but also to bask in the glow of their charisma. Houston was a beloved figure for the emotion she poured into her performances, even when they were erratic and under par, as they often were in her final years. You felt you were getting the whole person. Seeing a hologram of Houston nodding her head in an imitation of depth of feeling just isn't the same, and the audience knew it. 'I would like to sing some love songs. Is that all right with you?' she asked. Very few felt the need to answer her.* [WH6]

When it comes to reviving these cultural icons then the uncanny valley is a matter not only of appearance but of presence, and even of co-presence, when it comes to meeting the affective and experiential demands of audiences (Matthews and Nairn 2023; McLeod 2015). This should not be surprising given how deeply connected notions of presence already are to the emotional, psychological and communicative impact of any performance, but we are only beginning to understand how these are experienced in the context of synthetic recreations. We advance the concept of 'contested presence' here to draw attention to the ethical, cultural and epistemological stakes of reanimating memory through synthetic media – foregrounding how presence itself becomes a product of technological design, power asymmetries and competing claims over narrative, identity and authenticity. As another commentator suggested in the Fisher coverage: '*A performance is a lot more than a physical resemblance*' [CF17].

As we noted earlier, 53 per cent of articles included commentary about the fidelity of productions (how realistic, or how authentic they were). 37 per cent of mentions were positive (it is realistic, it is authentic),[4] 18 per cent negative[5] and 45 per cent provided very mixed assessments. This reflects a fair amount of ambivalence about on the one hand how '*striking*' these remediations were, but on the other their '*creepy*', '*ghostly*' or '*weird*' qualities. This echoes our findings from Chapter 3:

4 '*For my birthday Kanye gave me the most significant gift of my life. A special surprise from heaven. A hologram of my dad. It's so realistic! We saw him again and again, full of emotion,*' Kim wrote on Twitter [RK7], '*With such skill and precision you will have to look at it a couple of times to work out that it is, in fact, not real*' [BL10].

5 '*A hologram is a clinical presentation, a loop of exaggerated tics. Besides, I couldn't, even for an instant, suspend disbelief and think he was up there*' [T6], '*There is a whole doctorate paper to be written on the levels of reality and sad, self-lying artificiality at play there*' [T6].

> '*Her movements are surprisingly lifelike but her skin looks like it has never even heard of a pore.*' [AH2]
>
> '*A visually striking effort, yet implausible.*' [RK11]
>
> '*It's an impressive bit of techno-syncopation, but their [the dancers] flesh and blood corporeality only points up her essential alien weirdness.*' [WH10]

McLeod describes this ambivalence well when he notes that audiences are attracted to the familiarity of these representations, while at the same time being 'repulsed' by their seemingly 'artificial, trans- or post-human unfamiliarity' (McLeod 2015). In Figure 5.3 the presence of terms such as 'ghost/ly' 'creepy/creepiness' and weird/er/est/ly/ness', as well as 'amazed/ing' and 'uncanny/iness' can be tracked across our larger sample (n. 793):

The recreations of Shakur, Fisher and Reczek are considered especially 'ghost'-like, and 'weirdness' is correlated with Houston and Kardashian in particular. The Kardashian case study is framed as '*bizarre*' also, but not out of keeping with the '*circus*' [RK2] of his '*eternally weird*' family [RK17].

In our sample the way the past is understood to haunt the present – in a spectral or intangible way – can be understood as hauntological: '*Many of the dead stars being resurrected today certainly didn't realise that they might undergo a digital second coming*' [F4]. Remnants of these digital icons – their aesthetic and the narratives they connect us to – resurface, and linger even though they can no longer be fully realized. In this sense synthetic recreations might be considered 'functional specters' (Gruvæus 2023: 108) in that they serve a purpose in making those connections. More broadly, digital technologies, and perhaps especially AI, can be understood as hauntological given how they reproduce the ghosts of past human labour, decisions and patterns, and how tied they are to our uncertainty about the future. Code, according to Wendy Hui Kyong Chun (2011: 50), 'channels the ghost that we imagine runs the machine – that we see as we don't see – when we gaze at our screen's ghostly images'. These 'ghostly images' – and the feelings of dubiety and apprehension their 'creepiness' produces – pervade reporting with a sense that 'new time-spaces' are emerging (Kitchin 2023: 44).

In reanimating past human actions and behaviours for new contexts these approaches can also be understood as attempts at (digital) necromancy; ways of communicating with or raising the dead, often through what are understood

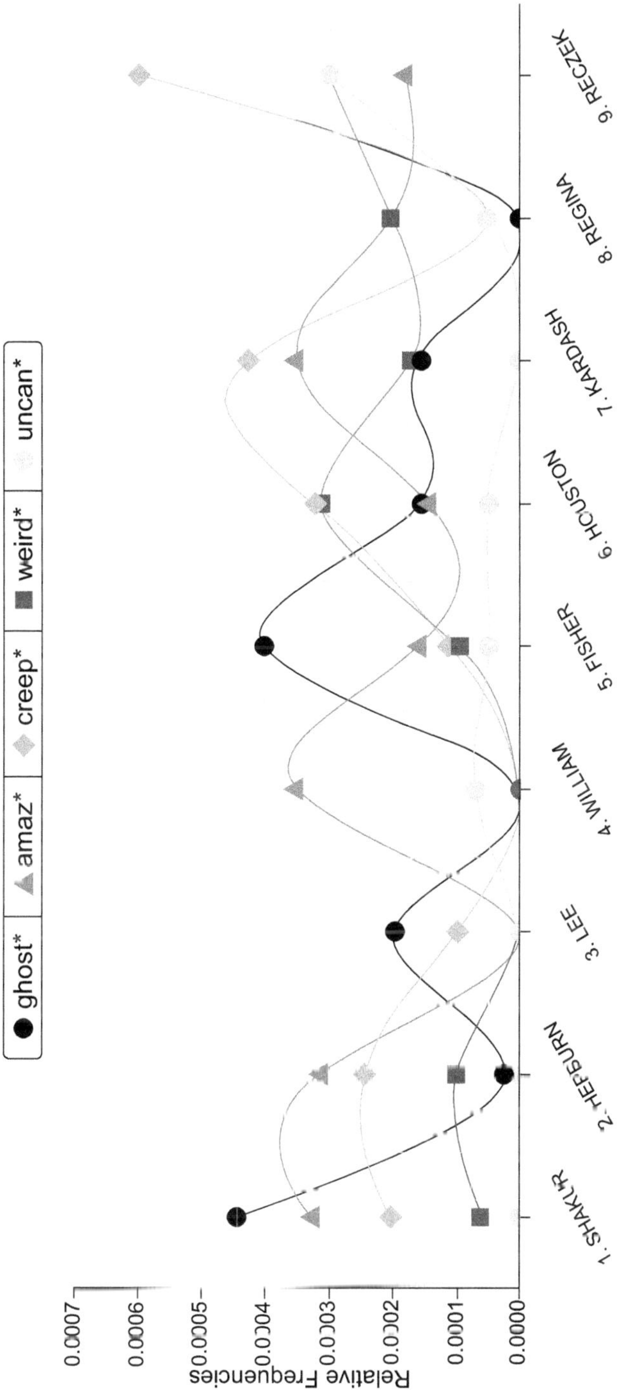

Figure 5.3 Key terms relating to ghostliness or creepiness or weirdness across the cases.

to be magical practices. That new technologies are somehow 'magical'[6] is a frequent trope in discourses about them, and we see this reflected across our sample, with regular references to '*magic*' and '*trickery*' across cases, and the occasional reference to the '*phantasmagorical*' [WH6]. In large part these are expressions of awe at technologies which often seem opaque, securing them an almost mythical status as a result. This echoes Alexandra Sherlock's assessment that to the vast majority of the public digital approaches remain 'incomprehensible,' which 'leaves the door wide open for mythical interpretation' (Sherlock 2013). In our study the 'desire to see the impossible' (Kopelman and Frosh 2023) imbues the technologies with magic. We interpret this as evidence of a '21st century fascination with the techno sublime' which 'celebrates and fetishizes' advances in technology (McLeod 2015; see also, Milne 2020; Recuber 2023), perhaps especially now algorithmic processes (Kopelman and Frosh 2023; Nagy and Neff 2024). As becomes apparent here with reference to the 'sublime', faith and spirituality often seep into discourses about technology,[7] and these connections have been a focus of some scholarly enquiry (Noble 1997; Geraci 2006, 2012; Musa Giuliano 2020).[8]

The trope of digital 'magic' is one we should problematize however given the work it can do to obscure and decentre the more problematic aspects of these technologies. Timothy Recuber (2023: 44) makes the case that focusing on the more 'enchanting' or 'reenchanting' aspects of technologies obscures their more disenchanting elements 'like the labour conditions used to create them, their vacuuming up and selling of user data, or the hidden algorithms secretly dictating what we see and hear while using them'. As Peter Nagy and Gina Neff propose in relation to what they call 'the conjuration of algorithms', technology companies' repetition of such tropes serves three purposes: 'To conceal the design of technologies, create confusion around the capabilities of technologies, and produce dazzling effects of technologies' (2024). Those dazzling effects mean audiences and users are less likely to see through deceptions and produce an image of the future in which algorithms provide

6 'Any sufficiently advanced technology is indistinguishable from magic' (Clarke 1962).

7 The idea of 'apocalyptic AI', for example (Geraci 2012).

8 McLeod sums them up perfectly when noting of holograms that they 'play with various quasi-spiritual notions as they question the boundaries between the material and the virtual, the human and the post-human, the living and the dead, the temporal and the eternal' (McLeod 2015).

an 'infallible panacea' (Nagy and Neff 2024). In this book we have worked to make these effects visible, but it is noteworthy that in our exploration here of media discourses – themselves heavily reliant on input from sources in the technology industry – such obliqueness should be prevalent. In the next section we further unpack the ethical parameters of these discourses.

Ethical issues

> *Just because we should revive someone digitally, should we?* [AH20]

In this section we turn our attention more expressly to ethical issues referenced in the reporting (in 73 per cent of articles). We do so across two subsections. Firstly, we consider perspectives on the ethics of memory and the (digital) maintenance of 'legacies'. Here we work across the themes of consent or permissions (referenced in 45 per cent of articles), memory or legacy, (36 per cent) and debates about profiteering (29 per cent) that were identified in our study. Secondly, we turn our attention to the implications of digital afterlives for the future of labour, and of creative work in particular (raised in 21 per cent of articles).

Memory and legacy

> *She is a symbol of Brazilian popular music. She is Elis Regina. And she has been dead for 41 years.* [ER4]

There is much coverage in our dataset on topics of memory and legacy, where there is an evident tension between a desire to extend the creative imaginary these artists have facilitated, and deep concern about tarnishing it in some way, especially through exploitation or profiteering, as we go on to discuss. The quotation at the start of this section comes from our Elis Regina case study where discussions about cultural and collective memory seemed to be particularly pointed. Elis Regina's image and voice were articulated across the sample as having a significant '*immortalising*' function when it came to Brazil's national memory: '*To see Elis Regina again on Brazilian screens has been for many an emotional peak … capable of appealing to the deepest part of a nation's memory*' [ER4]. However, the way her image and voice were being '*AI-fueled*'

[ER1] in the advert was subject to considerable criticism, both because people felt '*artificial resuscitation*' [ER1] was disrespectful to a national '*icon*' and given the specific political and historical context underpinning the depiction. In particular, the partnership with Volkswagen was referenced multiple times as problematic given Regina's opposition to the 1964–85 military regime (with which Volkswagen collaborated), as is summarized here:

> *But there are those who have been indignant: the fact that the technique allows it does not mean that it does not qualify as exploitation; in this case, of a deceased woman whose political and artistic concerns would never have made her lend herself to the promotion of a multinational company, and even less so with a song originally composed as a reflection on the opaque legacy of the military dictatorship for her generation.* [ER4]

The advert's '*digital trickery*' [ER4] is here seen as itself opaque and politically muddled; as well as inconsistent with Regina's own outlook. Such inconsistencies present '*ethical quandaries*' [ER1], and in this instance even led to the Brazilian National Council for Advertising Self-regulation opening an ethics investigation. This too was widely reported in our sample.

Debates about maintaining consistency with an artist's beliefs, talents or character were common in our sample, and were often collocated with observations about respect, legacy and fidelity.

> '*While death is unfortunate and inevitable, it brings a certain solemnity and gravitas to an artist's work that is inimitable. This zombification is incredibly disrespectful.*' [TS17]

> '*There's nothing special enough here to justify Hepburn's return, and the flavour of distaste lingers longer than chocolate ever could.*' [AH8]

> '*No matter what they take from me, sings Whitney Houston in one of her most famous songs, they can't take away my dig-ni-ty. Can I be frank, girlfriend? Right now they are having a damn good try.*' [WH10]

29 per cent of articles in our subset criticized these approaches for profiteering, or cashing in on, the fame and image of the deceased artist. This is referred to as, amongst other things, '*selling out*' [RW7], '*greed*' [TS17] and '*money spinning*' [WH3] and, alarmingly for some commentators, '*suggests that musicians are more valuable dead than they are alive*' (TS17). In the case of

Elis Regina one report queries '*who authorized it, and for how much?*' [ER4]. The commercial potential of these practices is clear to see; there are profits to be made from ticket sales, selling products, and of course, for the technology companies that support these endeavours. It was widely reported, for example, that the stock price of Digital Domain – the company that generated the Tupac hologram – went up by more than 60 per cent when news of the Coachella performance went viral (McLeod 2015). As long as these practices seem ripe for monetization the 'drive' towards them will clearly be strong (Frew et al. 2023).

Of course, as Jason Stanyek and Benjamin Piekut (2010: 17) point out 'there is nothing new about selling the dead to the living', indeed, 'in late capitalism, the dead are highly productive' (2010: 14). Each year, Forbes publishes its list of the highest paid dead celebrities, which in 2024 was topped by Michael Jackson at $600 million earned that year. Stars' earnings from Broadway shows, visitors to their estates, posthumous album releases and brand collaborations are detailed in the Forbes list, and regularly amount to tens of millions of dollars for artists. Stanyek and Piekut draw attention to the collaborative nature of 'intermundane' practices across 'bio- and necroworlds', which co-labour and co-produce 'social, economic, cultural, and affective' value (2010: 14). Their notion of 'inter-handling' (2010: 14), that is, arrangements that are not one-sided or necessarily exploitative but collaborative instead, is provocative.

'Selling out' was a particular criticism in the Audrey Hepburn and Bruce Lee case studies, where it was felt that the presentation in each advert was at odds with the respective star's public image and persona. Bruce Lee had been '*Digitally reincarnated to sell something he abstained from*' [BL2], which undermined the idea that the recreation had been done as a form of tribute: '*Not a tribute, only a commercial*' [BL3]. Audrey Hepburn was considered to have been '*disinterred for promotional purposes*' [AH1] provoking very strong negative reactions and the charge that she had become a '*posthumous saleswoman*' [AH2]. The following quote depicts well the sense of incongruity which annoyed many critics in this case: '*This week Audrey Hepburn became the latest Hollywood great to be brought back to life. Except poor, lovely, gamine Audrey is advertising a chocolate bar*' [AH9].

In the Hepburn sample there was an intriguing – and no doubt gendered – sense of conflict between her '*demure*', '*classy*', '*charming*' and '*elegant*' persona and the '*glassy-eyed, chocolate-loving robot*' [AH2] she became through reanimation. There was perhaps less surprise when it came to the Shakur case study where a resigned sense was evident that '*a subculture that workshops materialism was perhaps bound to materialize the immaterial*' [TS14]. Ng and Bax (2023) have described the way these practices are inserted into a 'capitalism of immateriality' facilitated by the capacity of digital data to be owned, transferred, copied and shared. Writing about ABBA Voyage they are particularly interested in the ways pastness, and indeed time itself, becomes commodified through its externalization as code: 'pastness becomes capital which can be packaged, circulated and sold' (Ng and Bax 2023: 14). Their notion of externalization – and the possibilities that are opened up through code for transferability, copying, storage and malleability – as well as the insertion of these activities into the market, begin to suggest questions about control and ownership (Ng and Bax 2023: 8). These were a feature of the articles in our sample; it is widely understood that '*the image rights and posthumous fortunes of the departed can lay legal and ethical minefields for brands*' [AH1], and that these practices amount to a '*Moral minefield*' [RW4].

In our sample, 45 per cent of articles mentioned consent or permissions for use of an artist's image or voice data. In most cases, permissions had been granted by the family and this was often reported in articles:

> *The team didn't want to replace him … The studio hired a new voice actor to record fresh lines of dialogue but then used Respeecher – an AI voice cloning software – to change the voice to match Reczeks and make it sound like him. Reczeks sons 'were very supportive' of the decision, the developer adds.* [MR1]

In a couple of our case studies however (e.g. Bruce Lee) issues of consent and rights were complicated by the family dynamics at play, and questions about a person's estate were sometimes not yet settled, raising concerns about who can and cannot give permissions for these posthumous representations. As Harris (2013) notes, families tend to be cast in the role of posthumous 'managers' for these artists, becoming at once both the 'stewards' and 'beneficiaries' of their legacy (Harris 2013). There is clearly potential then for conflicts of interest. When reporting familial consent there was often a stated (perhaps overstated) case made that an artist would have been '*proud*' of the output.

Such statements were common in our sample, framing these uses of artists' images as somehow both carrying on a creative legacy and aligning with their personal beliefs (Mihailova 2021). Some reports are cynical about this however and cast doubt on how authentic this position could ever be, as we see here in the Hepburn case:

> *She is still a star even now, and her sons – who control her estate – authorised the use of her image. This week they said she would be 'proud' of her new role and that she 'often spoke about her love of chocolate and how it lifted her spirit'. One imagines the fee they received was also chunky and deliciously moreish.* [AH9]

In our smaller sample we could explore in more detail the ebb and flow of discussions about permissions, uses and rights and saw evidence that in the most recent cases these themes were being covered more substantively. This would seem to indicate journalists and commentators have become more attuned to these issues over time. In the Regina and Reczek cases it is interesting that this shift is also in the context of talking more about voice data. Perhaps more generative uses of voice data raise the ethical stakes when it comes to these activities then, as it did in our exploration of deathbots (Chapter 4).

We have found the notion of custodianship to be a helpful one in thinking about these cases as it encourages us to focus on ethics in relation to caretaking, responsibility and accountability, and with an emphasis on guardianship for the future rather than ownership in the present. Custodianship gives us a framework for considering how a memory or a digital persona might be handled for the benefit of others, even where the commercial imperative might suggest an alternative course of action. The Carrie Fisher case study allowed us to test this approach given its extensive emphasis on legacy and respect. As we have noted, in this instance filmmakers decided *not* to use a fully computer-generated synthetic afterlife but to use previously filmed outtakes instead. As a result, the production team were required to work around the footage that was available rather than crafting new content that might have better fit the storyline. This approach, perhaps far from ideal, was taken in consideration of the strength of fan sentiment about the franchise and Fisher's place within it, and so the filmmakers wouldn't find themselves being accused of mistreating Fisher's legacy: '"*I knew a CG Carrie would have been a disaster and I knew, even if it looked great, it would just feel wrong*"' [CF1]. As is befitting of a custodianship approach, this decision demonstrated consideration of the emotional impacts of synthetic recreations on those who would be encountering them within the Star Wars universe, alongside transparency about the decision. In this respect, we might also note it as a considered bit of 'inter-handling' (Stanyek and Piekut 2010) across and between differing parties and interests, something that – as we have seen in this section – is too often done in consideration primarily of legal and technical matters, rather than social, mnemonic or affective ones.

Implications for creative work

> *Death, once the finite end to a celebrity career, is now only a marker for the next stage.* [RW7]

One other aspect of debates about ethical issues that came through strongly (in 21 per cent of articles) was the theme of creative work and its futures in the context of these developments. The quote at the start of this section from the Robin Willliams case study is particularly pertinent in that respect, emerging in the context of discussions about the actor's express decision-making with regard to these approaches: due to the legal arrangements he put in place before his death '*the earliest anyone can see an unapproved advertisement with the comedian – or even a hologram of him in a film – will be 2039*' [RW1].

Debates about creative work are clearly vexed when it comes to considering the impacts of AI (De Cremer et al. 2023; Epstein and Hertzmann 2023; Jiang et al. 2023; Kidd and Nieto McAvoy 2025), extending to the uses that might be made of synthetically recreated artists. One critic sums up concerns neatly and comprehensively in our sample, in reference to the case of Elis Regina:

> *Writers fear that, at best, they will be hired to edit screenplays drafted by AI. They fear that their creative work will be swallowed whole into databases as the fodder for writing tools to sample. And they fear that their specific expertise will be pushed aside in favour of 'prompt engineers', or those skilled at working with AI tools. / And actors fret that they will be forced to sell their likeness once, only to see it used over and over by studios. They fear that deepfake technologies will become the norm, and real, live actors won't be needed at all. And they worry that not only their bodies but their voices will*

> *be taken, synthesised and reused without continued compensation. And all of this is on top of dwindling incomes for the vast majority of actors.* [ER8]

Across the board, from writers to actors to editors, there are concerns about how to continue making a living in a landscape where AI can support the creation and circulation of output across multiple platforms, and ad infinitum. Recuber noted in 2023 that 'if nothing else, death is about running out of new content' (2023: 206), but this ceases to be the case once 'new' nostalgia-laden outputs can be generated in the guise of novel compositions or amalgams. These assessments are evidently linked to concerns about profiteering that were discussed in the previous section:

> *But why stop there? We don't even need musicians! A projection of Michael Jackson could sell out dozens of shows at the O2 Arena in London! Millions of old ladies around the globe could toss their britches at a hologram of Elvis Presley! We could re-create Woodstock with Jimi Hendrix and Janis Joplin and sell beer for $15 a bottle!* [TS28]

They are also linked to broader concerns that these approaches might be used to keep costs, including remuneration for work, artificially low within these industries: '*Many are also worried about the AI advancements leaving them unemployed, as studios may attempt to cut their costs by replacing real-life talent with virtual assistance*' [MR3]. There are a number of assessments from commentators in our sample pre-empting massive improvement in these technologies in the years to come, which would foretell further challenges in the short to medium term. There is a generalized sense of '*inevitability*' and '*eventual acceptance*' in these assessments, given '*this is where the market is going*' [CF16].

> '*And what if technology advances to such a degree that concert-goers have no way of telling whether or not their hero is actually on the stage, or thousands of miles away sipping cocktails on the deck of his yacht?*' [TS18]

> '*As the technology gets better (and it will), at what point will it rival or even supersede the appeal of living artists?*' [WH19]

These approaches could also appeal greatly to content producers if it turns out there is less friction in working with code than with artists. This came across especially strongly in discussions about the Whitney Houston hologram which, it was asserted, might be preferable to working with the '*flesh-and-blood diva*' herself: the digital representation was '*a beacon of light who never gets tired, never throws a tantrum, and always delivers the same perfect performance night after night.* [WH19]. We noted in previous sections how these approaches interfere with experiences of temporality, and create them anew, and these themes emerge in relation to industry considerations too. The idea that producers might be able to continue promoting or casting '*golden ghosts*' [CF10], that is, artists forever considered to be 'in their prime' is clearly an '*intoxicating*' proposition [AH20]. One critic concludes on the basis of this observation that '*it's going to be hard for Hollywood … to resist experimenting*' [AH20].

Zelda Williams (Robin Wiliams' daughter) has said that ''*These recreations are … cobbled together from the worst bits of everything this industry is*' [MR10]. They resist our corpo-realities; aging, imperfection, roughness, wastage and they fetishize financial leanness, predictability and looking back. Might more artists be wise to consider legal arrangements such as those put in place by Robin Williams? The sense we get from our data is that for now, in the face of huge uncertainty about these approaches and the lack of established or even emergent norms in terms of how artists might prepare for them, '*people like Robin Williams will remain the exception*' [RW7].

Conclusion

In this chapter we have seen that the digital resurrection of deceased celebrities and cultural figures has significant ethical, societal and artistic implications. The news reports we have explored raise questions about what it means to remember cultural icons healthily, authentically and respectfully, and we have demonstrated that norms are still very much in flux; there is no consensus on many aspects of digital 'revival' within the context of the creative industries.

While these technologies offer new creative possibilities and can evoke powerful emotional responses, they also raise profound questions about the integrity of artistic expression and the nature of memory and human legacy in the context of algorithms. The allure of profit and a desire to preserve and extend legacies is clearly driving these practices, which raises concerns about exploitation, consent and extractivism that are becoming familiar territory in this book. We have demonstrated that using digital recreations for advertising and endorsements can be particularly problematic, especially when the chosen product or message conflicts with an artist's known values or public image. These practices raise questions about who benefits financially and whether familial consent guarantees a faithful representation of the deceased's wishes. The absence of established norms and legal guidelines leaves artists vulnerable to exploitation, with limited recourse for protecting their image and legacy after death. The lack of clear legal frameworks regarding the use of synthetic media for impersonation more generally further complicates matters of consent and control.

We have suggested that the notion of custodianship might be productive for considering the likely social, emotional and mnemonic impacts of these approaches, not least where a deceased person is in the public eye. That said – and although debates about digital resurrection are playing out very publicly for celebrities and artists – it is becoming clear from the empirical insights in this book that estate planning for algorithmic afterlives and post-mortem rights '*shouldn't be limited to those with celebrity clients*' [RK13]. As Tonia Sutherland notes however, the distribution of post-mortem rights and dignity are not without prejudice. Sutherland reminds us of the cases of Michael Brown and George Floyd – men whose deaths were captured digitally and whose families found they could not control the circulation of those images – which is a powerful reminder that a sense of agency is not experienced equally. At 'the intersection where race, records, and the digital afterlife converge' (Sutherland 2023: 8) there is much work to be done (as we go on to explore in Chapter 6).

We have also highlighted the tension between the 'magic' of digital technology and the ethical issues these approaches produce. The ability to manipulate time, age and appearance in digital recreations can create a sense of wonder and possibility, but this allure can also obscure ethical complexities and the labour practices involved in creating synthetic afterlives. We caution against uncritically embracing the 'techno sublime', urging a more nuanced and critical understanding of the potential consequences of reducing individuals to digital data. We have noted the lack of diverse voices in public discussions about digital resurrection, and argued for the inclusion of a broader range of perspectives, including unions, regulators and ethicists alongside the voices of technology companies and families.

This chapter has charted growing anxieties within the creative community about the potential for AI to displace human talent and devalue creative work. Writers, actors and musicians fear being replaced by cheaper and (infinitely) more 'productive' AI agents, leading to job losses and the erosion of artistic control. This concern is exacerbated by predictions of rapid technological advancements, and no doubt also the preponderance of technology industry voices in the discursive arena occupied by these practices. While these recreations can evoke a sense of connection with cultural figures they also risk distorting the meaning-making process associated with their death and legacy; the ability to endlessly manipulate and repurpose digital representations potentially undermines the significance of an artist's finite body of work. They run the risk of creating, or amplifying, erroneous or false cultural imaginaries. In Chapter 6, we explore this risk within the differently charged context of cultural heritage sites and museums.

6

AI afterlives in the museum

This chapter explores how museums and heritage sites are increasingly interacting with AI afterlives. It shines a light on debates about authenticity, connection and ownership in the digital work of cultural institutions, demonstrating the precariousness of cultural heritage as data, but also its potential; for re-examining, rebalancing, redefining and recontextualizing.

As we argue elsewhere (Kidd and Nieto McAvoy 2019), museums, galleries and heritage sites are critical sites for the exploration of digital innovation and human–computer interactions (Hornecker and Ciolfi 2019). Their significance lies in the fact that they offer distinctive material resources and house extensive textual and visual digital assets, including datasets. They also maintain a captive audience for the trial and evaluation of new approaches. These institutions operate at the intersection of the physical and the digital, where the materiality of collected, preserved and displayed artefacts increasingly coexists with large-scale digitization, 3D imaging and hybrid forms of storytelling. As such, they provide a unique laboratory for interrogating the points of tension, collapse and erasure between physicality and digitality, offering insights that extend across – and beyond – digital heritage research and practice. As custodians of communities' collective pasts, museums and heritage sites also need to negotiate what stories are told and how, which is a critical – and increasingly political – observation.

In this chapter, our research questions are as follows (1) How do AI afterlives sit within the digital turn of museums and heritage sites, and what kind of new opportunities and challenges do they present for the sector?; (2) How are AI afterlives supporting the role museums and heritage sites play in (re) mediating archives and contributing to communities' collective and cultural memory; and (3) can AI afterlives be supportive of (or totally incompatible with) museum's values, particularly where institutions respond to public service mandates?

We explore these questions in discussion of a range of datapoints (outlined in this section) and using a series of analytical examples which illustrate our arguments in the chapter. These are:

Example 1: The *Hello Vincent* installation at the Musée d'Orsay is built around the use of generative AI. Launched in 2021, *Hello Vincent* was trained on a corpus of 900 letters written by Vincent van Gogh, allowing visitors to 'chat' with the artist via a microphone and interactive terminal as he paints *Wheatfield with Crows*. The *Hello Vincent* project was part of broader programming around the *Auvers-sur-Oise: The Final Months* exhibition, which also included VR experiences such as *Van Gogh's Palette*. The development of *Hello Vincent* involved a wide range of collaborators, including tech startup Jumbo Mana, and was funded by PI France and the Grand-Est region, with technical support from the University of Paris-Saclay and the Jean-Zay supercomputer at IDRIS.

Example 2: USC Shoah Foundation's *Dimensions in Testimony* project (Figure 6.1) enables people to ask questions that prompt real-time responses from pre-recorded video interviews with Holocaust survivors and other witnesses to genocide. The project used advanced filming techniques to

Figure 6.1 *Dimensions in Testimony*. USC Shoah Foundation Behind the Scenes Interactive Image of Eva Kor provided by the USC Shoah Foundation – The Institute for Visual History and Education http://sfi.usc.edu.

capture 3D testimonies – although for now they are mostly displayed as 2D – and harnesses a range of specialized technologies so it can be accessed online, or through on-site installations in museums. It uses natural language processing to create an interactive biography. Despite these sophisticated technical possibilities however, the project is grounded in its commitment to testimony and oral history, as the name suggests. The idea is to facilitate conversations where users can ask questions that are pertinent to them. There are a host of additional resources available online to support these interactions – for example, if teachers want to use *Dimensions in Testimony* in class.

Example 3: A series of works by multi-disciplinary media artist Nora Al-Badri. In *Neuronal Ancestral Sculptures Series* (2020), Al-Badri explores speculative archaeology and decolonial museum practices through generative adversarial networks (GANs). Al-Badri's (GAN)-generated 'technoheritage' is trained on thousands of scraped images of Mesopotamian, Neo-Sumerian and Assyrian artefacts to generate synthetic images that act as speculative, machine-generated heritage. These images function as both new artefacts and living memories, exploring visual language, materiality and cultural memory through AI. In *The Post-Truth Museum* (2021–3, Figure 6.2), Al-Badri uses AI and deepfake technology to animate the faces of prominent European museum directors, placing critical and unlikely admissions about imperial plunder, restitution and institutional shame in their mouths. Through these synthetic confessions – drawn from activist and scholarly voices – the piece challenges institutional authority and reframes museums as sites of postcolonial reckoning.

Example 4: *The Living Museum* is an AI-powered digital interface created by Jonathan Talmi, an independent AI engineer. *The Living Museum* allows users to create personalized exhibits and 'chat' with museum objects by animating them through large language models (LLMs). Built on open data from the British Museum's online collections (but unaffiliated), it creates interactive dialogues using each object's metadata to 'bring museum subjects to life'. The experience aims to make cultural heritage more engaging by enabling visitors to feel the 'presence' of artefacts and explore history through conversational AI (see Figure 6.3).

Example 5: Launched in October 2024, *Nature Perspectives* collaborated with the University of Cambridge's Museum of Zoology on a project that brought museum specimens to life using generative AI (see Figure 6.4).

Figure 6.2 Nora Al-Badri, film still *The Post-Truth Museum*, 2024. Reproduced with permission from Nora Al-Badri.

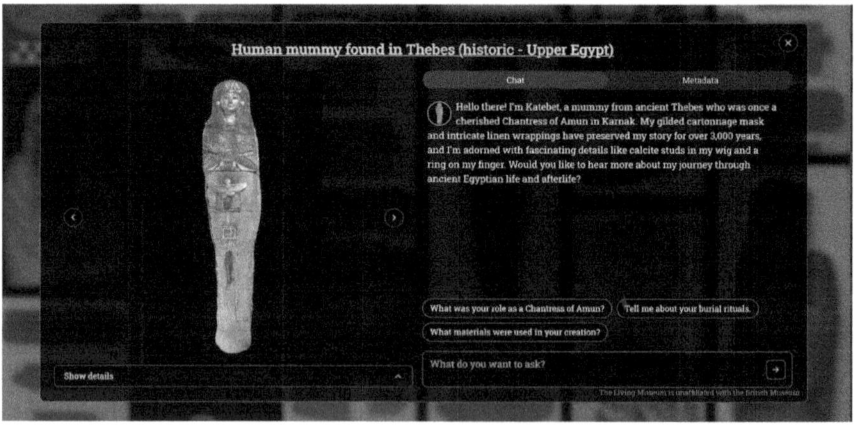

Figure 6.3 *The Living Museum*, a 'chat' with the Mummy of Katebet (screenshot). Reproduced with permission from Jonathan Talmi.

Figure 6.4 Chatting with a dodo at the Museum of Zoology, *Nature Perspectives*. © Jacqueline Garget from University of Cambridge.

> This initiative enabled visitors to engage in two-way conversations with thirteen different exhibits – including a dodo skeleton, a fin whale, a red panda and a cockroach – via QR codes that opened a chat interface on their mobile devices. These AI-powered interactions claimed to provide personalized, multilingual responses, simulating each specimen's unique voice and perspective. The project aimed to deepen public engagement with biodiversity and foster empathy towards non-human life by giving these animals a voice. It also served as an experiment to explore how AI can enhance museum experiences and influence visitors' perceptions of the natural world.

We also make reference to the *Dali Lives* installation which we introduced in Chapter 1.

The discussion of these examples is both theoretically informed and empirically grounded in participatory work with cultural professionals carried out as part of our Leverhulme Trust-funded Synthetic Pasts project.

In this work we have responded to calls for more inclusive, practitioner-led engagement with AI in the cultural and heritage sectors, acknowledging the critical need for those working within institutions to reflect not only on how AI might be integrated into their practices, but also on when and why it might be resisted. This work builds on our earlier research into the sector's rapid 'pivot to digital' during the COVID-19 pandemic (Kidd, Nieto McAvoy and Ostrowska 2022), which revealed both the creativity and the strain involved in adapting to new technological circumstances and demands. That study highlighted how digital adoption often occurred under conditions of urgency and uncertainty, with limited time for critical reflection. Our current project has extended those discussions, focusing on the longer-term implications of emerging AI technologies, particularly in how they reshape memory work, historical interpretation and user engagement.

Through interviews and workshops with fifty-four museum and heritage professionals – including curators, archivists and digital specialists – we have identified deep concerns around the use of AI to 'revive' historical figures and the ethical implications of relying on third-party platforms to facilitate digital interactions. Institutions are keenly experimenting with AI, but are concerned not to undermine their status as 'pillars of trust' within society (NEMO 2023). These conversations have underscored the sector's need for context-sensitive resources to support responsible engagement with AI. While toolkits such as those developed by the AI in Museums group (e.g. Murphy and Villaespesa 2020) provide valuable guidance, none yet address the specific complexities of AI Afterlives in heritage contexts. In response, we have developed a resource to help cultural professionals navigate these emerging practices. Co-designed with sector partners and led in collaboration with Alison John from creative studio yello brick, *The Responsible AI Afterlives Workbook* invites reflection, aiming to support institutions in balancing innovation with their core commitments to ethical stewardship. It advocates collaborative value-based approaches that serve as our entry point to explore these issues here, offering an analytical (rather than normative) framework (Kidd et al. 2025).

Insights from these interactions suggest that while AI afterlives are framed as providing new opportunities for the sector, (1) they sit within a much longer history of museums' changing relationships with technologies and their search for more open, participatory and meaningful experiences for users; (2) there is still a gap between claims made by developers, and evidence showing that objectives for these practices ever materialize; and (3) there is potential here, but given the challenges of generative AI – in terms of bias, representation and ownership – these potentials are currently limited, and laden with risk.

Before we go on to present our analysis it is important to set out some contextual and conceptual grounding for our approach in this chapter. Firstly, we consider AI afterlives here as *performative*, in that we investigate what they do rather than how they are constituted technically. We acknowledge that AI is used as an umbrella term that encapsulates different practices, and are alert to the discourses – claims made and language used – of museums, developers, media coverage and the participants in our research, interrogating them within wider genealogies of human–computer interaction in museums. Secondly, we do not claim to be comprehensive in our analysis of AI afterlives here and are aware of the rapidly shifting environment in which we are researching and writing. We have decided to work with examples that we think are a good entry point for broader discussions, each raising different, albeit overlapping, issues and concerns. These examples also usefully highlight the specificity and contextual nature of these practices, for example, varied motivations and strategies for creating AI afterlives, as well as the inevitable trade-offs that are involved.

Finally, our approach here, as it has been throughout this book, is ambivalent; we are not techno-sceptics but neither are we all out techno-enthusiasts. While critical of the many shortcomings of these technologies, we recognize that there are some interesting uses of AI afterlives that precisely respond to other ethical considerations that museums are grappling with. AI afterlives can be part of a radical reimagining and critique of the very concept of a museum, becoming a 'pathway' through which stories can flow, and around which dialogue can happen (Newell, Robin and Wehner 2017). They can enable people to (at least notionally) explore more radical visions of the future. Such visions may serve to deprioritize or unsettle the status quo – be that the dominant political consensus or the deeply embedded museological one. In this way, these approaches can align well with museums' activist aspirations (Janes and Sandell 2019). What is most interesting to us here is the way AI afterlives resurface theoretical and practical debates about the nature of memory and the role of institutions tasked with the job of keeping it alive for the communities they serve.

In the next section, we briefly examine how AI is currently being used in museums and give an overview of the theoretical framework that guides the remaining sections of this chapter.

Bringing collections 'back to life'

Museums and heritage site practitioners have begun exploring and incorporating AI in a variety of ways, from their backstage operations through to crafting visitor experiences (Thiel and Bernhardt 2023; Münster et al. 2024). Behind the scenes, museums are increasingly leveraging AI for collections management and care, machine vision is being explored to automate cataloguing and object recognition tasks, promising scalability and efficiency (Ciecko 2020), and AI is surfacing patterns across large datasets that would be otherwise impossible to detect manually. The promises of automation and efficiency come with critical caveats however, particularly in relation to sustainability and long-term maintenance. Within visitor experience design, AI has been applied to power chatbots (Gaia et al. 2019), generate deepfakes of historical figures (Kidd and Rees 2021), animate interactive exhibits (Cuseum 2019) and deploy humanoid robots such as Pepper, introduced at six Smithsonian sites (Styx 2024).

These technologies are often associated with claims of enabling personalized experiences, and deepening audience interaction (Li et al. 2024). Importantly, AI has the potential to broaden accessibility, offering alternative formats and multilingual interactions that could make cultural heritage more inclusive for diverse audiences. AI-generated content, particularly within the realm of AI afterlives – where visitors converse with AI-simulated historical figures or objects – promises to create immersive, interactive and emotionally engaging encounters that could make history more relatable and memorable (He et al. 2025). We saw as much in our own interactions with cultural professionals which suggested that they have high hopes for AI to support new forms of storytelling. This includes the exploration of alternative histories and the representation of marginalized voices, particularly through sparking conversations about gaps and absences in the historical record.

These potentials resonate with evolving conceptions of the museum as a more open, dynamic and collaborative space; as 'participatory' (Simon 2010), 'interactive' (Ntalla 2017), 'transmediated' (Kidd 2014) and 'post-digital' (Parry 2013b). Such shifts reflect broader ambitions to move away from authoritative, one-directional models of communication (Black 2012), to relinquish unilateral control (Adair et al. 2011) and to foster shared authorship and more democratic forms of cultural production (Sanderhoff 2014). However, the enthusiasm surrounding AI in cultural institutions must be tempered by a recognition of persistent challenges. There are clear ethical and epistemological considerations for museums as they further integrate artificial intelligence and automation. In the context of concerns about disinformation and declining levels of trust in public institutions and the media (OECD 2024), cultural institutions – and cultural professionals – continue to enjoy very *high* levels of trust and confidence (NMDC 2022). There are deep concerns within the sector that increased uses of AI (and in particular generative AI, with its well-known issues with 'hallucination') might in time undermine that trust, with questions about distortion and disinformation looming large; as institutions risk a 'loss' or 'lack' of control over narratives or narrowing their scope of inquiry (terms used by our research participants). There are concerns that the delegation of culture to computational systems might lead to (perhaps alarming) new cultural forms that intervene in definitions of fact and fiction, past and present, real and fake, and that complicate the already blurred line between authentic and inauthentic objects in museums given the increasing presence of (digital) copies and remediations (Brenna et al. 2019). New verification protocols will no doubt need to be established, but it is not at all clear yet how these might operate (Fletcher 2018).

In this book we have repeated concerns about bias and the perpetuation of inequality in AI systems (Mitchell 2019; Azar et al. 2021; Recuber 2023) and these too are a concern in museums (Jaillant et al. 2025; Tiribelli et al. 2024), with the potential to undo progress that has been made in mitigating these concerns. Limited diversity – including in the teams working on AI – and incompleteness in datasets can constrain AI's ability to accurately and fairly represent diverse cultural heritages (Jaillant et al. 2025). AI systems face difficulties accurately capturing complex cultural and historical nuances, risking superficial or inaccurate portrayals (He et al. 2025). Concerns relating to data privacy and rights (including copyright of existing or AI-generated outputs) are also in the mix. Participants in our research highlighted tensions where personal values (such as familial objections to the reuse of historical figures' data) might conflict with professional imperatives for public engagement. Broader concerns were raised about whether AI systems, often built on questionable training data, align at all with the missions and values of publicly funded institutions.

AI afterlives clearly present particular challenges for museums then. Questions about the dignity and autonomy of the deceased persist, as do concerns about the potential for exploitation and misuse of personal data by AI companies who might be involved as third party data stewards to these practices. As noted in Chapter 4, it is important to consider cultural and religious connotations when using AI to represent deceased individuals (Savin-Baden and Burden 2018) and particular caution is due in historical contexts where there are risks associated with creating an 'idealized specter' of deceased persons through AI, leading to a distorted understanding of their life and legacy, as we saw in Chapter 5 (Bao and Zeng 2024). There may be a tension between the need to respect the wishes of families and the goal of providing historical resources for broader audiences, and there may also be questions about who owns and controls the digital remains of the deceased, and who has the right to alter or manipulate those data (Fabry and Alfano 2024).

Beyond these ethical concerns, operational and practical challenges were also highlighted by our participants. Institutional onboarding is uneven across and within organizations, potentially undermining internal coherence and public messaging when it comes to uses of AI (James et al. 2019). Our participants noted the significant resource demands of AI projects – requiring financial investment, technical expertise and considerable energy consumption – which they want to see carefully weighed against any potential benefits. Sustainability concerns were closely tied to skill gaps, with many institutions facing the need for upskilling or risking long-term dependency on third-party providers. Furthermore, the sustainability and upkeep of AI experiences pose long-term tensions: projects that appear innovative at launch may struggle without ongoing support, technical maintenance and regular content updates.

Across both backend and visitor-facing applications, scholarly work emphasizes the importance of critical evaluation. For example, AI is hailed as a way to capture user data to deliver personalized recommendations that can enhance a museum visit (Capece et al. 2024), with user profiles and interests recognized as fundamental to a meaningful Cultural User eXperience (CUX) (Konstantakis et al. 2018). However, as we have argued elsewhere (Kidd and Nieto McAvoy 2019), purely data-driven solutions often fail to capture nuances in use or the long-term impact of these initiatives, although they might be enough to justify further funding. Questions remain about what kinds of impact museums should seek to measure. As institutions experiment with playful and provocative narratives that blur fact and fiction, for example, closer attention to visitor responses will be critical in understanding shifts in the perceived role of heritage organizations more broadly.

Our research participants highlighted that questions about why AI is being used in museums and heritage sites – and whether it genuinely serves audience-centred, story-led, multimodal practices (Kidd and Nieto McAvoy 2019) – should remain central to future evaluations. Claims about the benefits of using AI often adopt the logics and languages of technologists and corporations, which clearly have differing agendas to heritage institutions. AI is frequently promoted as a cost-effective solution to institutional challenges, but efficiency and scalability are not necessarily appropriate models for museum practices, which often thrive on hyper-local, tailored and community-specific programming (Merritt 2025). Critical, reflective frameworks such as the Smithsonian's AI Code of Ethics, alongside broader sector toolkits, such as the Arts Council England Responsible AI Practical Toolkit, offer promising starting points, suggesting sustained attention to the risks, unintended consequences and environmental impacts of AI that are crucial to developing sustainable cultural futures.

Against this backdrop, the sections that follow examine a series of interrelated issues around authenticity, ownership, affect and stewardship which emerged in our workshops and interviews, and which, we argue, will become central to discourses about AI afterlives in museums and heritage contexts. Situated at the intersection of data, death and the past, these notions are mobilized in ways that are often rhetorically persuasive but conceptually ambiguous. AI-driven experiences promise both affective connection and (perhaps under certain conditions) historical fidelity, yet frequently obscure the tension between them. We explore how authenticity is invoked and negotiated in these encounters, particularly in relation to storytelling, emotional resonance and the curatorial framing of synthetic figures. What emerges is a complex interplay between creative mediation and epistemic responsibility, raising critical questions about whether – and how – these experiences reconcile emotional accessibility with historical complexity, and what kinds of ownership, both material and narrative, are being asserted or contested in the process.

From auras to avatars

Projects like *Dalí Lives* (which we briefly introduced in Chapter 1) and *Hello Vincent* (introduced earlier) foreground the revival of historical figures through AI, offering emotionally engaging, avatar-led interactions that personalize visitor experience. The Dalí Museum promotes its experience as enabling learning 'from the person who knew him best', while the Musée d'Orsay presents *Hello Vincent* as a unique opportunity to converse with Van Gogh – though ethical concerns quickly surfaced, particularly regarding how the AI responded to questions about the artist's suicide (Solomon 2024). Similarly, *The Living Museum* and *Nature Perspectives* experiment with conversational interfaces powered by LLMs to animate artefacts and even non-human entities, such as the extinct dodo, aiming to foster affective, more-than-human relationships with cultural and natural heritage. In each case, AI is employed not only to animate collections but also to reframe them as interactive and emotionally resonant, inviting users to engage in dialogue across temporal, human and species boundaries.

These AI afterlife experiences are often framed as playful or emotionally engaging, as 'interpretative representations' that 'exist primarily for entertainment rather than as true reflections of reality' (Brailsford 2024). But this distinction is rarely foregrounded within the encounter itself. The language used to describe these avatars – 'digital facsimiles', 'resurrections' – collapses interpretative and ontological categories. The suggestion, intentional or not, is that users are speaking with *the person*, rather than an interface constructed from probabilistic associations and curated archives. Part of the strategy is to present the AI afterlife as grounded in historical and archival authority. Users are told that *Dimensions in Testimony*, for example, is based on hours of recorded interviews with Holocaust survivors, positioning its AI-recalled responses as direct extensions of lived experience and testimony.[1] Similarly, we are told on the Musée d'Orsay's website that *Hello Vincent* draws on Van Gogh's extensive correspondence, with art historian Dr Wouter van der Veen overseeing the historical accuracy of the training material, reinforcing the impression that users are engaging with a well-informed, credible version of the artist. In *The Living Museum*, publicly available object metadata from the British Museum is used to generate dialogues that are rooted in documented provenance and curatorial descriptions. This dual framing – as both imaginative interaction and factual engagement – blurs the boundaries between education and simulation, inviting users to trust the avatars as historically truthful while interacting with them in modes that are often informal and affective. As a result, the authority of the AI avatar rests not only in the technology, but in its alignment with existing archival and scholarly sources, reinforcing a sense of authenticity even within speculative and conversational formats.

When thinking about AI and deepfakes, authenticity is often identified as a key issue, but it remains a complex and contested concept in cultural heritage and historical memory. Traditionally linked to the material originality of an object and reinforced by ethical codes from ICOMOS (International Council on Monuments and Sites) and UNESCO, authenticity is increasingly recognized as ideologically shaped and open to multiple interpretations (Nakonieczna and Szczepański 2024). Museums have historically mediated authenticity through practices of reproduction and reinterpretation (Parry 2013a; Lowenthal 1990), highlighting tensions between storytelling and historical evidence (Economou et al. 2018; Kidd 2019). New technologies – digitization, 3D, AR, VR and now AI – introduce further challenges. Critics argue that digital reproductions risk dehumanizing heritage and diminishing the unique 'aura' associated with physical encounters (Benjamin 1969). Yet, as Yip and Kenderdine (2018) show, the relationship between originals and copies is evolving, with digital reproductions contributing to an artefact's 'cultural career' (Latour and Lowe 2010) and able to support sensorial, emotional and memory based engagement. And while scholars emphasize that authenticity is socially constructed and negotiated, shaped by relationships among objects,

1 Within heritage and memory studies, there is a rich scholarship on the Holocaust which falls out of the scope of this book and our expertise.

places, communities and perceptions of 'pastness' (Jones 1990), there is a risk that copies become uncritically accepted as fact (Amakawa and Westin 2018), and further complicate perceptions of cultural heritage.

AI-generated content, including deepfakes and synthetic media, further intensifies concerns about authenticity, authority and truth as we have seen throughout this book. For example, generative AI raises alarms about manipulated historical events and fabricated personas (Chesney and Citron 2019; Ajder et al. 2019; Rini 2019; Vaccari and Chadwick 2020; Lees et al. 2021; Lees 2023). AI's role in remediating older media highlights both continuity and transformation (Bolter and Grusin 2000), questioning conventional notions of historical evidence and introducing predictive logics into reconstructions of the past. The remediation of archives through AI increasingly frames pastness as a curated phenomenon rather than an emergent one, raising ethical concerns about the creation of 'false memories' (Murphy and Flynn 2022; Richardson-Walden and Makhortykh 2024), as we have explored elsewhere (especially Chapter 4).

Deepfakes, in particular, challenge museums' traditional custodianship models. Kidd and Rees (2021) frame deepfakes as a form of 'difficult heritage', reflecting new levels of procedural sophistication and raising ethical concerns about misinformation, reputational harm and the blurring of truth and fiction (Fletcher 2018; Anderson 2019; Mihailova 2021). While museums historically engaged in traditions of illusion and artifice (Parry 2013a; Lowenthal 1990), deepfakes' ambiguous materiality complicates acquisition, provenance and stewardship practices (Kidd and Rees 2021). They exist on a material continuum (Galani and Kidd 2020) yet still provoke unresolved questions about what constitutes a collectable artefact in an algorithmic age.

Nonetheless, museums can use these tensions productively, promoting critical engagement with emerging media forms, fostering public education around authenticity and modelling ethical literacy. Similar debates about immersive media highlight the risks of confusing interactivity with authenticity (Tsai 2019) and warn against uncritical acceptance of technological reconstructions (Amakawa and Westin 2018). While fakes can distort historical understanding, they also reveal evolving cultural constructions of authenticity. In her work, for example, Nora Al-Badri creates what Snow (2021) has called 'deepfakes for good'; in Al-Badri's *The Post-Truth Museum*

(2021–3), the museums directors' synthetic admissions – fabricated yet rooted in archival truth and activist discourse – destabilize the authority of museums as neutral spaces of knowledge and expose the ideological underpinning of claims to authenticity. Rather than deceiving, these synthetic voices expose the constructed nature of institutional narratives, using (deep)fakeness to provoke critical reflection on who gets to speak for the past and how that past is remembered, and highlighting how the perception of authenticity is strongly mediated by institutional authority. As Westling notes (2019), audiences' trust often depends more on the credibility of presenting institutions than on the intrinsic veracity of content.

The idea of 'legitimate use' determines whether synthetic or remediated materials are accepted as authentic. In a different project – the *Nefertiti Hack* – Al-Badri (with Jan Nikolai Nelles) deliberately destabilizes conventional understandings of authenticity by claiming to have secretly scanned the bust of Nefertiti at Berlin's Neues Museum and releasing the high-resolution 3D model online. Whether the scan was truly captured covertly or sourced through other means remains ambiguous – and intentionally so. This ambiguity becomes central to the work's critical force: the potential 'hoax' draws attention not to deception, but to the politics of access, ownership and institutional control over cultural heritage (Voon 2016). By circulating a digital copy of an object often withheld from public reproduction, the project questions who has the right to possess and disseminate cultural artefacts. In this way, the authenticity of the scan matters less than the critique it enacts, using the aesthetics of fakery to challenge the authority of museums and their claims to custodianship.

Bringing deepfakes into the museum context – such as in the exhibition *Deepfake: Unstable Evidence on Screen* at the Museum of the Moving Image[2] – grants these synthetic media a form of cultural legitimacy, positioning them not merely as tools of deception but as artefacts worthy of curatorial attention and critical reflection (Kidd and Rees 2021). By framing deepfakes within a museum setting, the exhibition elevates them from viral content to objects of aesthetic, historical and ethical inquiry, conferring a kind of institutional authenticity on a technology otherwise associated with manipulation

2 Further information is available at https://movingimage.org/event/deepfake-unstable-evidence-on-screen/.

(Mihailova 2021). Projects like *Dalí Lives* and *Hello Vincent* further illustrate how deepfakes and synthetic media gain legitimacy through their presence in a museum. It could be argued that here authenticity does not derive from strict historical accuracy or factual representation, but from the emotional resonance and perceived intimacy these avatars offer to visitors (Hamilton 2024). As Hank Hine of the Dalí Museum put it (Dali Museum 2019), the goal of *Dalí Lives* is to create a sense of 'emotion' and 'connection' that allows audiences to relate more directly to the artist and his work. The *Dimensions in Testimony* project enables a personalized interaction with Holocaust survivors and other witnesses to genocide, which – despite being curated – feels 'real' to users through its affective immediacy. In both cases, authenticity becomes less about verifiable truth and more about affective plausibility, grounded in institutional framing and user experience. These synthetic figures are not so much validated by their historical fidelity as by their ability to produce a sense of co-presence and engagement, suggesting that in the museum context emotional connection can sit in tension with factual accuracy.

Affective Encounters

The emphasis on affective and personalized connection is central to how AI afterlife projects are conceptualized and promoted, often framed as enhancing access, empathy and emotional resonance. As we have suggested, the rhetoric of 'presence' and 'co-presence' plays a key role here, with developers and institutions emphasizing the emotional realism of these avatars as a means of fostering meaningful encounters. Yet this presence is carefully curated and technologically constrained. While developers like Jumbo Mana and institutions such as the Dalí Museum stress that these experiences are not attempts at 'rebirth', but cultural tools grounded in archival or biographical material, they nonetheless invite users to relate to the avatars as emotionally available and, implicitly, historically truthful interlocutors. This dual framing – as both interpretive representation and historically grounded simulation – creates an ambiguity. The use of terms such as 'digital facsimile' or 'digital twin' (Brailsford 2024), even when paired with caveats about speculative reconstruction, reinforces a sense of authenticity that users may not be fully equipped to question. Despite institutional efforts to contextualize these encounters, the emotional immediacy of a conversation with 'Van Gogh' or 'Dalí' may override critical distance, particularly in museum contexts where authority is already assumed. What emerges, then, is a tension between the desire to create affective connections and the ethical complexities of presenting algorithmically generated responses – however historically informed – as emotionally and epistemically equivalent to direct human testimony. This tension becomes even more acute when engaging with traumatic pasts, as seen in *Dimensions in Testimony*, where live in-person interpreters often mediate the exchange between user and AI avatar, revealing both the potential of these encounters and their fragility.

The presence – or rather, co-presence – engineered by AI afterlives is a central appeal of these experiences, but it also demands further scrutiny. The perceived intimacy of interacting with an AI-powered avatar, particularly one modelled on a historical figure, encourages users to form emotional connections that mirror, and at times exceed, traditional forms of engagement with museum collections. This design is deliberate. As noted earlier, creators speak openly of their aim to foster empathy, affect and access – Hank Hine's assertion that visitors 'want a way in' is emblematic of this affective turn (Dalí Museum 2019). Yet, the success of these interactions depends as much on their emotional charge as on their perceived authenticity. Projects like *Dalí Lives* and *Hello Vincent* carefully walk the line between imaginative speculation and historical veracity, building user trust through credible archival or biographical foundations. The emotional responses they elicit are not merely reactions to narrative content but to the *presence* of the figure – animated, articulate and seemingly responsive.

This affective presence is reinforced by the invocation of authenticity through source material, which we noted previously. These choices are not neutral. they frame the avatars as not only emotionally responsive but also epistemically trustworthy. The museum visitor is encouraged to relate to these figures not as fictionalized constructs but as legitimate, even authoritative, bearers of history. We advanced in Chapter 5 the concept of 'contested presence' as the unstable and negotiated forms of engagement enabled by AI Afterlives. It captures the tension between the emotional immediacy and immersive realism these technologies offer, and the layers of abstraction, remediation and erasure that underpin them. In this sense, presence is a site of negotiation – between historical fidelity and affective storytelling, between embodied memory and datafied simulation, between institutional authority and community voice. In the case of AI Afterlives in the museum, 'contested presence' is shaped not just by algorithmic logic but also by curatorial framing and infrastructural politics.

This is particularly fraught in projects dealing with traumatic histories. In *Dimensions in Testimony*, for instance, interactions with survivor avatars are on occasion mediated by interpreters, who translate audience questions into prompts that the AI can process. This step is necessary not only due to technological constraints but also to safeguard the coherence and sensitivity of the exchange. Nonetheless, the risk remains that fully automated or unmoderated interactions with AI avatars – particularly those modelled on deceased individuals – may simplify or even trivialize complex historical narratives. As Kubota-Hiramoto (2018) observed in his analysis of the same project, while the avatars preserve the intonation and silence of real testimony, the absence of genuine responsiveness can be jarring. 'The more one becomes emotionally attached to the survivor's story … the more one feels abandoned in the end,' he writes, recalling how a survivor's harrowing account of losing her father continued without pause, leaving him feeling unexpectedly vulnerable (Kubota-Hiramoto 2018: 347). The affective power of the medium is therefore ambivalent: immersive, yet incapable of true reciprocity.

This ambivalence becomes a critical point of analysis when assessing claims about user agency, emotional resonance and educational impact, as well as the facilitation of empathy. As projects like EMOTIVE[3] have shown, the affective dimensions of digital heritage are difficult to measure, even as they are increasingly central to institutional narratives of success (Perry et al. 2018; see also, Kidd 2019; Huws et al. 2019). The assumption that personalization and interactivity necessarily lead to deeper understanding or agency is one that has already been challenged in immersive media research (Gröppel-Wegener and Kidd 2019). Nevertheless, such assumptions persist in the framing of AI-driven experiences. Deepfakes and LLM-powered avatars are often promoted as solutions to declining attention or engagement, yet the evidence supporting their transformative potential remains largely anecdotal.

3 https://emotiveproject.eu/ (accessed 16 September 2025).

Rather than producing radically new forms of cultural participation, many of these systems risk replicating traditional didactic models – wrapped in a more responsive, emotionally suggestive interface.

The characterization of these projects as 'synthetic resurrection' or 'digital afterlife' (Savin-Baden and Burden 2018) introduces deeper ethical considerations. Morris and Brubaker (2024) distinguish between AI-generated representations created with a person's consent (first-party ghosts) and those made without it, often after death (third-party ghosts). While first-party ghosts may support legacy and end-of-life planning (including public use in museums as in *Dimensions in Testimony*), other AI afterlives sit on a spectrum of consent as we analysed in Chapter 5. Tessa Solomon (2024) poses this challenge directly: 'Does being the custodian of a collection permit stewardship of a soul?', complicating claims of cultural accessibility with unresolved concerns around posthumous representation, historical distortion and the instrumentalization of the dead, which differ strongly across cultures and beliefs around death (Savin-Baden and Burden 2018), as we will go on to explore. AI afterlives offer access, playfulness and perhaps emotional attachments and increased learning, but also raise enduring questions about what is being accessed, who is speaking and how those voices are framed, remembered and emotionally received.

Flattening history

As we have noted, one of the defining objectives in AI afterlife projects is to create emotionally available, approachable avatars, engineered to foster personal connection with users. This design choice, however, carries significant risks. As Martin Pagh Ludvigsen (from GS&P) noted of *Dalí Lives*, the deepfake version of Salvador Dalí was made deliberately 'optimistic' and 'positive', acknowledging that meeting the real Dalí might have been 'less pleasant' (Solomon 2024). Similarly, the Musée d'Orsay's *Hello Vincent* adjusted its conversational Van Gogh model after visitors frequently asked about his suicide, steering the AI towards more life-affirming responses (Solomon 2024). While these interventions seek to enhance accessibility and emotional resonance, they actively curate affective narratives, smoothing over historical complexity and, at times, glossing over more difficult pasts.

Such strategic emotional framing recalls broader debates in memory studies about the co-construction of memory and its mediation through technological systems (Smit et al. 2024; Hoskins 2024). The construction of 'amenable' figures risks producing a form of what Smit et al. (2024) term 'stochastic remembering' – not a retrieval of historical truth but a pattern-based simulation that blurs 'historical authenticity and digital reimagination'. Although projects like *Dimensions in Testimony* demonstrate how AI can preserve dynamics and silences in survivors' voices (Kubota-Hiramoto 2018), they also highlight vulnerabilities, such as the abandonment Kubota-Hiramoto (2018) refers to and we noted earlier. Emotional engagement, while powerful, thus risks being underpinned by flattened or selectively curated narratives.

The simplification inherent in many AI afterlife projects stems partly from the technical constraints of generative models. AI's statistical logic treats the past as a 'line of best fit' (Mackenzie 2015 as in Walden-Richardson and Makhortykh 2024), resulting in what Schuh (2024) describes as 'temporal compression', flattening historical nuance and favouring recent, dominant patterns of memory. These developments challenge traditional frameworks of historical accountability and complicate collective historical consciousness. Moreover, the selective portrayal of figures like Dalí invites critical questions about the politics of remembrance. While the Dalí Museum frames the deepfake as celebrating the artist's creative spirit, it implicitly silences less convenient aspects of his legacy, such as his public support for Francisco Franco's regime – a political history that might resonate differently depending on audience context, but that is quite problematic nonetheless. Such omissions align these projects with broader patterns observed in heritage practices, where commemorations – like statues or portraits – are subject to contestation, as we discuss later.

The broader epistemological implications of AI-mediated memory are substantial. Generative systems lack the 'chain of evidence' that underpins traditional historical validation (Schuh 2024), and while capable of producing novel combinations, they prioritize plausibility over truth (Hicks et al. 2024). Although fictionalized histories and speculative heritage have long operated within recognized genres that signal their constructedness (Parry 2013a), AI-generated narratives increasingly circulate without such framing, complicating interpretation. As Chris Gilliard (2024) notes, AI invites users to 'ignore the machinery that crushes our reality into small parts and reconstitutes it into strange shapes', drawing attention away from the sociotechnical infrastructures shaping memory. AI's 'ways of seeing' (Offert and Phan 2024) and its 'radical alterity' (Richardson-Walden and Makhortykh 2024) fundamentally challenge anthropocentric notions of authorship and historical authority.

In this context, AI afterlives not only foreground the aesthetic and emotional textures of remembrance but also reconfigure critical questions about agency, authority and the ethics of memory-making in the digital age, especially as commercial interests exert influence over these 'mnemotechnologies' (Prey and Smit 2018). As oral historian Tomoko Kubota-Hiramoto (2018: 347) notes, *Dimensions in Testimony* 'ruthlessly flattens the subjectivity which oral historians value so deeply'. However, Kubota-Hiramoto (2018) also notes that the interactive exhibition engaged museum visitors across age groups, with children in particular showing unexpected enthusiasm for discussing war memories through technologically mediated encounters with projected survivors, suggesting a promising strategy for intergenerational remembrance.

Ghosts in the gift shop

AI afterlives increasingly serve as mechanisms for drawing audiences into cultural institutions, leveraging emotional appeal, novelty and personalization. These systems often act as entry points – interactive hooks intended to boost footfall and engagement. Public reception has generally been positive: 'When it is Van Gogh, people like it,' observed Agnès Abastado, head of digital development at the Musée d'Orsay (Small 2023). Similarly, Cuseum (2019) posed the question, 'How much more likely would you be to visit a museum if you could have a conversation with a legendary artist?', suggesting that deepfake driven experiences could enhance interactivity, relevance and even contribute to fundraising through personalized interactions. While there is anecdotal evidence suggesting that *Dalí Lives* and *Hello Vincent* have been significant drivers of museum attendance – claims were made, for instance, about record-breaking visitor numbers at the Musée d'Orsay – formal evaluations of their long-term impact remain limited. This reflects a wider challenge in assessing the benefits of new media in museum settings, where rhetorical claims often outpace empirical validation.

The appeal of such projects aligns closely with broader promotional strategies. As Mihailova (2021) notes, *Dalí Lives* emerged from a 'marriage of advertising agency tools and museum curatorial practices', introducing deepfakes into the museum through the lens of commercial branding. Both Dalí and Van Gogh have long been subject to popular, though sometimes controversial, immersive experiences and their respective afterlife projects reflect the global commodification of their images. Even as the Musée d'Orsay emphasizes its public mission – 'Our goal is to make the collection speak to everyone' – these initiatives are inevitably entangled with the logic of visibility, attention and audience capture (as we saw in Chapter 5).

There are clear limits to innovation and the technological possibilities driving these experiences, which have been discussed at length in relation to earlier digital experiences in museums. Perry et al. (2018) argue that virtual museums, for example – those designed to replicate physical institutions in digital space – often fall short of their transformative potential, tending instead to reproduce traditional, didactic models of education. As a result, these environments are frequently perceived as 'immature cultural constructs', lacking the resonance and relevance expected by visitors who are already familiar with more sophisticated forms of digital interaction in other domains. This critique aligns with broader findings across museum and HCI research which suggest that deep, meaningful immersion is most effectively achieved when technology recedes into the background, allowing content and experience to take precedence. As Ciolfi (2015), Poole (2017), Kidd et al. (2019) observe, the most powerful encounters often occur where the technology becomes 'invisible' – facilitating engagement rather than becoming the focus of it.

Dali Lives has clearly capitalized on the novelty of deepfake technology, while *Dali Asks* and *Hello Vincent* are framed in all the promotional narratives as products of generatively produced synthetic media. Technology is thus front and centre in how these AI afterlives are being framed. *Dimensions in Testimony* stands apart in both ethos and trajectory. Rather than riding the current wave of AI enthusiasm, the project emerges from a longer-standing commitment to preserving living archives of Holocaust survivor testimony, with roots in oral history and memory studies rather than in technology-led innovation. Developed over more than a decade, the initiative has incrementally adopted new technologies as they have become available – not for spectacle, but in pursuit of durability and fidelity. For example, the use of volumetric 3D recording anticipates future advances in rendering and interaction, effectively 'future-proofing' the archive by capturing data that might support richer engagements over time. Crucially, these interactions are carefully curated: survivors and their families have consistently insisted that their voices remain intact, unedited and unmanipulated. This ethos is reflected in the design of the experiences, many of which rely on trained interpreters who mediate between the audience and the AI system, translating user queries into inputs the model can process. The aim here is not entertainment or emotional immersion for its own sake, but the safeguarding of testimony in a form that balances accessibility with ethical and epistemic care.

Nora Al-Badri's artistic practice exemplifies a critical engagement with technology, using AI not merely as a tool for promotion but as a means to interrogate and challenge institutional narratives. *The Post-Truth Museum* (2021–23) confronts the authority of cultural institutions, highlighting the constructed nature of historical narratives and the potential of AI to question established power structures, and in another work – *Babylonian Vision* (2020) – Al-Badri critiques the gatekeeping of cultural heritage and the biases inherent in museum collections. The resulting 'technoheritage' challenges traditional notions of authenticity and ownership, suggesting alternative ways of engaging with the past. Rather than allowing technology to obscure or simplify complex histories, her projects make the technology visible, using it to expose and question the underlying structures of cultural institutions. This approach aligns with broader calls in memory studies for epistemic disobedience and the decolonization of knowledge production as we will go on to discuss further.

Whether visible or invisible, the affective affordances of AI afterlives respond to the constraints and conventions of their design. These are not neutral mediations, but highly curated, affectively charged performances shaped by institutional agendas, technological limitations and promotional logics. This promotional orientation also connects to broader infrastructural goals, including data extraction. *Hello Vincent*, for example, was developed in collaboration with tech startup Jumbo Mana, whose stated mission is to 'bring virtual characters to life' for use in sectors like customer service. In this context, user interaction becomes both a mode of engagement and a source of valuable behavioural data.

As Mihailova (2021) points out, the presence of AI afterlives in museum spaces must therefore be understood not only as cultural experimentation but also as a convergence of curatorial ambition and platform capitalism.

Haunted data: Decolonizing knowledge in AI afterlives

As AI becomes increasingly entangled in cultural heritage practices, questions emerge about its potential to contribute to unearthing hidden stories of marginalized communities and filling gaps in the archive, or whether it instead reproduces existing hierarchies of knowledge and authority. Framed as innovative tools for engagement and access, AI afterlives often draw on deeply partial and politicized data sources as we will go on to explore. AI afterlives may enable imaginative 'what if' histories, but they also risk flattening historical complexity through polished, probabilistically optimized outputs, as we saw earlier. Digital resurrection technologies risk commodifying or spectacularizing the dead. When reanimating racialized and marginalized bodies, it can also echo long-standing forms of violence – such as slavery – and the epistemic injustice embedded in both analogue and digital archives (Sutherland 2023). Apparently less contentious reanimations, such as those of objects and animals, also raise a set of ethical and epistemological issues.

Experiences like *The Living Museum* and *Nature Perspectives* illustrate how AI is mobilized to make non-human entities 'speak', often in the hope of provoking empathy or altering perception. *The Living Museum* enables users to interact with objects from the British Museum based on publicly available metadata. While instructive and fun to play with, its answers to users' questions are an example of how colonial perspectives can be reinforced. Asked whether the moai would want to be repatriated to their original home at the sacred site of Orongo in Rapa Nui (Easter Island), the Hoa Hakananai'a moai answers, 'My presence here allows many to learn about the rich culture of Easter Island, though I understand the pain of being removed from my original sacred site.'[4] Projects like *Nature Perspectives* present themselves as advancing more-than-human engagement, yet they expose the limits of generating alternative epistemologies through archival data. As the museum's assistant director put

4 Authors' interaction with *The Living Museum* on 30 April 2025.

it, 'Can we change the public perception of a cockroach by giving it a voice?' – a gesture that reveals a fundamentally Western epistemological framing, where voice is equated with subjectivity and moral value.

These approaches risk projecting human logics onto more-than-human entities, privileging recognizable speech over other forms of relational knowing. In doing so, it can inadvertently marginalize non-Western relational and non-anthropocentric epistemologies and ontologies (Abdilla et al. 2020) in which non-human beings are already recognized as communicative, agentive and sacred, without needing to be made audible or legible – least of all through AI. Rather than disrupting anthropocentric knowledge systems, these interventions can reinscribe them, reducing more-than-human presence to computable form. As Puig de la Bellacasa (2017) argues, care in more-than-human relations requires attentiveness to the epistemic conditions through which such voices are made to speak – conditions that AI systems, drawing from institutional archives, rarely interrogate. The result is not an expansion of ontological plurality, but a recording of existing structures under the guise of technological innovation. By treating the act of giving voice as ethically and epistemologically neutral, these projects risk reinscribing the very hierarchies they seek to undo, offering a form of technological ventriloquism that centres Western frameworks of intelligibility and care.

To understand AI afterlives, then, is also to understand the histories of the archives they draw from, and to critically examine what kinds of memory-making are enabled or foreclosed. Their promise lies less in their capacity to tell new stories and more in their ability to provoke new questions: who owns cultural memory, how is it made and for whom? The archive has long been recognized not simply as a repository of knowledge but as a mechanism through which power is exercised, shaping what can be said, remembered and legitimized (Foucault 1972; Derrida 1996). Far from neutral, archives historically served as instruments of governance, particularly within imperial contexts, where they structured racialized and gendered hierarchies through their very form and content (Stoler 2002). The act of archiving, Achille Mbembe (2002) suggests, is both one of preservation and of violence – of encoding and effacing – rendering the archive a space where access, secrecy and exclusion are structurally intertwined. This growing body of work urges a redefinition of the archive as a contested terrain, where power, identity and memory are actively negotiated rather than passively stored. Community-driven models emphasize collaboration and care to counteract the extractive tendencies of dominant archival paradigms (Prescott et al. 2020; Reid 2002). Saidiya Hartman's (2008) notion of 'critical fabulation', highlights how speculative narratives can serve to surface what has been structurally excluded from the archive. Can AI and generative AI afterlives challenge these epistemic structures?

The introduction of AI into these already fraught archival spaces intensifies longstanding tensions. Media archaeology, particularly through Wolfgang Ernst (2013), shows how digital memory systems privilege computational efficiency and technical standardization, flattening the textured temporality of lived experience into structured, searchable data. In cultural heritage contexts, such dynamics are not merely technical but deeply epistemological: what becomes machine-readable is also granted institutional legitimacy, often to the exclusion of Indigenous, subaltern or otherwise marginalized ontologies. As the *Living Archive of Aboriginal Knowledge* and initiatives like *Provisional Semantics* reveal, efforts to digitize or remediate memory risk reinscribing colonial logics unless rooted in practices of relationality, reciprocity and community stewardship. As Prescott et al. (2020), Reid (2002), and Dalal-Clayton and Rutherford (2024) show, archival records – particularly those concerning racialized makers and colonized communities – are often marked by institutional neglect, inaccuracies and the prioritization of dominant narratives. Rather than offering restitution or inclusive memory, AI afterlives risk enacting a second erasure – under the guise of presence and preservation – by reinforcing extractive logics and reinscribing misrepresentation, calling into question who controls the means of representation and whose stories are sanctioned in the process (Sutherland 2023).

Broader critical scholarship on data systems has called attention to how digital infrastructures are entangled with structures and logics of colonialism, racism and economic extraction (Couldry and Mejias 2018; Zuboff 2019), reproducing racial hierarchies and reinforcing systemic inequalities (Browne 2015; Noble 2018; Benjamin 2019; Offert and Phan 2024). AI in artistic and cultural settings also reproduces epistemic coloniality through aesthetic experiments devoid of social accountability (Baradaran 2024; Hakopian 2024). These critiques intersect with calls for data justice and data sovereignty, particularly in Indigenous contexts (Abdilla et al. 2020). Efforts to resist these dynamics increasingly converge with ecological concerns, as the resource-intensive nature of AI raises urgent questions about environmental justice, linking epistemic and ecological sustainability (Abdilla et al. 2020).

These concerns echo warnings in memory studies against allowing AI to erase or distort marginalized histories. Scholars such as Richardson-Walden and Makhortykh (2024) argue for more inclusive and pluralistic models of memory-making that acknowledge the alterity of AI systems, while Kidd and Nieto McAvoy (2023) question whether synthetic media can yet offer genuinely meaningful, non-reductionist contributions to historical practices. The epistemic ambivalence of AI afterlives lies in this contradiction: they appear to offer access, but often within the epistemological confines of the dominant record. As Mignolo's (2010) concept of 'epistemic disobedience' makes clear, decolonial interventions must challenge – not merely extend – the frameworks of Western-centric knowledge systems. Instead, AI systems are often built on data mostly sourced from Euro-American archives, classified through Western taxonomies, and programmed in English, reinforcing what Schuh (2024) describes as the marginalization of statistically invisible or non-hegemonic epistemologies.

Another issue is whether algorithmic logic allows for disobedience. As noted elsewhere in this book (and in Kidd and Nieto McAvoy 2023), algorithmic remediation operates best in abstraction, with programmers excluding atypical data to ensure predictable, persuasive results (Markham 2020: 10). This uniformity reveals AI's stochastic mechanisms as culturally coded, shaped by historical, institutional and geopolitical forces rather than unpredictability. Despite data mashups and seemingly unique outputs, remediation leaves little room for 'disobedience' against algorithmic power as we have noted (Quadflieg et al. 2022). In their effort to produce coherent, affectively resonant experiences, they risk eliding complexity, reinforcing dominant tropes or even creating false or distorted memories (Murphy and Flynn 2022, Hoskins 2024). Reparative approaches that use AI not only to avoid but also actively counteract bias (Jackson and Courneya 2023) can potentially challenge forms of hegemonic collective memory (Smit et al. 2024). This might entail embedding 'diverse and potentially dissenting perspectives' into training datasets and computational logic (Richardson-Walden and Makhortykh 2024), and ensuring communities retain control over their 'memory capital' (Schuh 2024). Without such commitments, even the expansion of datasets risks replacing one dominant narrative with another, rather than transforming how memory itself is structured and valued.

Still, AI afterlives may serve as sites of epistemic friction. Nora Al-Badri's *Post-Truth Museum* (2021–3) and *Neuronal Ancestral Sculptures Series* (2020) explore the aesthetic and ethical implications of synthetic cultural memory. Similarly, *Looty*, a digital restitution project led by Chidi Nwaubani, uses LiDAR scanning to recreate looted objects such as the Rosetta Stone, releasing them as NFTs and redistributing proceeds to support African artists. These projects do not simply critique institutional biases – they perform alternative forms of archival and curatorial labour, interrogating who gets to narrate cultural memory and through what media.

Some interventions also advocate for alternative temporality and epistemic frameworks. For instance, the *Ancestra AI* project by AIxDesign proposes 'slow AI' as a response to Silicon Valley's extractive ethos, drawing on non-Western models of governance, archiving and data ethics. These speculative and experimental practices resonate with calls for a 'slow archive' (Christen and Anderson 2019), which values relational, reciprocal and community-grounded knowledge practices. Salvaggio (2024) proposes looking for the 'ghosts' in generative AI, not in its visible outputs but in the absences and silences it carries. Digital memory-making cannot be disentangled from histories of race, power and structural violence (Sutherland 2023).

Tensions remain, as efforts to decolonize archives demand careful, community-led engagement with records of marginalized histories, yet these are often undermined by the push towards open-access digitization, which can reproduce extractive logics and overlook the ethical and epistemological implications of mass data dissemination (Dalal-Clayton and Rutherford 2024). AI afterlives may not, in themselves, constitute acts of epistemic disobedience – but they expose the scaffolding of dominant memory frameworks, and in doing so, open space for critique, reimagination and contestation.

Ambiguous afterlives: Unpacking the discourses of AI in the museum

Thinking with AI afterlives seems to crystallize a host of long-standing concerns within the cultural and heritage sectors – concerns that have circulated for some time, but which take on new dimensions in the context of digital technologies and automation. Questions about what is remembered, how and by whom; concerning ownership, legacy and sustainability; and around distortion, exploitation and exclusion – these are not new, but are more (or differently) complicated when reanimation, reworking and reinvention become technically possible, and even routine.

There are tensions here, but they can be productive ones. AI invites us to reflect again on what it means to care for the past, to engage with its fragments, and to co-produce its meaning in the present. Museums, in this light, may serve less as authoritative custodians and more as sites of negotiation, and of critical experimentation, where publics can encounter shifting ideas of authenticity, presence and memory. Rather than adopting AI uncritically, institutions might instead stay with that ambiguity, asking what these tools make possible – and at what cost. The challenge, then, is not only technical but epistemological. What counts as knowledge in these contexts? Whose stories are being told, and whose are being synthesized, approximated or left out? While there is potential for AI to amplify underrepresented voices, it is worth questioning what kinds of representation are on offer, and whether those persons being represented recognize themselves in the outputs.

The widespread adoption of generative AI, particularly following the launch of ChatGPT, has increased the need for guidance to support non-specialists – including creatives and NGOs – in adopting AI responsibly. Recent policy initiatives reflect growing concern with AI's societal impacts, particularly within the cultural heritage sector. UNESCO's Recommendation on the Ethics of Artificial Intelligence (2021) and the European Parliament's Resolution on AI in education and culture (2021) directly address the use of AI in preserving, managing and interpreting tangible and intangible heritage. Sector-specific frameworks, such as the AI+Museum Network Toolkit (Murphy and Villaespesa 2020) and the Smithsonian Institution's AI Ethics Framework, further support heritage institutions in adopting AI responsibly. In parallel, broader initiatives – such as UK Research and Innovation's Principles for Trusted Research and Innovation, the SAFE-D Principles[5]

5 The SAFE-D principles are: Sustainability, Accountability, Fairness, Explainability, Data Responsibility (https://www.gov.uk/government/publications/ministry-of-justice-ai-and-data-science-ethics-framework/safe-d-principles-text-only#what-are-the-safe-d-principles).

developed by the Alan Turing Institute (Leslie et al. 2023), and the Horizon Institute's Responsible Innovation Prompts – emphasize ethical responsibility and stakeholder engagement across AI applications more generally.

Common recommendations emphasize transparency, explainability, regulatory compliance, human oversight and alignment with institutional values. Key priorities include mitigating bias, ensuring data diversity, building capacity, anticipating risks and environmental impacts, and fostering collaboration across diverse – sometimes competing – stakeholder groups to develop ethical, fair and responsible AI systems. Of course, as we noted in the book's introduction, many of the principles for responsible AI adoption – such as transparency, accountability and dignity – are vague enough to be interpreted and operationalized in different ways by different stakeholders and industries (Jobin et al. 2019). While sound, they might not be realistic both at a practical and theoretical level. For example, in relation to 'transparency', we might ask what does it mean to be transparent when the technologies themselves are opaque, especially when using commercial tools that obscure internal workings? Often, digital experiences are created by external third-party developers that might – or might not – have a clear and open record of their process (Hamilton 2024). In our research participants reminded us of how difficult it is to subvert users' expectations – the often-unconscious contracts visitors make with cultural objects they interact with – through transparency, and the difficulty of getting such messages across, despite consistent use of explainers, disclaimers and caveats. 'Accountability' in AI-driven cultural projects is also complex, as responsibility is distributed across developers, institutions and users. While firms like Goodby Silverstein & Partners acknowledge the need for regulation (Solomon 2024), and Jumbo Mana aligns its work with national data sovereignty goals (Les DeepTech), such projects often blur ethical boundaries – particularly in publicly funded museums. In the case of the concept of 'dignity', Rueda et al. (2025) note that it is 'an elusive concept with multiple philosophical interpretations' and that its repeated use in AI literature 'can be counterproductive for AI ethics'. It is not only the principles that remain vague, but the term AI itself, something that we remain attentive to in our analysis.

The cultural sector's engagement with AI must also be understood within a longer tradition of policy ambiguity. As argued in studies of cultural policy, concepts such as 'value' and the 'cultural industries' have long functioned as flexible, malleable signifiers, useful for advocacy but often detached from practical change (Gray 2015; Nieto McAvoy and Allan 2023). The same dynamics appear to be at play in AI-related discourse: policy keywords – 'innovation', 'impact', 'inclusion' – are deployed strategically but ambiguously, serving political agendas while leaving underlying inequalities and structural barriers intact (Hayden 2012; Gillespie and Nieto McAvoy 2016; Belfiore 2021). Without addressing underlying power structures and entrenched inequalities, as well as critically interrogating whose interests AI adoption serves, there is a risk that digital transformation in museums remains performative rather than transformative.

Discourses, framing and expectations matter. AI might deepen engagement with collections, or it might risk distancing visitors from the material traces of the past. It might surface new narratives or entrench familiar exclusions. It might fill perceived 'gaps' in historical records, but such acts of completion always carry interpretive weight; while they should be treated as speculative rather than corrective, the onus is often on the user to make that distinction. As such, user experience should not be reduced to interaction design or emotional impact alone. How AI shapes the kinds of questions visitors are invited to ask – or not ask – is just as crucial. The uncanny valley may not only be aesthetic but also epistemological: where do we locate discomfort, and what might that discomfort reveal?

In all of this, collaboration remains essential, not only as a practice but also as a mode of thinking. Bringing together institutions, technologists, communities and researchers can create a space for shared learning, contested meanings and ethical reflection. Rather than aiming for consensus or closure, such exchanges might support an ongoing inquiry into what AI does – and what it could become – within the shifting terrain of memory, culture and care. Collaboration however is a fraught goal when thinking about AI:

> A *collaboration* implies a give and take, a set of *mutual* compromises. But nobody is asking AI – its industry, interfaces, data collection practices, its *infrastructure* – to compromise with *us*. (Salvaggio 2024)

On the one hand, scholars often place AI as one in a long history of technologies with which to mediate memory, creativity, identity and care, relativizing the moral panic about its capabilities. But in the midst of all the discursive confusion, being transparent about the limitations of algorithmic logics is not so easy. We might want to think carefully about what we are giving up when adapting to the limitations imposed by AI. As Salvaggio (2024) notes, adapting memory to fit into the infrastructures of AI – and not just the infrastructures of the archive – might not be a compromise custodians of our collective pasts should be willing to make.

Conclusion

As experimenting with algorithmic afterlives becomes an increasingly mundane practice, museums, heritage sites and archives must grapple with the ethical, cultural and technical implications of engaging with datafied remains. There is a rare and timely opportunity for these institutions to get ahead of the curve – not simply by adopting new technologies, but by critically shaping their development through collaborative, context-aware approaches such as co-design. Yet, in doing so, they must ask: what kind of continuance is being crafted here, and for whom?

Custodianship, traditionally understood through legal and familial lenses, is shown to be more complex and contested in these emerging contexts. As new, often collaborative, forms of data embodiment arise, we are prompted to reconsider who the rightful custodians are. Might we require a more distributed model – one that includes not only families and estates but also communities, cultural institutions, data stewards and even technology companies? The role of these technology companies, in particular, demands closer scrutiny. Are they collaborators, curators, data sources or something else entirely? And if we agree they bear responsibility, how is that responsibility conceptualized and enacted? Similarly, the role of regulation – still vague and uneven – raises pressing questions about institutional preparedness. Should heritage organizations now be considering the inclusion of data trustees to navigate these terrains responsibly?

A more robust regulatory framework for AI – particularly generative AI – is likely to emerge in the coming years, with consultations already underway in the UK and elsewhere. In parallel, we may also see increasing regulatory attention towards the ethical management of digital remains. Despite these developments, museums will undoubtedly continue to engage with emerging technologies; they have long demonstrated agility and a capacity for innovation, particularly when working in collaboration. Their appeal as partners lies not only in their expertise but also in the rich collections and datasets they steward. Yet this trust – carefully cultivated over time – should not be jeopardized. It is essential that these institutions do not retreat from their ongoing commitments to inclusivity, accessibility and the diversification of narratives. To do so would risk both cultural and reputational harm. As French and Villaespesa (2019: 101) argue, there is a pressing need for museums to become 'informed consumers of these emerging technologies'.

7

Conclusion: Rethinking memory, mourning and mediation in the age of synthetic media

In this book, we have traced the complex and often disquieting terrain of synthetic media, exploring their profound implications for memory, mourning and meaning-making in the digital age. Through a close examination of emergent technologies – from genealogical deepfakes to AI-generated deathbots and cultural 'revivals' – we have demonstrated how algorithmic systems are actively reshaping the ways in which individuals and societies remember, grieve and reimagine both personal and collective pasts. We have shown that these AI afterlives are not neutral or purely technical phenomena; rather, they are deeply embedded within sociotechnical, economic and cultural structures that demand critical scrutiny.

At the heart of our argument is a concern with how memory is being operationalized under platform capitalism. The chapters collectively reveal a shift from memory as a fluid, affective and socially situated process to one increasingly defined by automation, commodification and algorithmic logics. Whether in the personal realm – through platforms like *MyHeritage* and *HereAfter* – or in the public domain of the creative industries and cultural institutions, the practices we have explored show how AI afterlife technologies are rarely about preserving memory in any authentic sense. Instead, they often function to repackage the past in ways that serve the agendas of visibility and profit.

Our analysis also makes clear how these technologies invite users to engage in acts of remembrance that are shaped as much by illusion as by information. The appeal of synthetic media lies in its promise of connection – of seeing a loved one smile again, or hearing a favourite artist sing once more – but that promise is often underwritten by processes of distortion, data abstraction and erasure. The affective power of such encounters obscures the extent to which synthetic afterlives depend upon reductive templates, proprietary systems and extractive logics. They invite forms of mourning that are increasingly prescripted and removed from the interpretive labour of genuine remembrance.

Building from these observations, we argue for more cautious and reflexive engagement with the past's digital reanimation. As norms around death, memory and digital identity continue to evolve, it will be crucial to more robustly foreground questions of ethics, authorship, consent and context, and to think more creatively about how these opportunities are presented and framed. In their current manifestations, AI afterlives risk enacting a politics of memory that prioritizes spectacle over substance, efficiency over empathy and reproducibility over respect. They reconfigure what is remembered, how it is remembered and who has the power to remember in ways that are deeply consequential.

If the future of memory is increasingly being shaped algorithmically, then the challenge before us is not simply technical but profoundly cultural and ethical. We must ask what it means to remember well in a 'synthetic' age and insist on forms of digital commemoration that honour the complexities of grief, the integrity of the individual and the social richness of human memory. Only through such a critical lens can we begin to resist the flattening effects of synthetic media and reclaim a more human and plural vision of digital afterlives in the AI era.

Mapping AI afterlives in this book

In Chapter 2, we established a theoretical framework to underpin our exploration of AI afterlives in the chapters that followed. Synthetic media was defined and examined, with a focus on its influence in shaping how memory is created, stored and retrieved in digital spaces. We discussed the growing prominence of generative AI, deepfakes and virtual performers, alongside the ways these technologies are increasingly integrated into personal and cultural memory-making. The chapter also explored ethical concerns surrounding the manipulation of memory, particularly in relation to death and mourning. This foundation served as a basis for understanding how synthetic media not only alters personal recollections but also affects our broader cultural memory and social connections. Our overview of algorithmic culture emphasized the pervasive influence of algorithms in everyday life, raising important concerns about data privacy, bias and the opacity of AI processes that influence how we remember the past.

Chapter 3 then turned to the ethical and social ramifications of AI in personal memory-making, focusing on genealogy platforms like *MyHeritage* and its *Deep Nostalgia* feature. This case study highlighted how AI systems are used to 'revive' deceased ancestors, raising critical questions about the authenticity of digital afterlives. By animating still photographs of the deceased, the platform generates a sense of immediacy and connection, but as we argued, these outputs become increasingly detached from their original source materials. This chapter introduced the notion of 'algorithmic nostalgia' – the idea that AI-driven media can distort and homogenize personal memories through the standardization of facial expressions and movements, and we also highlighted the potential for 'deceptive genealogy' where boundaries between authentic and artificial memories become blurred. The chapter raised ethical concerns about the commodification of memory, especially when driven by social media and data extraction practices, building on the theoretical ideas established in Chapter 2 about how memory is influenced by technology.

Further developing the discussion about personal memory in Chapter 3, Chapter 4 examined how digital afterlife platforms – in our case *Almaya*, *HereAfter*, *Seance AI* and *You, Only Virtual* – use AI to capture and curate personal memories, often through the creation of 'deathbots'. These platforms enable users to preserve and interact with the memories of deceased loved ones, but, as we argued, rely on an overly simplistic understanding of memory and connection. The chapter critiqued how these platforms downplay the complex emotional and social factors that shape memory formation. We highlighted the 'platformization' of memory, showing how the business models of these platforms oversimplify memory making processes in order to create scalable, profitable services. Despite the promise of digital immortality, we demonstrated that these services fail to live up to their idealized vision, exposing a considerable gap between their marketed benefits and the actual experiences users encounter.

Chapter 5 shifted the focus from personal memory to cultural memory, exploring the role of synthetic media in the creative industries, particularly the use of AI to 'revive' cultural figures. Through a series of case studies – from the Tupac Shakur hologram to the voice cloning of Polish actor Miłogost Reczek – we analysed public narratives about AI's role in cultural memory-making. We argued that while these AI recreations may foster a sense of connection with cultural 'icons', they can also distort the public's understanding of those icons' death and legacy. As in earlier chapters, we showed that the manipulation of digital likenesses raises significant ethical questions, and seeds particular anxieties within the creative industries where writers, actors and musicians fear being replaced by AI that can endlessly replicate and generate new works, often at a lower cost. This fear, combined with the rapid pace of technological progress, signals broader concerns about the devaluation of artistic labour and cultural narratives. The discussion drew on insights from earlier chapters about the platformization of memory and the challenge of creating convincing and respectful representations of persons past.

Chapter 6 shifted to consider approaches to collective memory in the heritage sector. Unlike personal memory, which is often tied to individual experiences, practices of memory curation in museums and heritage sites involve complex negotiations of collective memory, and of power. We argued that the use of synthetic media in these contexts to create immersive, interactive representations of historical events and figures promises to offer radical reimaginings of memory practices, blurring lines between storytelling and simulation, emotional resonance and historical fidelity, and innovation and commodification. The analysis draws on participatory research and workshops with heritage professionals, showing that while there is enthusiasm for AI's potential, concerns about disinformation, sustainability and third-party control are widespread. The chapter questions whether AI-generated interactions risk flattening complex histories, particularly through curated avatars that prioritize emotional connection over uncomfortable truths. Examples like *Hello Vincent* and *Dalí Lives* were contrasted with the more ethically grounded *Dimensions in Testimony* initiative and artist Nora Al-Badri's experimental projects. The chapter situates AI afterlives within longer traditions of archival critique, colonial histories and debates about who owns and curates memory. It also exposed the ambiguity of 'responsible AI' discourses.

Across the chapters we see how AI-driven technologies and synthetic media are reshaping both individual and collective memory. From personal genealogical experiences to broader cultural memory-making in the creative industries and heritage sectors, we have highlighted the ethical, emotional and social challenges that emerge as we increasingly rely on digital technologies to preserve and 'revive' the past. Across all chapters, we emphasize the need for critical reflection on how AI afterlives influence our understanding of memory, identity and legacy, while urging more nuanced and informed approaches to the use of these approaches which start with the question 'where we *can* revive a face, a voice, a gesture – should we?'

Limitations of the study

While this book provides a wide-ranging and theoretically informed exploration of AI-driven afterlives and synthetic memory practices, it is not without its limitations. The study focuses primarily on English-language materials and Western-centric platforms, particularly in the creative and heritage sectors. This inevitably limits the cultural diversity of perspectives represented, as we reflect further in our Data Coda (Chapter 8). Synthetic media practices in non-Western contexts – where conceptions of memory, death and digital identity may differ significantly – remain underexplored. Further research is needed to examine how these technologies operate within different cultural, religious and geopolitical frameworks. We are also very aware of temporal constraints on our investigation given the pace of innovation in generative AI and memory technologies. Platforms such as *MyHeritage*, *HereAfter* and *Seance AI* are constantly evolving their services, and new applications are emerging all the time. As such, this book captures a snapshot in time rather than a definitive account. Future developments may introduce new capabilities or ethical frameworks that shift the terms of debate here.

Research in the fields of digital culture and digital memory is also clearly impacted by limited access to proprietary data and algorithms, with the danger that access to data impacts the kinds of research deemed possible. Many of the platforms studied in this book operate as commercial black boxes, offering limited transparency about how their underlying algorithms function or how data is processed. This restricts the extent to which we can fully interrogate the technical mechanisms driving synthetic memory outputs. While sociotechnical walkthroughs and document analyses have provided insight, they cannot replace full access to systems. Much of the analysis – especially in the chapters on *Deep Nostalgia* and AI 'revivals' in the creative industries – relies on media discourse, platform documents and user-generated content (e.g. tweets). While these are rich sources, they capture how synthetic media are talked about, rather than the full spectrum of emotional or interpersonal experiences users may have in relation to them. Future ethnographic or interview-based work could help illuminate these more intimate dynamics, and is a priority for us in the next stages of our inquiry.

Lastly, the book adopts a critical lens, emphasizing risks such as data exploitation and memory distortion. While necessary, this focus may understate the agency of users or the potential for creative, therapeutic or restorative uses of synthetic media. We have referenced these potentials at various points in the book, but there is room for further inquiry into how communities might actively shape or subvert these technologies in meaningful ways.

Synthetic pasts: Contributions and implications

The book's arguments resonate far beyond the specific use cases we have examined, offering vital insights for scholars, practitioners and citizens concerned with how technology, memory and mortality intersect.

Academically, this research contributes to a growing body of interdisciplinary work in (digital) memory, heritage, media and critical algorithm studies by offering a sustained, empirically grounded and theoretically rigorous examination of how synthetic media are reconfiguring mnemonic practices. In particular, it moves beyond celebratory or deterministic accounts of digital innovation, attending instead to the cultural politics, ethical ambiguities and emotional labour entailed in algorithmic remembrance. It pushes these fields forward with a robust new conceptual vocabulary – terms such as *synthetic pasts*, *remediated memory*, *algorithmic nostalgia*, *deceptive genealogy* and *contested presence* – which can aid future analyses of AI-driven memory systems. It also underscores the importance of integrating affective and sociotechnical perspectives when studying emerging media, revealing how emotional experiences of loss and remembrance are increasingly entangled in opaque infrastructures of digital design and data extraction.

Across the chapters one contribution of note is the extension of remediation theory into the domain of synthetic media and AI-mediated memory practices. We suggest that synthetic media do not only refashion older media forms but also fundamentally reconfigure relationships between presence, temporality and memory. AI afterlife technologies remediate social practices of mourning and cultural memory, introducing new forms of immediacy and presence that are entirely simulated. These processes challenge existing frameworks by collapsing distinctions between the living and the dead, past and present, real and artificial. Our contribution, therefore, is to theorize remediation as a mnemonic and affective process – one increasingly entangled with algorithmic systems and commercial platform logics. In doing so, we situate the remediation of memory within the ethical and epistemological conditions of algorithmic culture.

The book encourages a more robust confrontation of synthetic media not merely as a technical novelty or cultural trend, but as a force reshaping epistemological and ontological boundaries. In so doing it also offers a way to begin imagining synthetic media differently, as Ferrari and McKelvey (2022) propose: 'Although we cannot foresee the future worlds of synthetic media, we can strive to develop a theoretical repertoire to imagine them.' On the one hand, the pervasive use of synthetic media exposes how quickly human narratives can be manipulated, simplified or commodified, and these concerns must be taken seriously. Yet on the other hand, we have seen that the same tools that distort can also amplify, offering unique opportunities to engage new publics with memory work across geographies, and across time. They can enable innovative forms of storytelling, stimulate affective connections with lost histories, and offer marginalized communities alternative frameworks to engage with memory work beyond the institutional confines of Western dominated archival spaces and logics, even when considering all the caveats of the technology. We like to envisage the (future) creation of synthetic pasts through the harnessing of community-driven approaches to AI, perhaps using smaller, slower, specific and culturally situated datasets to innovate, visualize the intangible and reimagine the absent; uses which go beyond providing simulacra, becoming prompts for deeper and more consequential memory work. The challenge is not to reject synthetic media outright then, but to reclaim their development and application for purposes that prioritize dignity, nuance and multiplicity. How we interact with synthetic media going forward is going to necessitate that we embrace 'ambiguity, irresolution, [and] multivalence' (Horning 2025) which we understand as a good thing in these contexts given the need to emphasize memory as itself equivocal and faltering. Synthetic media's significance may rest less in their storytelling potential than in their capacity to prompt critical questions – who gets to tell what stories and for whom?

Our work also has implications for how we might think about how AI operates and how it is perceived. In line with broader approaches to thinking about and with AI (e.g. Bajohr 2025), we interrogate dominant narratives that treat AI as primarily technical, computational or efficiency-oriented on the one hand, or as an existential challenge that could surpass or fundamentally alter the human condition on the other. This entails recognizing that AI reshapes not just information flows or artistic practices but also our conceptual vocabularies, requiring scholars to revise how authenticity, memory and meaning, for example, are theorized in light of AI's logics and affordances. Our analysis highlights that AI is not a neutral tool acting on (biased) data, but a cultural apparatus deeply embedded in meaning-making processes, shaped by assumptions about personhood, history and social value from both developers and users. In attending to the emotional and mnemonic dimensions of AI, we challenge prevailing paradigms that privilege scale, optimization and automation over careful reflection, contextual sensitivity and (more-than) human complexity, probing epistemological, aesthetic and affective frameworks. Our work suggests that to offer critiques of AI going forward, one must interrogate not only what it *does* but also how it frames, filters and forgets, and therefore what it *does not do* – the data and decisions that haunt (Salvaggio 2024), the silences it reproduces, the histories it excludes and the structures it privileges.

Socially, the implications of the book's arguments are profound. As synthetic media become more accessible and more deeply embedded in everyday life – from memorial chatbots to AI-generated celebrity performances – they will shape public understandings of death, identity and history in subtle yet far-reaching ways. These systems not only mediate how individuals grieve but also influence what and who is deemed worthy of remembrance. They risk reinforcing cultural biases, perpetuating misinformation and narrowing the scope of collective memory by privileging data-rich subjects and market-friendly narratives. We therefore interrogate the public, corporate and official discourses about AI, examining how they construct narratives of inevitability, innovation and neutrality, while often masking the ideological, economic and epistemological assumptions that underpin the development and deployment of these technologies. We argue that ambiguity in these contexts benefits rather than hinders these exploitative practices. As Bory points out, it falls to us as media and communications scholars to identify and understand 'how corporate narratives are driving the symbolic and cultural integration of new intelligent systems in society' (Bory 2019). This involves a rethinking of what is meant by ethics, legacy and dignity in relation to algorithms – terms too often shaped by corporate logics rather than collective deliberation. Our approach is in keeping with that of 'AI justice' perhaps (Munn 2023), experimenting with what that might mean in the context of memory and historical interpretation.

Building on Shoshana Zuboff's call to protect our 'elemental epistemic rights' from 'capitalist surveillance', Tackett (2021) wonders if this should extend to the dead also: 'Do we need a necroethics?' Cyberthanathology is fraught with theoretical and practical ethical issues (Beaunoyer and Guitton 2021); at the very least, some argue, digital remains also deserve to be treated with dignity and have their moral rights recognized (Lambert et al. 2018), just as physical corpses do (Öhman and Floridi 2017). This is complicated by what Gruvæus (2023) terms 'peak death' – a cultural moment in which death ceases to be final in the ways traditionally understood in modern, secular Western societies. AI now enables the creation of 'ghosts' that continue to functionally participate in the world of the living, through AI simulations, digital avatars and synthetic media that simulate the dead and blur the boundaries between life and digital presence. If AI afterlives are understood as 'functional ghosts' or 'functional spectres' (Gruvæus 2023), their function lies in preserving, simulating and mediating presence – offering continuity, dialogue and memory beyond death. They serve as interfaces between past and present, enabling the living to interact with curated traces of the dead for purposes ranging from education, mourning and commemoration, to entertainment, affective connection or institutional storytelling. Yet their functionality also includes unsettling effects: they reconfigure authorship, challenge cultural understandings of death and reveal the politics embedded in who is remembered, how and by whom.

Practically, the findings have relevance for technologists, policymakers, archivists and professionals in the cultural and creative sectors. The research invites these actors to think critically about the design, governance and ethical oversight of AI-driven memory systems. It calls for greater openness around data provenance, clearer consent mechanisms rooted in the ethos of custodianship and stewardship, and a commitment to continue interrogating the situated and co-constructed dimensions of memory work, which cannot be replicated through automation alone. Importantly, it also creates space for public dialogue about what a slower, more considered digital afterlife might entail – one that recognizes the plurality of mourning practices and relations with the deceased, as well as with the living, across human, more-than-human and planetary engagements. As we further our research in this area we are actively pursuing these connections; publishing policy papers, collaborating with industry and practitioners to produce resources, contributing to calls for evidence and carrying out public engagement on these themes.[1]

The book's contributions matter because they intervene at a moment when technological capabilities to simulate the past are accelerating, yet our regulatory, cultural and ethical frameworks for responding to them remain underdeveloped. By critically interrogating the promises and perils of synthetic media, this book not only maps an emerging field of inquiry but also issues a broader call: to resist the erosion of memory's complexity and to envision imaginative sustainable futures grounded in care, complexity and multi-directional and interdependent world-making.

Paths ahead

Our study of AI afterlives opens up multiple avenues for future research at the intersection of synthetic media, digital memory and AI-driven afterlives, and it suggests innovative ways this research might be designed. As the technologies

1 Up-to-date information about these activities can be found on our website www.syntheticpasts.com.

examined continue to evolve, so too must the critical and methodological frameworks used to study them. Here we identify future directions for our work as we continue to engage with disciplines, scholars and approaches that were out of scope for this book.

Future research on AI afterlives will benefit from engagement with a growing body of scholarship that calls for more cross-cultural and transnational approaches to digital commemoration. Media mediate our shared human condition – birth, death, embodiment, memory and imagination – shaping how we experience and make sense of existence across time, space and culture (Frosh 2018). As current discourses remain shaped predominantly by Western norms surrounding death, identity and technology, there is an urgent need to explore how synthetic media intersect with diverse memory practices – including ancestral veneration, collective mourning and posthumous rituals – that diverge significantly from Euro-American paradigms. Such research can help to decolonize this emerging field and support more pluralistic frameworks of digital remembrance.

Efforts to advance data justice and data sovereignty align closely with now longstanding movements in a range of contexts, for example, in the work of human rights organizations and social justice groups, as well as in heritage institutions and archives. Frameworks on Indigenous data sovereignty emphasize the importance of communities retaining control over their own data and cultural memory (Walter et al. 2022; Kukutai 2016; Carroll 2021). These concerns are echoed in heritage studies that advocate for a redistribution of epistemic authority from Eurocentric institutions towards source communities, proposing rematerialization, reparative justice and affective engagement with contested objects, as well as alternative frameworks that centre Indigenous epistemologies and collaborative curation (e.g. Brown and Peers 2005; Lonetree 2012; Rassool 2015; Modest and Augustat 2023, Hicks 2020). A data justice approach focused on access, representation and the right to refusal would further support critical evaluation of synthetic media practices that reanimate the past without consent. These intersecting perspectives also find resonance in critiques of racialized surveillance and technological infrastructures that risk reinforcing colonial logics (Benjamin 2019; Browne 2015). These critiques converge on a shared demand that resists extractive practices and foregrounds the relational, contested and situated nature of memory: to build infrastructures – digital or material – that are accountable to diverse communities, sensitive to epistemic harm and capable of supporting plural and contested pasts.

Relatedly, ethnographic and participatory methodologies are essential for capturing the lived experiences of users engaging with synthetic afterlife technologies. While this book has focused on discourse, platform design and media representation, future research might explore how individuals and families navigate these tools in practice; particularly during emotionally charged moments such as bereavement or cultural remembrance. Investigating how users negotiate meaning and agency in real time would yield rich insight into the emotional and social dimensions of synthetic memory, and what becomes of forgetting, silence and the natural limits that give memory its depth and meaning.

While our current analysis has begun to engage with questions of surveillance and biometric technologies, this remains a significant area for future work, particularly given the implications for AI afterlives. Research in surveillance studies offers critical insights into how synthetic reconstructions of human presence – such as avatars and interactive installations – are entangled with histories of racialization, visibility and control. These technologies operate not in neutral space, but through inherited regimes of vision and categorization that shape what can be preserved or animated. Biometric systems have been shown to be embedded within racialized logics of power, and facial recognition technologies to perpetuate social hierarchies under the guise of technical neutrality (Browne 2015; Benjamin 2019). Such critiques are particularly relevant when considering the reanimation of historical figures or marginalized subjects within cultural institutions. The appropriation of personal data, even posthumously, has been identified as a key mechanism of surveillance capitalism (Zuboff 2019), while the opacity and extractive nature of AI training datasets raises significant ethical and epistemic concerns (Crawford 2021; Crawford and Paglen 2019). These insights call attention to the implications of using archival or biometric material in ways that may commodify or distort memory. Artists and theorists have proposed alternative frameworks, such as 'queering the biometric norm,' to reimagine how museums might critically examine and resist dominant visual regimes. Bringing surveillance studies more centrally into the conversation around AI afterlives offers an opportunity to rethink the politics of recognition and memory and to make visible how power is encoded in technologies designed to simulate presence.

Something we find particularly intriguing is how smiles function within affective surveillance systems – not as spontaneous expressions, but as standardized indicators of compliance and emotional legibility. These systems, shaped by culturally biased emotion taxonomies, instrumentalize facial expressions to reinforce normative and corporate-friendly behaviours, which can be read through historically encoded logics of control, disproportionately affecting those already marginalized (Benjamin 2019). Smiles in synthetic media, particularly when embedded in AI-generated avatars or reanimations, are far from neutral indicators of friendliness or authenticity – they are affective tools deeply entangled in histories of power, surveillance and racialized control (Sutherland 2023). Our inquiries into these practices (and discourses) would benefit from engaging more closely than we have here with science and technology studies (STS) as well as actor-network theory (Stark 2019). Lauren Lee McCarthy's performance works (e.g. *LAUREN*) expose how friendly, emotionally intelligent interfaces can mask coercive systems of data extraction and behavioural surveillance. In the context of AI afterlives, smiling avatars – such as those in *Dalí Lives*, *Deep Nostalgia* or the puppeteering of celebrities – are not merely affective gateways, they are curated affective regimes that seek to build emotional connection while potentially flattening historical complexity or contested legacies, as we have argued throughout the book.

AI afterlives foreground critical tensions between embodiment and disembodiment also, particularly as they produce datafied versions of human lives, rendering memory, identity and presence into computational forms. As we have noted data acts as proxy flesh, offering a facsimile of presence and co-presence. Feminist posthumanism offers a vital lens for interrogating these tensions, challenging techno-utopian narratives that sever data from flesh. The figure of the cyborg (Haraway 1985), the posthuman subject (Braidotti 2013) and the digitally mediated avatar each destabilize boundaries between human and non-human, past and present, life and simulation. These theoretical provocations are particularly resonant when considered alongside the historical treatment of human remains in museums (Biers and Stringer Clary 2023). Bodies, removed from their social, spiritual and geographic contexts and reframed as objects of scientific or cultural knowledge, have long embodied tensions between presence and absence, materiality and meaning, which we wish to explore further. The museum, like the algorithm, extracts and reconfigures; whether through display or datafication, both render human lives into curated forms that are disconnected from their lived complexity. Linking AI afterlives and museological practices makes visible a shared logic of archival capture and representational control. If the cyborg once offered a hopeful reimagining of hybrid subjectivity, its institutional deployment today – whether reanimations of ancestors and celebrities, deathbots or digital facsimiles of artists and historical figures – risks reinscribing disembodied authority unless critically contextualized. Posthumanist frameworks instead push us to recentre the body, not as a static biological entity but as a relational, affective and contested site of memory and meaning. In this light, both skeletal remains and synthetic avatars demand attention to the ways institutions handle personhood, consent and epistemic justice across material and digital domains.

We also think the potential implications of 'model collapse' – a phenomenon gaining traction within AI's discursive arena as we write – are intriguing when it comes to our interactions with the past. As synthetic media increasingly populate the internet and themselves become data to train generative AI systems, it may become increasingly challenging to find, create or even imagine contexts for mnemonic work that do not in some way reflect back synthetic systems, media and agencies (Ananny 2024). Many feel this risk is overstated and not purely an AI problem, but the line between fabricated and historically grounded content is likely to become harder to trace in the years to come, undermining the epistemic authority of digital heritage outputs and digital memories. Mitigating these effects calls attention to the importance of archival integrity, provenance and human-centred curation, including: ensuring access to high-quality, diverse and contextually grounded source materials; embedding critical metadata and narrative framing into datasets; and maintaining transparent boundaries between real and synthetic content. How this works in practice and can be incentivized is an open question however given that implementation will require collaboration between technologists, corporations, researchers, citizens and cultural practitioners.

The creative and resistant potentials of synthetic media remain an area open to further exploration and critical inquiry too. A number of artists, like

Nora Al-Badri (*The Post-Truth Museum*, *Neuronal Ancestral Sculptures*) and Chidi Nwaubani (*Looty*), critically interrogate AI not as a neutral tool but as a site of cultural, political and historical contestation. Stephanie Dinkins's *Conversations with Bina48* explores intergenerational dialogue and racial identity through AI, while Mimi Ọnụọha's *The Library of Missing Datasets* exposes structural absences in data collection and classification. Trevor Paglen and Kate Crawford's *Training Humans* and *ImageNet Roulette* reveal the racialized and gendered logics of machine vision datasets. Lauren Lee McCarthy, in works like *LAUREN*, uses performative AI interfaces to question intimacy and surveillance. Hito Steyerl's *How Not to Be Seen* offers a biting critique of visibility and control in the digital realm, resonating with broader concerns about synthetic media. Amir Baradaran (*Towards a Decolonial I in AI*) and Ian Cheng (*BOB*) use speculative aesthetics to reflect on subjectivity and memory in algorithmic systems, while Kate Crawford and Vladan Joler's *Anatomy of an AI System* maps the extractive infrastructures sustaining AI. Collectively, these practices contribute to ongoing debates about epistemic justice, data sovereignty and the politics of representation, complicating dominant narratives and enriching the critical discourse around AI afterlives. Beyond critique, how might artists, archivists and communities harness these technologies to honour the dead, preserve endangered histories or confront structural erasures? Exploring alternative imaginaries for synthetic pasts – ones grounded in care, justice and co-authorship – will be crucial for shaping more equitable digital futures.

As synthetic memory systems grow in power and influence, the responsibility to shape them wisely does not lie with technologists alone. It is a challenge for scholars, artists, ethicists and citizens alike; to ensure that in digitizing the past, we do not lose what makes remembering human. Our own work models a hybrid, interdisciplinary approach that combines empirical analysis with creative and speculative thinking, and will be further expanded in the coming months and years to include further collaborative, community-engaged and critical interventions. Scholars must question dominant epistemologies in relation to AI, tracing absences in training data and actively working to surface alternative memory practices, particularly those of historically marginalized communities. AI afterlives invite us to imagine immortality in data, but they also demand that we confront the limits of simulation.

Between presence and commodification: Ambivalence in AI afterlives

Public discourses often present the further development of synthetic media and AI systems as inevitable (Bareis and Katzenbach 2021; McKelvey et al. 2024), foreseeing their eventual domestication within our public and private (intimate) lives, where the geopolitics of AI intersect with cultural power and ideological influence in evermore intricate assemblages. In life a great many algorithmic processes pass us by 'without being noticed' (Beer 2017). Stopping and noticing algorithms and AI, making them visible and holding their impacts up for analysis – as we have done in this book – is an ethical, epistemological and even ecological imperative. As Simon Cottle notes, such attention can help us to 'move beyond instrumental rationality to integrative intelligence and ecological relationality' helping us to 'envision and reorient society to a better world' (Cottle 2025: 364). It can also help us to better understand and interrogate 'the longstanding relationship between capitalism and computation' and to consider 'the knowledge-systems that have been privileged and the indigenous epistemologies that have been ignored' (Munn 2023: 874).

Ambivalence and ambiguity have been central to our discussions, as epistemological entry points also. The smile, like the digitally mediated face more broadly, exemplifies the technological ambivalence of our time, where utopian hopes for connection and empathy coexist with dystopian concerns about manipulation, surveillance and erasure (Davis 2012); as Bode et al. (2021) argue, the human face is increasingly troubled in its roles as biological fact, image, social marker and commodity. Deepfakes and digital expressions thus emerge not as neutral representations, but as 'culturally, technologically, institutionally, and historically situated phenomena' (Bode et al. 2021, 850). AI afterlives are saturated with technological ambivalence, where conflicting promises and perils coexist within the same systems. Beyond the affective ambiguity of the smile, these tensions emerge in multiple dimensions. Authenticity is one: synthetic avatars are framed as historically grounded and emotionally truthful while being, at the same time, fabrications generated by probabilistic logics, raising the question of whether emotional resonance can substitute for historical accuracy. Another is presence: AI reconstructions aim to offer intimate, immersive experiences, yet they rely on disembodied data, severed from context, culture and corporeality. Agency also becomes ambiguous, as users are invited into personalized interactions that simulate choice and dialogue, though the parameters of these exchanges are tightly constrained by training data and curatorial design. Moreover, remembrance and forgetting collide: AI systems are heralded for preserving memory and enabling eternal return, but they also risk erasing nuance, context and silence, generating reductive or fictionalized pasts as well as reinforcing extractive epistemologies, techno-solutionism or the commodification of grief and memory. These tensions are not confined to institutional settings such as museums but emerge across everyday digital practices – from personalized memorials and chatbot companions to algorithmic genealogies – where synthetic memory work is increasingly normalized. In these spaces, AI afterlives operate at the intersection of affect, remediation and automation, revealing how memory is being reshaped by systems that are simultaneously intimate and industrial, emotive and extractive. These ambivalences are not flaws to be resolved, but constitutive features of AI afterlives that demand ongoing critical interrogation.

8

Data coda

One of our ambitions as we work with AI afterlives has been to centre responsible design, transparency and ethics as sincere critical and methodological commitments. We wanted to be clear in the book how our approach to data has been informed by these principles, and felt it would be worthwhile doing so in a fully reflective chapter. We have called this a 'coda' to reflect the distinct work this chapter does as an important addition – but an addition none-the-less – to the book's main structure. This data coda offers a detailed overview of our varied approaches to AI afterlives so that readers can understand and evaluate them, and as a means to demonstrate the broad range of tools researchers now have available to them as they navigate increasingly intricate digital phenomena.[1] Our hope is to suggest ways that researchers can embrace methodologically curious and innovative projects in the fields of memory and heritage studies in future. As scholars familiar with these disciplines we understand that they are not typically informed by mixed and interdisciplinary approaches, but we contend there is a need for these in order to make sense of increasingly complex and multi-faceted sites of study. In our work, we have tested an expansive suite of social science and creative research methods, including (but not limited to) social media analysis, platform analysis, text analysis and visualization, user walkthroughs, co-production and collaboration with artists. We have worked across these methods in ways that are both quantitative and qualitative, and our understanding of their capabilities (and limitations) is informed by interdisciplinary insights.

In the book's introduction (Chapter 1), we referenced Samuel Merrill's (2025) work to champion 'hybrid methodologies' in the study of social and cultural memory, and we feel this is a helpful way of reflecting on our approach. Merrill's

1 Our approach to transparency here is informed by Bonini and Treré (2024).

reference to 'hybridity' goes beyond suggesting the combination of methods from different fields – although this is a factor – gesturing to the ways analyses can benefit from being situated in relation to ontological assumptions (Merrill 2025). Like in Merrill's work, our own approach has recognized the complexity (and sometimes disorder) of temporality, spatiality, materiality and agency in our data, it has examined how memory-related objects change or move through processes like remediation, and we have worked with computational 'collaborators' as we go on to detail. We are drawn to the concept of hybridity, particularly because, as Maurizia Boscagli argues, hybrids 'refuse to occupy their assigned space in the grid of meaning and value' (2014: 11). Hybridity foregrounds ideas of 'flux', 'in-betweenness' and 'liminality' (Chadwick 2013: 5), opening up possibilities for novel methodological combinations and shifting power relations (Galani and Kidd 2020). In line with Nick J. Fox and Pam Alldred (2017), our study adopts a mixed approach to create 'research-assemblages' that acknowledge and navigate the micropolitics inherent in methods. In this chapter we are committed to critically visibilizing these assemblages.

The book's arguments are built on a series of empirical investigations carried out between 2021 and 2025 as follows:

- A social media analysis of 6,935 posts on Twitter (now X) alongside a platform analysis of the *MyHeritage* genealogy service. *Underpinning Chapter 3.*
- Sociotechnical user walkthroughs of four 'deathbot' platforms, alongside systematic textual analysis of those platforms' official public documents. *Underpinning Chapter 4.*
- Content and textual analysis of news reporting on nine historical case studies spanning more than a decade (2012–23), amounting to 793 international reports. *Underpinning Chapter 5.*
- Thematic analysis of nineteen interviews as well as discussions and outputs from three workshops with a further thirty-five cultural professionals. *Underpinning Chapter 6.*

Our use of these humanities and social science research methods – which we introduce in more detail in the remainder of this chapter – has been coupled throughout with other kinds of investigation. We have embraced *making* both as a creative practice and as a method – producing, for instance, a series of digital stories and a highly visual web presence (www.syntheticpasts.com).

These outputs embody our critical-creative approach and are informed by the work of scholars across intersecting fields. We have been guided by Jenna Ng and Oliver Tomkins, whose 2023 video essay and theorization of *The New Virtuality* has been crucial to our approach; by Lev Manovich, whose artistic practice and foundational contributions to new media studies continue to provide an essential frame; and by Joanna Zylinska, whose 'hybrid' mode of enquiry productively weaves together philosophy and artistic practice.

Throughout the project, we have produced many generative AI images and videos, positioning ourselves as researcher-users of different platforms and devices. This has been a way of visualizing our findings and concerns about AI afterlives – using content generators such as Gemini, Magic Media, DALL-E4 and Stable Diffusion. We have created deathbots, virtual avatars, online installations, a Twine game, and even a digital Ouija board as mechanisms for staging and visualizing our research themes. Alongside this, we have undertaken extensive desk research, engaging with publicly available chatbots and avatars and examining the diverse ways others are deploying these technologies.

We have also collaborated with artists in a variety of ways. In 2024 we worked with Mark Stuart-Smith[2] on an installation of *Black Box* on The Strand in London as part of King's College London's *Fake or Real?* exhibition. The artwork, a response to the themes of our Leverhulme Trust funded Synthetic Pasts project, consisted of a carved wooden sculpture of a head, begun when the artist was sixteen years old, and reworked and reanimated for the exhibition (see Figure 8.1). The head rotated inside a miniature simulacrum of the place where it was first carved, highlighting the role of authenticity in how we interact with images, and with memory.

We also worked with creative studio yello brick[3] who produced a series of playful encounters for use in our workshops as a way of generating discussions amongst participants. *Who Owns a Memory?* for example, featured two audio recordings – one playable on a Panasonic cassette deck, the other on an iPhone – and a series of scripted prompts to encourage interaction around, and then reflection on, themes of memory, authenticity and ethics (see Figure 8.2). According to feedback, these thought-provoking and playful interventions

2 More about Black Box and Mark's work can be found here: https://markstuartsmith.co.uk/.
3 More about yello brick's work can be found here: https://www.yellobrick.co.uk/.

Figure 8.1 Mark Stuart Smith's *Black Box* installed in London, 2024–5. Reproduced with permission from Mark Stuart Smith.

helped create space for more collaborative and generative discussions and activities amongst our workshop participants.

The use of these creative approaches has opened up new ways of thinking both about and through the issues we foreground in this book, and we continue to extend and deepen these collaborations.

Finally, we have also used a number of social media platforms to explore the issues associated with AI afterlives. Later we detail our use of Twitter (now X[4]) to glean insights into personal memory-making in the orbit of AI afterlives, but we have also used Instagram and WhatsApp as a way of communicating about our research. Instagram's highly visual aesthetic and vernacular speaks well to the substance of our research inquiry (Gibbs et al. 2015; Leaver et al.

4 Beyond clarifying that Twitter is now known as X, we feel it is appropriate to refer to the platform here as Twitter given this best reflects the character of the platform at the time the research was carried out (2021). Since Elon Musk acquired Twitter in 2022 it has of course changed profoundly, with many researchers, ourselves included, now minded not to use it at all.

Figure 8.2 *Who Owns a Memory?* activity, designed by yello brick, 2024. Reproduced with permission from Alison John, yello brick.

2020; Hu and Kidd 2024), but our use of WhatsApp has been more extensive, amounting to many thousands of messages over the course of the last four years as we shared news stories, images, observations and reflections. Like Bonini and Trere (2024: 180) we understand our WhatsApp communications with one another to be 'field notes' and fundamental to our thinking about AI afterlives.

In the following sections we introduce more formally the methods we have used chapter by chapter, reflecting on what these approaches made possible, as well as their challenges and limitations. We then close with a reflection on research ethics.

Deep Nostalgia social media analysis (Chapter 3)

Discussions in Chapter 3 were oriented around the launch of *MyHeritage*'s *Deep Nostalgia* feature, 25 February 2021. In order to understand how people were using *Deep Nostalgia* and sharing the outputs produced we carried out an analysis of all Twitter data (now X) on the hashtag #DeepNostalgia during the two-week period that followed. The Twitter data were sourced from Vicinitas.[5] The resulting dataset (n. 6,935) was quantitatively analysed using available metadata from Twitter, before a randomized sample was extensively and qualitatively analysed thematically (n. 347, reduced to n. 316 once tweets that were no longer available were excluded[6]). This smaller sample worked as a 'thickening strategy' for the analysis in recognition that 'data abundance' is not in itself an indicator of research quality or insightfulness (Latzko-Toh et al. 2016).

The quantitative analysis of manifest data included date, language, type of media, type of tweet and number of replies, retweets and quoted tweets. During the inductive and qualitative analysis of the smaller sample, we coded for emotional resonances (did *Deep Nostalgia* elicit nostalgia, and were emotional responses explicit or signalled with emojis), attitudes towards the animation of bodies in *Deep Nostalgia* (e.g. was it 'creepy' or 'amazing'), assessments of the ethical and technological ramifications of this bit if kit, and the overarching tone of tweets. We also carried out an analysis of any visual materials in the post. This more nuanced manual qualitative analysis meant we were able to remain attentive to each tweet's context and the juxtaposition of elements it contained. So, for example, tweets containing combinations of text, videos (mostly shares from the *Deep Nostalgia* feature) and emoji could be considered in their entirety, or if a post was a response tweet we could refer back to the original for context, as well as exploring any comments or discussion that followed.

We acknowledge that any study of data of this type, and in this way, is bound to be limited. In our analysis, we have needed to remain mindful that a 'Twitter public' is not by any means a representative societal cross-section (and an X public even less so), and that choosing this network rather than any other will have skewed the population in our study. It also no doubt impacts the ways issues were debated, given that Twitter users tend to be disproportionately white, male and managerial or professional in occupation (Sloan 2017). Indeed, those

5 Changes in the Twitter API mean accessing historical data is problematic without the use of commercial data services. Such data sets are likely to be imperfect, but are the fullest that can be accessed, and have become a standard (e.g. in Ruffer et al. 2020).

6 At 5 per cent we reached saturation point. The mixed-methods analysis was informed by Snelson et al. 2016, and the protocols for the thematic analysis followed Nowell et al. 2017.

who work or research in the technology sector tend to be over-represented on Twitter – as was the case in our sample – and this too may have impacted the character of the discussions.[7] There were practical reasons for our choice of this social network however. Chief amongst these was the fact that *MyHeritage* was using Twitter as a way of launching the feature, but acquiring a dataset was also more straightforward than it would have been for Facebook, the other network *Deep Nostalgia* users were encouraged to share their creations through.[8]

These data did uniquely reveal the confluence of public and professional discourses circulating around the launch of *Deep Nostalgia*, but they told us less about the company's motivations and the platform's dynamics. To complement the social media study then, we also carried out a systematic platform analysis of the *MyHeritage* genealogy service. This included a close critical reading of language used on the platform and by the D-ID studio that created the underlying technology, plus a document analysis of Terms and Conditions in relation to data use, as well as relevant Privacy Policies (D-ID 2021a, 2021b, 2023a, 2023b, 2023c; MyHeritage 2022a, 2022b, 2023a, 2023b, 2023c).

Together, the social media and platform analyses gave us as rounded a snapshot as was possible – at the time of the *Deep Nostalgia* launch – of the 'offer' being presented by *MyHeritage*, and how users were responding to it in real time. Chapter 3 details findings from those analyses. The discussions reflect on AI afterlives in the context of firstly, *MyHeritage* as above all else a genealogy platform, secondly, *Deep Nostalgia*'s particular formulation of remediated memory, and thirdly, social platforms and their role in networking, normalizing and standardizing digital memory work.

'Deathbots' platform analysis (Chapter 4)

In Chapter 4, our investigation broadened to include four commercial platforms purporting to create more fulsome AI afterlives. These platforms

7 80 per cent of users in our sample were individuals – 55 per cent of whom were members of the public, 18 per cent described themselves as working or interested in technology and 27 per cent described themselves as professionals, mostly journalists, writers, academics, researchers and cultural and heritage workers.

8 *Deep Nostalgia* users can download the video or copy the link to share on other platforms.

were: *Almaya*, *HereAfter*, *Seance AI* and *You, Only Virtual*. To better understand these platforms we used a branched approach to data gathering. Firstly, we carried out sociotechnical walkthroughs of the platforms as user-researchers (following Light et al. 2016; Ritter 2022; Troeger and Bock 2022; Duguay and Gold-Apel 2023). This was done methodically such that the operation and utilization of each could be thoroughly interrogated. The analysis revealed how each interface structures user interaction, in so doing 'incentivising, modulating and/or encouraging particular kinds of interactions and in-app activities' (Ash et al. 2024: 99). During this process, we recorded details about all stages of platform interaction: registration and entry, everyday use, as well as suspension of an account, closure and leaving (following Ash et al. 2024). In doing so, we were able to position ourselves as real-world users of these services as we felt and experienced those touchpoints.

Using our own data in this way meant, in three platforms, taking on the role of living persons archiving our own life stories and personas as if for people to interact with after our demise (so, the platform was mimicking us). In the last case study (*Seance AI*), we interacted with the platform in the role of 'loved ones' initiating a séance with a person hybridized from our own extant datasets. We spent approximately two days working with each platform. For *Hereafter AI* and *Almaya* we contributed approximately twenty video or audio memories each, for *Seance AI* we uploaded a series of our own WhatsApp messages and email texts, and for *You, Only Virtual* we used those same textual resources, plus a series of lengthy voice notes. Our rationale for this methodological choice – using our own data rather than working with those of research participants – was grounded in our own dubiety about these processes, as well as our desire to better understand the 'feel of algorithms' in these contexts (Ruckenstein 2023).

Following this, we carried out an analysis of official public documents related to each platform. These were manually collated from the platforms on 9 September 2024, resulting in ten documents as shown in Table 8.1. These documents were deemed meaningful for the analysis because they gave us access to the structural, informational and legal architectures crafted by these platforms, and within which all users should operate.

As scholars have noted, documents have a distinctive ontological status, and rather than being read straightforwardly as representing an

Table 8.1 Documents in the Analysis

Platform	Document	Date published (where available)	Word count
Almaya	Terms and Conditions	26 December 2022	6,576
Almaya	Privacy Policy	23 November 2021	8,195
Almaya	FAQs		1,161
Hereafter.ai	User Agreement	15 June 2023	5,441
Hereafter.ai	FAQs		685
Seance AI	Terms and Conditions		565
Seance AI	Privacy Policy		345
Seance AI	FAQs		257
You, Only Virtual	Terms of Service	01 June 2024	6,152
You, Only Virtual	Privacy Policy	01 June 2024	5,590
TOTAL			**34,967**

organizational or social 'reality', should be understood as constituting a 'documentary reality' written with a distinct readership in mind, and produced within certain organizational, regulatory and cultural conditions (Atkinson and Coffey 1997). The documents analysed in this study are used to accomplish very specific objectives relating to the provision and use of services, and rules and conditions associated with those. Many are Terms and Conditions and Privacy Policies which act as very particular kinds of legal documents relating to agreements between businesses and customers. In the case of Terms and Conditions they constitute a contract which should be accepted by all users, one which offers clarity about rights, responsibilities and roles for all parties, details protections such as copyright conditions and age limits, and (it is hoped) supports trust and confidence. Privacy Policies have a rather different orientation towards data, explaining how these will be collected, why and for what purposes. In such policies, users should be informed how data will be protected, sold or shared, and what their rights are should they wish to exercise them. Where companies' services interact with third-party providers, these entanglements should also be detailed in the Privacy Policy. Ideally, these service level documents will be clear, concise and use unambiguous language, but as any user of digital services can attest, this is not always the case.

Our ten documents amounted to a dataset of 34,967 words. Once collated, we first carried out an analysis using Voyant Tools, a 'web-based reading and analysis environment for digital texts'.[9] Voyant Tools is an open-source project designed both to suit the needs of Digital Humanities scholars and to be publicly available (examples of use include Lell 2022; Schumann 2022; Zaidi and Allahdad 2023). It is a powerful tool for exploring word trends in large bodies of textual data, including incidences of key terms, collocations, sentiment, links between keywords and repeat phrases. Exploring each of our documents in this way made visible what was being emphasized in each, and across them all. We followed this quantitative analysis with a manual qualitative analysis of the full sample using thematic coding to identify patterns inductively, but in a systematic way. This closer reading revealed how values and data practices were articulated (following Scharlach et al. 2023), and where these documents' shortcomings were. Signing up for accounts and carrying out the sociotechnical walkthroughs before doing the textual and thematic analyses meant we were already familiar with the contexts within which these documents should be applied, and we were able to strive for sensitivity in how we worked with them. We were thus able to produce empirical knowledge and understanding systematically (Bowen 2009) which underpinned the findings recounted in Chapter 4. These reflect on the platformization of memory, specifically in the context of grief and debates about posthumous personhood.

Stage and screen content analysis (Chapter 5)

In Chapter 5, our focus turned to an exploration of nine case studies where high-profile public figures (often cultural 'icons') had been 'revived' using varied forms of synthetic media; from the Tupac Shakur 'hologram' in 2012, through to the voice cloning of Miłogost Reczek in 2023. Our emphasis here was on understanding the ebb and flow of public debates about these technologies, as well as on who has shaped those debates.

To support the analysis we carried out a systematic content analysis of news reports from international English language publications. These were sourced via LexisNexis and included newspapers, online publications and

9 More about Voyant Tools can be found here: https://voyant-tools.org/.

magazines and trade press. In each case, the most relevant keywords were chosen for the retrieval of a dataset, and these keywords are highlighted in bold in Table 8.2. Once cleaned (duplicates and mismatches removed), that dataset amounted to 793 reports. The breakdown of cases and reports was as follows:

In total, this longitudinal study captured debates spanning more than a decade (eleven years and eight months). For each case study, the specific timeframe was selected to capture the start of media debates about that case, plus a period of two months following that story breaking. In this way we could examine both how debates about each case, and about the issues in more general terms, were shifting over time.

The analysis of those reports was then carried out in two stages. Firstly, the full sample for each case was analysed using Voyant Tools (introduced in the previous section). Given the varied sizes of the datasets in our sample, frequency of key terms gave us a picture of discourse around each of these cases, but had limited comparative use value when it came to establishing how that discourse differed across cases, or over time. Relative frequencies represent a more meaningful picture in this regard, and it is these that readers will see in the graphs in Chapter 5.

To complement this arguably more remote exploration of the nine case studies,[10] we then went on to perform a detailed content analysis on a smaller subset of data for each (as outlined in Table 8.2). This analysis charted which sources were being used in the reporting as well as which themes and frames were being activated. We coded thematically for debates about embodiment, fidelity, emotions and attitudes towards the technology, as well as carrying out a detailed appraisal of ethical issues which cropped up in each report.

The two stages of this analysis allowed us to combine a deductive process – using broad top-down categories suggested by our research questions and in the literature – with insights arising from the corpus itself through the inductive and iterative process of thematic analysis (Braun and Clarke

10 Lell (2022) refers to her use of Voyant Tools to analyse legal texts as a form of 'distant reading' (borrowing from Moretti's work in literary history) using computational means, which can allow researchers to see data in new ways, and make longer term trends in language use visible.

Table 8.2 Breakdown of Case Studies by Number of Reports in the Sample

Cases (keywords in *italics*)	n. reports (words)	Sub-sample (n. reports)
Debates about the *Tupac 'hologram'* between 15/04/2012 and 14/06/2012	413 [239,129]	30
Debate about Audrey *Hepburn*'s revival for *Galaxy* chocolate advertisement between 24/02/2013 and 23/04/2013	41 [41,197]	20
Debates about *Bruce Lee*'s 'resurrection' for *Johnnie Walker* advertisement between 10/07/2013 and 09/09/2013	11 [10,251]	10
Debates about *Robin Williams'* attempt to lock down his *image* for twenty-five years after death between 29/03/2015 and 28/05/2015	20 [14,264]	10
Debate about a possible AI or *CGI* revival for *Carrie Fisher* in the Star Wars franchise, between 09/12/2019 and 08/02/2020	51 [62,599]	20
Debate about the *Whitney* Houston *'hologram'* between 25/02/2020 and 24/04/2020	93 [77,511]	20
Debates about the Robert *Kardashian* AI *'hologram'* between 29/10/2020 and 28/12/2020	126 [94,113]	20
Debates about the *AI* revival of Brazilian singer *Elis Regina*, between 14/07/2023 and 13/09/2023	20 [19,896]	10
Debates about the 'voice cloning' of Polish actor *Miłogost Reczek* for the *Cyberpunk* video game, between 12/10/2023 and 11/12/2023	18 [16,815]	10
TOTAL	**793 [575,775]**	**150 (19%)**

2006). The findings (recounted in Chapter 5) reveal who is speaking and shaping debates about synthetic media in the context of cultural memory and creative practices, which themes, values and related discourses are activated, and how discussions about ethics play out in the orbit of these high-profile cases.

Cultural sector interviews and workshops (Chapter 6)

In Chapter 6, we shifted our investigation to collective memory practices, and particularly those facilitated by museums and heritage institutions. Working in interaction and collaboration with cultural heritage professionals has been a part of our research process for many years, and it has continued to be a regular touchpoint while writing this book. Indeed, we might note cultural sector interactions as where we started in our investigation of these issues, as we go on to outline.

In 2021, at the height of the second COVID-19 lockdown in the UK, we set out to do some research to understand how cultural heritage professionals were responding to the pandemic. We were particularly interested in the perspective of those working in digital roles given how prominent they were in the 'digital pivot' of institutional efforts and attention during that period (to use the lexicon of that period). As a part of that endeavour, our Research Associate – Dr Ania Ostrowska – interviewed nineteen digital cultural professionals from all over the UK. These interviews, the transcripts of which were thematically coded and reported in a series of publications (Kidd et al. 2021, 2022) made several things very clear to us at that time. Firstly, digital cultural professionals were navigating a suite of sometimes competing demands, which they often felt they were not being adequately supported to negotiate. Many were working in institutions that did not have a digital strategy or guidelines, and adequate structures and accountability measures were rarely in place. There was a sense from our participants that – especially at that time – they were at the sharp end of the institution, having to very visibly make decisions or statements that might leave them vulnerable. Secondly, and most pertinent for the themes of this book, there was a looming anxiety evident in those discussions about questions of data use and integrity, and working with third party providers of digital data services. These concerns were amplified by a sense that institutional drivers to engage with emerging technologies were not always couched within principles of 'care' and durability. As we have continued to observe in our interactions with the sector, these concerns are nowhere more vexed than in work with AI.

Following from these insights, and as we began the Leverhulme Trust Synthetic Pasts project in 2024, we decided to pick up some of these themes and address the question of AI afterlives more specifically – in a sector-facing work package. This began with a series of workshops, and resulted in a published resource for cultural professionals interested in working with *AI Afterlives: The Responsible AI Afterlives Workbook* (launched 2025). At these workshops – held in Cardiff, Wales and London, England[11] – thirty-five

11 All attendees were offered £30 as remuneration for their time.

cultural heritage professionals shared their thoughts and experiences with us, working collaboratively to co-imagine what responsible values-informed approaches to AI afterlives might look like. These workshops were supported by Research Associates Dr Bethan Jones and Dr Rio Creech-Nowagiel, and delivered in partnership with yello brick.

Chapter 6 is underpinned by insights from these work packages. In it, we show that while there is enthusiasm for AI's potential, concerns about disinformation, sustainability and third-party control are widespread. The chapter questions whether AI-generated interactions risk flattening complex histories, particularly through curated avatars that prioritize emotional connection over uncomfortable truths. We also use a number of illustrative examples, situating AI afterlives within longer traditions of archival critique, colonial histories and debate about who owns and curates memory.

Ethics

Given the emphasis in this book on exploring technology's impacts on how we understand and work with our past(s) – touching on the societal, cultural, material and affective dimensions of human existence – we have felt a critical compulsion in our work to robustly reflect upon ethical considerations arising from our own uses of these technologies. This includes reflection on: our software and hardware choices; our interactions with public data, as well as data from 'the public'; our development and design work; and how our research might interact with, and perhaps even inform, technological innovation.

As researchers attentive to critiques of digital infrastructures and data power, we remain cautious about engaging with some of the platforms we examine in this book, and mindful of how significantly certain services – perhaps most notably X – have transformed over the course of our study. We understand that our behaviours and experiences on these platforms shape the value we ascribe to them, and that as users we are subject to the same algorithms, echo chambers and personalization that shape access to digital content more generally. We recognize too that our own interactions with these technologies cannot fully reflect the multiplicity of ways they are experienced by others. Indeed, as researchers based in (largely) English-speaking regions of the

Global North (in Wales and England, in the UK) we have been acutely aware of our positionality when conducting this research. Our perspectives, shaped by our cultural, economic and social contexts, no doubt influence the ways we have interpreted data and engaged with non-Western or non-English speaking outputs in this book. It is possible that we have inadvertently projected our own values, assumptions and biases in this work, overlooking important nuances in global approaches to AI afterlives, including those reported in scholarship not in English. The many hours we have spent reflecting on our positionality in relation to our site(s) of study have made us mindful of the limitations of our research, but perhaps also more keenly aware of where its actual strengths and contributions are.

As is to be expected we have obtained ethical approval from our Departmental Ethics Committee for the various work packages underpinning this book. We have remained mindful of the ethical implications of using publicly available data, and we have prioritized data integrity and transparency when handling that data (Yadlin-Segal et al. 2020). In Chapter 3 – the social media study – we used data from members of the public, but in Chapter 4 we stopped short of recruiting participants, opting at this stage of our research to volunteer ourselves as data subjects for the creation of deathbots. Beyond more normative considerations (privacy, consent) we have committed to an ongoing process of reflection throughout the lifecycle of our project, so our approach to these concerns can be considered more than merely a 'performance' constructed for an ethics committee (Hughes 2005; see also, van den Hoonaard and Hamilton 2016; Kasstan et al. 2023). Where appropriate (including in our creative and collaborative work, some of which underpins Chapter 6) we have used UKRIs AREA Framework for responsible innovation (UKRI 2023), which we have found to be both thought-provoking and enabling.

One area of our work where we have been acutely aware of AIs representational, historical and cultural biases is in our use of generative AI tools to produce (largely image-based) outputs that speak to our research themes, some of which can be seen on our project website. Through such use we have been able to note – and trace over time – how these systems limit diverse representations and offer imbalanced perspectives, rendering visible, if one cares to look for them, the biases present in their training data. It is clear to us that research into or about 'the past' which is based on AI outputs is particularly prone to misrepresentation, loss of complexity and loss of context (Nieto McAvoy and Kidd 2026). Our practical and empirical insights have critically informed our understanding of the issues in this book, and made us more diligent, for example, when we have been comparing materials and interpretations, or deciding whether and how to use images to represent our research, for example, in publications or at conferences (Pickering and Kara 2017). In our practical engagements with generative AI we have been learning in real time – as have others – how to think about ethics, not least in relation to how these models are trained on data scraped from public sources without remuneration (Ferrari et al. 2023), and given the varied ways we have become enmeshed in these developments ourselves – as users, creatives and researchers.

We are also acutely aware of the ethical dimensions of working across disciplines in the ways that we have. Disciplinary norms often dictate standards for research design, data usage and participant treatment, as well as academic integrity and societal responsibility. Blending fields with different norms, methodologies and values clearly raises tensions, not least in the potential for misinterpretation or the oversimplification of complex ideas. But we are unapologetic about that. Working in this way has been invaluable for us in that it has allowed us to 'see' AI afterlives from multiple angles, and to hold them up for analysis in more creative ways. It has enabled us to reduce our blind spots, or at least find new ways of interrogating them, and to communicate our research and envisage its real-world applications in more dynamic terms. In the coming months and years it is this that we will turn our attention to.

Bibliography

Abbott, R. B., and E. Rothman. 2023. 'Disrupting Creativity: Copyright Law in the Age of Generative Artificial Intelligence'. *Florida Law Review* 75 (6): 1141–201.

Adair, B., B. Filene and L. Koloski. 2011. *Letting Go? Sharing Historical Authority in a User-Generated World*. The Pew Center for Arts and Heritage.

Ahmend, S. 2004. *The Cultural Politics of Emotion*. Edinburgh University Press.

Airoldi, M. 2022. *Machine Habitus: Toward a Sociology of Algorithms*. Polity Press.

Ajder, H., G. Patrini, F. Cavalli and L. Cullen 2019. *The State of Deepfakes: Landscape, Threats, and Impact*. Deeptrace AI.

Amakawa, J., and J. Westin. 2018. 'New Philadelphia: Using Augmented Reality to Interpret Slavery and Reconstruction Era Historical Sites'. *International Journal of Heritage Studies* 24: 315–31. https://doi.org/10.1080/13527258.2017.1378909

American Alliance for Museums. 2021. Museums and Trust. https://www.aam-us.org/2021/09/30/museums-and-trust-2021/ (Accessed 24 March 2025).

Ananny, M. 2024. 'Making Generative Artificial Intelligence a Public Problem. Seeing Publics and Sociotechnical Problem-Making in Three Scenes of AI Failure'. *Javnost - The Public* 31 (1): 89–105.

Anderson, C. 2019. 'A New Hermeneutics of Suspicion? The Challenge of Deepfakes to Theological Epistemology'. Cursor_ Zeitschrift Für Explorative Theologie. https://doi.org/10.21428/fb61f6aa.771d30b7

Andrejevic, M., and N. Selwyn. 2022 *Facial Recognition*. Polity.

Angel, M., and A. Gibbs. 2006. 'Media, Affect and the Face: Biomediation and the Political Scene'. *Southern Review: Communication, Politics and Culture* 38 (2): 24–39.

Angwin, J., J. Larson, S. Mattu and L. Kirchner. 2016. 'Machine Bias – There's Software Used across the Country to Predict Future Criminals. And It's Biased against Blacks'. *ProPublica*, Online Edition. https://www.propublica.org/article/machine-bias-risk-assessments-in-criminal-sentencing

Annabell, T. 2023. 'Scrolling Back: Remediation within and through Digital Memory Work'. *Memory, Mind & Media* 2 : e10. doi:10.1017/mem.2023.6

Arnold, M., M. Gibbs, T. Kohn, J. Meese and B. Nansen. 2018. *Death and Digital Media*. Routledge.

Arnold-de-Simine, S. 2019. 'The Stories We Tell: Uncanny Encounters in Mr Straw's House'. *International Journal of Heritage Studies* 25 (1): 80–95.

Arora, N., S. Rana, V. Sharma and H. Hon Tat. 2024. 'Strategic Implementation and Ethical Navigation of Deep Fake Technology in Digital Marketing in Girish Lakhera'. In *Navigating the World of Deepfake Technology*, edited by Sanjay Taneja, Ercan Ozen and Pawan Kumar. IGI Global.

Asgari, Z., A. Naghavi and M. R. Abedi. 2022. Death and Dying in a Digitalized World. *OMEGA - Journal of Death and Dying* 90(4): 1951–62.

Ash, J., R. Kitchin and A. Leszcynski. 2024. *Researching Digital Life: Orientations, Methods and Practice*. Sage.

Assman, J. 2010. 'Communicative and Cultural Memory'. In *Cultural Memory Studies: An International and Interdisciplinary Handbook*, edited by Astrid Erll and Ansgar Nünning, 109–18. De Gruyter. https://doi-org.abc.cardiff.ac.uk/10.1515/9783110207262.2.109

Atkinson, P. A., and A. Coffey. 1997. 'Analysing Documentary Realities'. In *Qualitative research: Theory, Method and Practice*, edited by D. Silverman, 45–62. Sage.

Azar, M., G. Cox and L. Impett. 2021. 'Introduction: Ways of Machine Seeing'. *AI & Society* 36: 1093–104. https://doi-org.abc.cardiff.ac.uk/10.1007/s00146-020-01124-6

Bajohr, H. 2025. *Thinking with AI: Machine LEarning the Humanities*. Open Humanities Press.

Bao, A., and Y. Zeng. 2024. 'Embracing Grief in the Age of Deathbots: A Temporary Tool, Not a Permanent Solution'. *Ethics and Information Technology* 26 (7). https://doi-org.abc.cardiff.ac.uk/10.1007/s10676-024-09744-y

Baradaran, A. 2024. 'Towards A Decolonial I in AI: Mapping the Pervasive Effects of Artificial Intelligence on the Art Ecosystem'. *AI & SOCIETY* 39 (1): 7–19. https://doi.org/10.1007/s00146-023-01771-5

Barassi, V. 2024. 'Toward a Theory of AI Errors: Making Sense of Hallucinations, Catastrophic Failures, and the Fallacy of Generative AI'. *Harvard Data Science Review* (Special Issue 5). https://doi.org/10.1162/99608f92.ad8ebbd4

Barclay, K., and N. J. Koefoed. 2021. 'Family, Memory, and Identity: An Introduction'. *Journal of Family History* 46 (1): 3–12.

Bareis, J., and C. Katzenbach. 2021. 'Talking AI into Being: The Narratives and Imaginaries of National AI Strategies and Their Performative Politics'. *Science, Technology, & Human Values* 47 (5): 855–81. https://doi.org/10.1177/01622439211030007

Bassett, D. J. 2015. 'Who Wants to Live Forever? Living, Dying and Grieving in Our Digital Society'. *Social Sciences* 4: 1127–39. https://doi.org/10.3390/socsci4041127

Bassett, D. J. 2022. *The Creation and Inheritance of Digital Afterlives: You Only Live Twice*. Springer Nature.

Baym, N. K. 2015. *Personal Connections in the Digital Age* (2nd ed.). Polity.

BBC. 2024. 'Google to Fix AI Picture Bot After "Woke" Criticism'. https://www.bbc.co.uk/news/business-68364690

Beaunoyer, E., and M. J. Guitton. 2021. 'Cyberthanathology: Death and Beyond in the Digital Age'. *Computers in Human Behavior*, 122.

Beer, D. 2017. 'The Social Power of Algorithms'. *Information, Communication and Society* 20 (1): 1–13.

Belfiore, E. 2021. 'Is It Really About the Evidence? Argument, Persuasion, and the Power of Ideas in Cultural Policy'. *Cultural Trends* 31 (4): 293–310. https://doi.org/10.1080/09548963.2021.1991230

Bell, S. 2015. 'The dB in the .db: Vocaloid Software as Posthuman Instrument'. *Popular Music and Society* 39 (2): 222–40.

Bender, S. M. 2023. 'Coexistence and Creativity: Screen Media Education in the Age of Artificial Intelligence Content Generators'. *Media Practice and Education* 24 (4): 351–66. https://doi.org/10.1080/25741136.2023.2204203

Benjamin, R. 2019. *Race After Technology: Abolitionist Tools for the New Jim Code*. 1st edition. Polity.

Benjamin, W. 1969. 'The Work of Art in the Age of Mechanical Reproduction'. In *Illuminations*, edited by Hannah Arendt. Schocken Books.

Biçer, Ş., and A. Yıldırım. 2022. 'Digital Death and Thanatechnology: New Ways of Thinking about Data (Im)Mortality and Digital Transformation'. *OMICS* 26 (2): 88–92.

Biers, T., and K. Stringer Clary (eds). 2023. *The Routledge Handbook of Museums, Heritage, and Death*. Routledge.

Black, D. 2008. 'The Virtual Ideal: Virtual Idols, Cute Technology and Unclean Biology'. *Continuum* 22 (1): 37–50. https://doi.org.abc.cardiff.ac.uk/10.1080/10304310701612018

Black, G. 2012. *Transforming Museums in the Twenty-first Century*. Routledge.

Bode, K., and L. M. E. Goodlad. 2023. 'Data Worlds: An Introduction'. *Critical AI* 1 (1–2). doi: https://doi.org/10.1215/2834703X-10734026

Bode, L., D. Lees, and D. Golding. 2021. 'The Digital Face and Deepfakes on Screen'. *Convergence* 27 (4): 849–54. https://doi.org/10.1177/13548565211034044

Bolter J. D., and R. Grusin. 2000. *Remediation. Understanding New Media*. MIT Press.

Bond, L., S. Craps and P. Vermeulen (eds). 2016. *Memory Unbound: Tracing the Dynamics of Memory Studies*. New York and Berlin Berghahn Books.

Bonini, T., and E. Treré. 2024. *Algorithms of Resistance*. MIT Press.

Boon, M. 2010. *In Praise of Copying*. Harvard University Press.

Bortolotti, L. 2023. *Why Delusions Matter*. Bloomsbury.

Bory, P. 2019. 'Deep New: The Shifting Narratives of Artificial Intelligence from Deep Blue to AlphaGo'. *Convergence* 25 (4): 627–42.

Boscagli, M. 2014. *Stuff Theory: Everyday Objects, Radical Materialism*. Bloomsbury Academic.

Bosch, M., G. Fernandez-Borsot, I. Miró A. Comas and J. Figa Vaello. . 2022. 'Evolving Friendship? Essential Changes, from Social Networks to Artificial Companions'. *Social Network Analysis and Mining* 12 (39). https://doi-org.abc.cardiff.ac.uk/10.1007/s13278-022-00864-1

Bowen, Glenn A. 2009. 'Document Analysis as a Qualitative Research Method'. *Qualitative Research Journal* 9 (2): 27–40.

Boyle, J. 2024. *The Line: AI and the Future of Personhood*. MIT.

Braidotti, R. 2013. *The Posthuman*. Polity.

Brailsford, L. 2024. 'History Brought Back to Life with AI', 7 February. MoMoLab. https://momolab.nl/news/history-brought-back-to-life/

Braun, V., and Clarke, V. 2006. 'Using Thematic Analysis in Psychology'. *Qualitative Research in Psychology* 3 (2): 77–101.

Brenna, B., H. Dam Christensen and O. Hamran. 2019. *Museums as Cultures of Copies: The Crafting of Artefacts and Authenticity*. Routledge.

Brescó de Luna, I., and B. Jiménez-Alonso. 2024. 'Deathbots. Discussing the Use of Artificial Intelligence in Grief'. *Studies in Psychology* 45(1): 103–22. https://doi.org/10.1177/02109395241241387

Browne, J., S. Cave, E. Drage and K. McInerney. 2023. *Feminist AI: Critical Perspectives on Algorithms, Data and Intelligent Machines*. Oxford University Press.

Browne, S. 2015. *Dark Matters: On the Surveillance of Blackness*. Duke University Press. https://doi.org/10.1215/9780822375302

Brown, A. K., and L. Peers (eds). 2005. *Museums and Source Communities: A Routledge Reader*. Routledge. https://doi.org/10.4324/9780203987834

Bryan-Kinns, N., C. Ford, A. Chamberlain, S. D. Benford, H. Kennedy, Z. Li, W. Qiong, G. G. Xia and J. Rezwana. 2023. 'Explainable AI for the Arts: XAIxArts'. In *Proceedings of the 15th Conference on Creativity and Cognition (C&C '23).*

Association for Computing Machinery, 1–7. https://doi.org/10.1145/3591196.3593517

Buben, A. 2015. 'Technology of the Dead: Objects of Loving Remembrance or Replaceable Resources?' *Philosophical Papers* 44 (1): 15–37. https://doi-org.abc.cardiff.ac.uk/10.1080/05568641.2015.1014538

Bucher, T. 2018. *If…Then: Algorithmic Power and Politics*. Oxford Academic.

Burgess, J., K. Albury, A. McCosken and R. Wilken. 2022. *Everyday Data Cultures*. Polity.

Burlingame, K. 2022. 'High Tech or High Touch? Heritage Encounters and the Power of Presence'. *International Journal of Heritage Studies* 28 (11–12), 1228–41. https://doi-org.abc.cardiff.ac.uk/10.1080/13527258.2022.2138504

Cachoian-Schanz, D., and K. Schwerzmann. 2021. 'One Unique You: Affective Attachments and DNA-testing as Ethnotechnological Apparatus'. *Deanna Cachoian-Schanz* [blog], 17 December 2021. https://deannacachoian.net/2021/12/17/one-unique-you/

Calo, R. 2015. *Robotics and the Lessons of Cyberlaw*, 103 Calif. L. Rev. 513 (2015), https://digitalcommons.law.uw.edu/faculty-articles/23

Capece, S., C. Chivăran, G. Giugliano, E. Laudante, M. L. Nappi and M. Buono. 2024. 'Advanced Systems and Technologies for the Enhancement of User Experience in Cultural Spaces: An Overview'. *Heritage Science* 12 (1): 1–25. https://doi.org/10.1186/s40494-024-01186-5

Caramiaux, B. 2023. 'AI with Museums and Cultural Heritage'. In *AI in Museums: Reflections, Perspectives and Applications* (1st ed., Vol. 74), edited by S. Thiel and J. C. Bernhardt, 117–30. transcript Verlag. https://doi.org/10.14361/9783839467107

Carmi, E. 2021. 'A Feminist Critique to Digital Consent'. *Seminar.net* 17 (2). https://doi.org/10.7577/seminar.4291

Carroll, S. R., E. Herczog, M. Hudson, K. Russell and S. Stall. 2021. 'Operationalizing the CARE and FAIR Principles for Indigenous Data Futures'. *Scientific Data* 8 (1): 108. https://doi.org/10.1038/s41597-021-00892-0

Cassman, V. 2008. *Human Remains: Guide for Museums and Academic Institutions*. AltaMira Press.

Cave, S., and K. Dihal. 2020. 'The Whiteness of AI'. *Philosophy & Technology* 33: 685–703. https://doi-org.abc.cardiff.ac.uk/10.1007/s13347-020-00415-6

Chadwick, A. 2013. *The Hybrid Media System: Politics and Power*. Oxford University Press.

Cheney-Lippold, J. 2017. *We Are Data: Algorithms and the Making of Our Digital Selves*. NYU Press.

Chesney, R., and D. Citron. 2019. 'Deepfakes and the New Disinformation War: The Coming Age of Post-truth Geopolitics'. *Foreign Affairs*. Available at: https://www.foreignaffairs.com/articles/world/2018-12-11/deepfakes-andnewdisinformation-war?cid=otr-authors-january_february_2019-121118 (Accessed 15 June 2022).

Christen, K., and J. Anderson. 2019. 'Toward Slow Archives'. *Archival Science* 19 (2): 87–116. https://doi.org/10.1007/s10502-019-09307-x

Chrostowska, S. D. 2010. 'Consumed by Nostalgia?'. *SubStance* 39 (2) issue 122: 52–70.

Chun, W. H. K. 2008. 'The Enduring Ephemeral, or the Future Is a Memory'. *Critical Inquiry* 35 (1): 148–71.

Chun, W. H. K. 2011. *Programmed Visions: Software and Memory*. MIT Press.

Ciecko, B. 2020. *AI Sees What? The Good, the Bad, and the Ugly of Machine Vision for Museum Collections*. MW20 Online.

Ciolfi, L. 2015. 'Embodiment and Place Experience in Heritage Technology Design'. In *The International Handbook of Museum Studies: Museum Media*, edited by Michelle Henning, 419–46. Wiley.

Clarke, A. C. 1962. *Profiles of the Future: An Inquiry into the Limits of the Possible*. Phoenix.

Clegg, M. 2020. *Human Remains: Curation, Reburial and Repatriation*. Cambridge University Press.

Cleland, K. 2009. 'Intimate Encounters: the Mixed Reality Paradigm and Audience Responses'. *UC Irvine: Digital Arts and Culture*. http://www.escholarship.org/uc/item/1964v9cb

Conner, V. 2023. 'Fever Dreams and the Future of Nostalgia on TikTok'. *AoIR Selected Papers of Internet Research*. https://doi.org/10.5210/spir.v2023i0.13408

Cottle, S. 2025. *Communicating a World in Crisis*. Peter Lang.

Couldry, N., and U. A. Mejias. 2018. 'Data Colonialism: Rethinking Big Data's Relation to the Contemporary Subject'. *Television & New Media* 20 (4): 336–49. https://doi.org/10.1177/1527476418796632

Cranor, L. F. 2008. 'A Framework for Reasoning about the Human in the Loop'. In *Proceedings of the 1st Conference on Usability, Psychology, and Security (UPSEC'08)*. USENIX Association, Article 1, 1–15.

Crawford, K. 2021. *Atlas of AI*. Yale University Press.

Crawford, K., and T. Paglen. 2019. *Training Humans*. Fondazione Prada.

Cull, F. 2015. 'Dead Music in Live Music Culture'. In *The Digital Evolution of Live Music*, edited by A. Cresswell-Jones and R. J. Bennett, 109–37. Chandos Publishing.

Cuseum. 2019. '3 Things You Need to Know About AI-Powered "Deep Fakes" in Art & Culture'. https://cuseum.com/blog/2019/12/17/3-things-you-need-to-know-about-ai-powered-deep-fakes-in-art-amp-culture

Dalal-Clayton, A., and A. Rutherford. 2024. 'Provisional Semantics: Addressing the Challenges of Representing Multiple Perspectives Within Public Collections'. *Collections* 20 (1): 221–40. https://doi.org/10.1177/15501906241232427

Dali Museum. 2019. 'Dali Lives: Museum Brings Artist Back to Life with AI'. Art & Object. http://www.artandobject.com/press-release/dali-lives-museum-brings-artist-back-life-ai

Davies, D. J. 2005. *A Brief History of Death*. Blackwell Publishing.

Davis, F. 1979. *Yearning for Yesterday: A Sociology of Nostalgia*. Free Press.

Davis, J. L. 2012. 'Social Media and Experiential Ambivalence'. *Future Internet* 4: 955–70.

de Almeida, F., and S. Rafael, 2024. 'Data Sins: Speculative Design Unveiling Data Colonialism Through AI Imagery'. In *Design, User Experience, and Usability. HCII 2024. Lecture Notes in Computer Science*, Vol. 14712, edited by A. Marcus, E. Rosenzweig and M. M. Soares. Springer, Cham. https://doi-org.abc.cardiff.ac.uk/10.1007/978-3-031-61351-7_2

De Cremer, D., N. Morini Bianzino and B. Falk. 2023. *How Generative AI Could Disrupt Creative Work*. Harvard Business Review.

De Groot, J. 2020. 'Ancestry.Com and the Evolving Nature of Historical Information Companies'. *The Public Historian* 42 (1): 8–28. https://doi.org/10.1525/tph.2020.42.1.8

Dencik, L., E. Treré, R. Redden, and A. Hintz. 2022. *Data Justice*. SAGE.

Derrida, J. 1996. *Archive Fever: A Freudian Impression*. University of Chicago Press.

Dewdney, A. 2022. 'The Politics of the Networked Image'. In *The Networked Image in Post-digital Culture*, edited by A. Dewdney and K. Sluis. Routledge.

Dietrich, E., C. Fields, J. P. Sullins, B. van Heuveln, and R. Zebrowski. 2021. *Great Philosophical Objections to Artificial Intelligence: The History and Legacy of the AI Wars*. Bloomsbury.

Duguay, S., and H. Gold-Apel. 2023. 'Stumbling Blocks and Alternative Paths: Reconsidering the Walkthrough Method for Analyzing Apps'. *Social Media + Society* 9 (1). https://doi.org/10.1177/20563051231158822

D-ID. 2021a. 'D-ID's Pledge for the Ethical Use of Synthetic Media'. Available at: https://www.d-id.com/ethics/ (Accessed 24 April 2023).

D-ID. 2021b. 'Deepening Our Relationship with My Heritage, D-ID, 9 November'. Available at: https://www.d-id.com/deepening-our-relationship-with-my-heritage/ (Accessed 26 April 2023).

D-ID. 2023a. 'About D-ID'. Available at: https://www.d-id.com/ (Accessed 26 April 2023).

D-ID. 2023b. 'Live Portrait'. Available at: https://www.d-id.com/liveportrait/ (Accessed 26 April 2023).

D-ID. 2023c. 'Speaking Portrait'. Available at: https://www.d-id.com/speaking-portrait/ (Accessed 26 April 2023).

Dreyfus, J.-M., and E. Anstett (eds). 2016. *Human Remains in Society: Curation and Exhibition in the Aftermath of Genocide and Mass-Violence*. Manchester University Press.

Economou, E., H. Young and E. Sosnowska. 2018. *Evaluating Emotional Engagement in Digital Stories for Interpreting the Past. The Case of the Hunterian Museum's Antonine Wall EMOTIVE experiences*. IEEE.

El-Hadi, N. 2021. 'Faces of Histories'. *Real Life*. https://reallifemag.com/faces-of-histories/ (Accessed 17 April 2023).

Elder, A. 2020. 'Conversation from Beyond the Grave? A Neo-Confucian Ethics of Chatbots of the Dead'. *Journal of Applied Philosophy* 37 (1): 73–88. doi: 10.1111/japp.12369.

Ellis, D., and I. Tucker. 2021. *Emotion in the Digital Age: Technologies, Data and Psychosocial Life*. Routledge.

Epstein, Z., and A. Hertzmann. 2023. 'Art and the Science of Generative AI'. *Science* 380: 1110–11.

Erll, A., and A. Rigney. 2009. *Mediation, Remediation, and the Dynamics of Cultural Memory*. Walter de Gruyter.

Ernst, W. 2013. *Digital Memory and the Archive*, translated by Parikka, J. University of Minnesota Press.

Esposito, E. 2022. *Artificial Communication: How Algorithms Produce Social Intelligence*. MIT Press.

Esteve Del Valle, M., and R. Smit. 2021. 'Moonwalking Together: Tracing Redditors' Digital Memory Work on Michael Jackson'. *Convergence* 27 (6): 1811–32.

EU. 2023. 'Artificial Intelligence Act: Deal on Comprehensive Rules for Trustworthy AI'. *European Parliament News*, 9 December. Available at: https://www.europarl.europa.eu/news/en/press-room/20231206IPR15699/artificial-intelligence-act-deal-on-comprehensive-rules-for-trustworthy-ai (Accessed 19 December 2023).

Evans, T. 2011. 'Secrets and Lies: the Radical Potential of Family History'. *History Workshop Journal* 71 (1): 49–73. https://doi.org/10.1093/hwj/dbq065

Evans, T. 2020. 'How Do Family Historians Work with Memory?' *Journal of Family History* 46 (1): 92–106. doi: 10.1177/0363199020967384.

Fabry, R. E., and M. Alfano. 2024. 'The Affective Scaffolding of Grief in the Digital Age: The Case of Deathbots'. *Topoi* 43: 757–69. https://doi-org.abc.cardiff.ac.uk/10.1007/s11245-023-09995-2

Fawns, T. 2022. 'Remembering in the Wild: Recontextualising and Reconciling Studies of Media and Memory'. *Memory, Mind & Media* 1 (11): 1–9.

Fenwick, M., and P. Jurcys. 2023. 'Originality and the Future of Copyright in an Age of Generative AI'. *Computer Law & Security Review* 51.

Ferrari, F., and F. McKelvey, 2022. 'Hyperproduction: A Social Theory of Deep Generative Models'. *Distinktion: Journal of Social Theory* 24 (2): 338–60.

Ferrari, F., J. van Dijck and A. van den Bosch. 2023. 'Foundation Models and the Privatization of Public Knowledge'. *Nature Machine Intelligence* 5 (8): 818–20. https://doi.org/10.1038/s42256-023-00695-5

Fisher, M. 2012. 'What Is Hauntology?' *Film Quarterly* 66 (1): 16–24.

Fletcher, J. 2018. 'Deepfakes, Artificial Intelligence, and Some Kind of Dystopia: The New Faces of Online Post-Fact Performance'. *Theatre Journal* 70 (4): 455–71.

Ford, M. 2018. 'How the Supreme Court Could Re-write the Rules for DNA Searches'. *The New Republic*, 30 April. Available at: https://newrepublic.com/article/148170/supreme-court-rewrite-rules-dna-searches (Accessed 26 April 2023).

Foucault, M. 1972. *The Archaeology of Knowledge and the Discourse on Language*. Pantheon Press.

Fox, N. J., and P. Alldred. 2017. 'Mixed Methods, Materialism and the Micropolitics of the Research-Assemblage'. *International Journal of Social Research Methodology* 21 (2): 191–204. https://doi-org.abc.cardiff.ac.uk/10.1080/13645579.2017.1350015

French, A., and E. Villaespesa. 2019. 'AI, Visitor Experience, and Museum Operations: A Closer Look at the Possible'. *Humanizing the Digital: Unproceedings from the MCN 2018 Conference*, 13: 101–13.

Frew, M., T. Tzanidis and J. Flinn, 2023. 'Events and the Metaverse: A DARQ Future?' In C. Drakely, and T. Brown, *Virtual Events Management: Theory and Methods for Event Management and Tourism*. Goodfellow Publishers.

Friday, K. 2014. 'Learning from E-Family History: A Model of Online Family Historian Research Behaviour'. *Information Research: An International Electronic Journal* 19 (4). https://eric.ed.gov/?id=EJ1050454.

Frosh, P. 2018. *The Poetics of Digital Media*. John Wiley & Sons.

Gaia, G., S. Boiano and A. Borda. 2019. 'Engaging Museum Visitors with AI: The Case of Chatbots'. In *Museums and Digital Culture*, edited by T. Giannini and J. Bowen. Springer, Cham. https://doi-org.abc.cardiff.ac.uk/10.1007/978-3-319-97457-6_15.

Galani, A., and J. Kidd. 2020. 'Hybrid Material Encounters - Expanding the Continuum of Museum Materialities in the Wake of A Pandemic'. *Museum and Society* 18 (3): 298–301. (10.29311/mas.v18i3.3565)

Galvão, V. F., C. Maciel, R. Pereira, V. F. Galvão, C. Maciel, R. Pereira, I. Gasparini, J. Viterbo and A. C. Bicharra Garcia. 2021. 'Discussing Human Values in Digital Immortality: Towards A Value-Oriented Perspective'. *Journal of the Brazilian Computer Society* 27 (15). https://doi.org/10.1186/s13173-021-00121-x

Garde-Hansen, J., A. Hoskins and A. Reading (eds). 2009. *Save As… Digital Memories*. Palgrave Macmillan.

Garnham, I., and Smith, R. C. 2023. 'The Social Life of Algorithms: Tracing Notions of Algorithms Beyond Human-Algorithm Interactions'. In *HCI International 2023 – Late Breaking Papers: 25th International Conference on Human-Computer Interaction, HCII 2023, Copenhagen, Denmark, July 23–28, 2023, Proceedings*, Part III. Springer-Verlag, 273–89. https://doi.org/10.1007/978-3-031-48044-7_20

Garon, J. M. 2023. 'A Practical Introduction to Generative AI, Synthetic Media, and the Messages Found in the Latest Medium'. Available at SSRN: https://ssrn.com/abstract=4388437

Gellers, J. C. 2023. *AI Ethics Discourse: A Call to Embrace Complexity, Interdisciplinary and Epistemic Humility*. AI and Society. https://doi.org/10.1007/s00146-023-01708-y

Gensburger, S., and F. Clavert 2024. 'Is Artificial Intelligence the Future of Collective Memory?' *Memory Studies Review* 1 (2): 195–208. https://doi.org/10.1163/29498902-202400019

Geraci, R. M. 2006. 'Spiritual Robots: Religion and Our Scientific View of the Natural World'. *Theology and Science* 4 (3): 229–46. https://doi.org/10.1080/14746700600952993

Geraci, R. M. 2012. *Apocalyptic AI: Visions of Heaven in Robotics, Artificial Intelligence, and Virtual Reality*. Oxford University Press.

Gibbs, M., J. Meese, M. Arnold, B. Nansen and M. Carter. 2015. '#Funeral and Instagram: Death, Social Media and Platform Vernacular'. *Information, Communication & Society* 18 (3): 255–68.

Giesen, M. (ed.). 2013. *Curating Human Remains: Caring for the Dead in the United Kingdom*. Boydell Press.

Gillespie, M., and E. N. McAvoy. 2016. 'Digital Networks and Transformations in the International News Ecology: A Critique of Agent- Centred Approaches to Soft Power'. In *Routledge Handbook of Soft Power*, edited by N. Chitty, C. Hayden, L. Ji, and J. Simons, 203–18. Routledge.

Gilliard, C. 2024. *The Deeper Problem with Google's Racially Diverse Nazis*. The Atlantic. https://www.theatlantic.com/technology/archive/2024/02/google-gemini-diverse-nazis/677575/

Graham, R. 2023. *Investigating Google's Search Engine: Ethics, Algorithms, and the Machines Built to Read Us*. Bloomsbury.

Gramigna, R. 2024. 'Preserving Anonymity: Deep-Fake as an Identity-Protection Device and as a Digital Camouflage'. *International Journal for the Semiotics of Law* 37: 729–51. https://doi-org.abc.cardiff.ac.uk/10.1007/s11196-023-10079-y

Gray, C. 2015. 'Ambiguity and Cultural Policy | the Nordic Journal of Cultural Policy'. *Nordisk Kulturpolitisk Tidsskrift* 18 (1): 66–80. https://doi.org/10.18261/ISSN2000-8325-2015-01-05

Gruvæus, A. 2023. 'Beyond Peak Death? – The Advent of Digital Necromancy and Functional Ghosts'. *Journal of Futures Studies* 27 (3): 103–9.

Grønning, A. 2021. 'Micro-Memories: Digital Modes of Communication Across Three Generations'. *Memory Studies* 14 (4): 733–46.

Gröppel-Wegener, A., and J. Kidd. 2019. *Critical Encounters with Immersive Storytelling*. Routledge.

Hakopian, M. F. 2024. 'Art Histories from Nowhere: On the Coloniality of Experiments in Art and Artificial Intelligence'. *AI & SOCIETY* 39 (1): 29–41. https://doi.org/10.1007/s00146-023-01768-0

Halbwachs, M. 1925. *Les Cadres sociaux de la memoire*. Alcan.

Hall, G. 2025. *Masked Media: What it Means to be a Human in the Age of Artificial Intelligence*. Open Humanities Press.

Hamilton, B. 2024. 'Ethical AI Integration in Museums: A Critical Analysis of Current Frameworks and Future Adaptations'. Master's Dissertation. University of Queensland Australia. https://doi.org/10.13140/RG.2.2.16285.01760

Haraway, Donna J. 1985. 'A Manifesto for Cyborgs: Science, Technology, and Socialist Feminism for the 1980s'. *Socialist Review* 15 (2): 65–107.

Harbinja, E., T. Morse and L.Edwards. 2024. 'Digital Remains and Post-mortem Privacy in the UK: What do users want?' *BILETA 2024 Conference Paper*, 1–24. http://dx.doi.org/10.2139/ssrn.4813651

Harbinja, E. 2022. *Digital Death, Digital Assets and Post-mortem Privacy: Theory, Technology and the Law*. Edinburgh University Press.

Harbinja, E., L. Edwards and M. McVey. 2023. 'Governing Ghostbots'. *Computer Law & Security Review*, 48.

Hare, S. 2022. *Technology Is Not Neutral*. London Publishing Partnership.

Harrington, J. H. 2020. *Digital Remains*. New Degree Press.

Harris, M. 2013. 'The Hologram of Tupac at Coachella and Saints: The Value of Relics for Devotees'. *Celebrity Studies* 4 (2): 238–40. https://doi-org.abc.cardiff.ac.uk/10.1080/19392397.2013.791054

Hartman, S. 2008. 'Venus in Two Acts'. *Small Axe*, 12(2): 1–14.

Harvey, E., H. Sandhaus, A. Z. Jacobs, E. Moss and M. Sloane. 2024. 'The Cadaver in the Machine: The Social Practices of Measurement and Validation in Motion Capture Technology'. *ACM CHI Conference on Human Factors in Computing Systems (CHI'24)*. Association for Computing Machinery, New York, NY, USA, Article 768, 1–23. https://arxiv.org/pdf/2401.10877.pdf

Hayden, C. 2012. *The Rhetoric of Soft Power: Public Diplomacy in Global Contexts*. Lexington Books.

Hayles, N. K. 1996. 'Embodied Virtuality: Or How to Put Bodies Back into the Picture'. In *Immersed in Technology*, edited by M. Moser and D. LcLeod. MIT Press.

He, Z., J. Su, L. Chen and T. Wang, 2025. '"I Recall the Past": Exploring How People Collaborate with Generative AI to Create Cultural Heritage Narratives'. In *Proceedings of the 2025 ACM Conference on Computer Supported Cooperative Work (CSCW'25)*. Proc. ACM Hum.-Comput. Interact. 9, 2, Article CSCW108 (May 2025), 30 pages. https://doi.org/10.1145/3711006

Hepp, A., J. Jarke and L. Kramp. 2022. *New Perspectives in Critical Data Studies: The Ambivalences of Data Power*. Springer.

Hicks, D. 2020. *The Brutish Museums: The Benin Bronzes, Colonial Violence and Cultural Restitution*. Pluto Press.

Hicks, M. T., J. Humphries and J. Slater. 2024. 'ChatGPT is Bullshit'. *Ethics and Information Technology* 26, 38 (2024). https://doi.org/10.1007/s10676-024-09775-5

Hjorth, L., and S. Hinton. 2019. *Understanding Social Media*. Sage.

Hollanek, T., and K. Nowaczyk-Basińska. 2024. 'Griefbots, Deadbots, Postmortem Avatars: On Responsible Applications of Generative AI in the Digital Afterlife Industry'. *Philosophy and Technology* 37, article number 63.

Holmberg, T., A. Jonsson and F. Palm (eds). 2019. *Death Matters*. Palgrave Macmillan.

Hornecker, E., and L. Ciolfi. 2019. *Human-Computer Interactions in Museums*. Morgan & Claypool.

Horning, R. 2025. 'What Is Realism in the Age of AI?' *Aperture* 257.

Hoskins, A. 2011. '7/7 and Connective Memory: Interactional Trajectories of Remembering in Post-scarcity Culture'. *Memory Studies* 4 (3): 269–80.

Hoskins, A. 2018. *Digital Memory Studies: Media Pasts in Transition*. Routledge.

Hoskins, A. 2024. 'AI and Memory'. *Memory, Mind & Media* 3 (18). doi:10.1017/mem.2024.16

Hoskins, A., and H. Halstead. 2021. 'The New Grey of Memory: Andrew Hoskins in Conversation with Huw Halstead'. *Memory Studies* 14 (3): 675–85. https://doi.org/10.1177/17506980211010936

Hristova, S., S. Hong and J. D. Slack. 2021. *Algorithmic Culture: How Big Data and Artificial Intelligence Are Transforming Everyday Life*. Lexington Books.

Hu, N., and J. Kidd. 2024. 'Harnessing Instagram's "Platform Vernacular" during the COVID-19 Pandemic: A Case Study of Philbrook Museum of Art'. *Curator: The Museum Journal* 67 (2): 411–27.

Hugenholtz, P. B., and J. P. Quintais. 2021. 'Copyright and Artificial Creation: Does EU Copyright Law Protect AI-Assisted Output?' *IIC* 52: 1190–216.

Hughes, J. 2005. 'Ethical Cleansing? The Process of Gaining "Ethical Approval" for a New Research Project Exploring Performance in Place of War'. *Research in Drama Education: The Journal of Applied Theatre and Performance*, 10 (2): 229–32. https://doi-org.abc.cardiff.ac.uk/10.1080/13569780500103968

Hutson, J., and J. Ratican. 2023. 'Life, Death, and AI: Exploring Digital Necromancy in Popular Culture—Ethical Considerations, Technological Limitations, and the Pet Cemetery Conundrum'. *Faculty Scholarship* 478. doi: 10.54517/m.v4i1.2166.

Huws, S., A. John and J. Kidd. 2019. 'Traces - Olion: Creating a Bilingual "Subtlemob" for National Museum Wales'. In *The Routledge International Handbook of New Digital Practices in Galleries, Libraries, Archives, Museums and Heritage Sites*, edited by Hannah Lewi, Wally Smith, Dirk vom Lehn and Steven Cooke, 441–50. Routledge. doi:10.4324/9780429506765.

Jackson D., and M. Courneya. 2023. 'Unreliable Narrator: Reparative Approaches to Harmful Biases in AI Storytelling for the HE Classroom and Future Creative Industries'. *Brazilian Creative Industries Journal* 3 (2): 59–75. https://doi.org/10.25112/bcij.v3i2.3540

Jacobsen, B. N. 2023. 'Machine Learning and the Politics of Synthetic Data'. *Big Data & Society* 10 (1). https://doi.org/10.1177/20539517221145372

Jacobsen, B. N., and D. Beer. 2021a. 'Quantified Nostalgia: Social Media, Metrics, and Memory'. *Social Media and Society* 7 (2): 1–9.

Jacobsen, B. N., and D. Beer. 2021b. *Social Media and the Automatic Production of Memory*. Bristol University Press.

Jaillant, L., O. Mitchell, E. Ewoh-Opu and M. Hidalgo Urbaneja. 2025. 'How Can We Improve the Diversity of Archival Collections with AI? Opportunities, Risks, and Solutions'. *AI & SOCIETY* 40: 4447–59. https://doi.org/10.1007/s00146-025-02222-z

James, D., G. Davies, J. Kidd and A. John. 2019. *Awe or empathy, fast or slow? Articulating impacts from contrasting mobile experiences*. In Museums and the Web. Presented at the MW19, Museums and the Web.

Janes, R. R., and R. Sandell. 2019. *Museum Activism*. Routledge.

Jarrett, K. 2022. *Digital Labor*. Wiley.

Jelin, E. 2021. *The Struggle for the Past: How We Construct Social Memories*. Berghahn Books.

Jenkins, T. 2010. *Contesting Human Remains in Museum Collections: The Crisis of Cultural Authority*. Routledge.

Jiang, H. H., L. Brown, J. Cheng, M. Khan, A. Gupta, D. Workman, A. Hanna, J. Flowers and T. Gebru. 2023. 'AI Art and Its Impact on Artists'. In *Proceedings of the 2023 AAAI/ACM Conference on AI, Ethics, and Society (AIES '23)*, 363–74. Association for Computing Machinery. https://doi.org/10.1145/3600211.3604681

Jin, D. Y. 2021. *Artificial Intelligence in Cultural Production: Critical Perspectives on Digital Platforms*. Routledge.

Jobin, A., M. Ienca and E. Vayena. 2019. 'The Global Landscape of AI Ethics Guidelines'. *Nature Machine Intelligence* 1 (9): 389–99. https://doi.org/10.1038/s42256-019-0088-2

Jones, Mark. 1990. 'Why Fakes?' In *Fake? The Art of Deception*, edited by M. Jones, D. Lowenthal, and N. Barker, 11–15. Exhibition catalogue, British Museum.

Jørgensen, S. M. H., S. Vitting-Seerup and K. Wallevik. 2017. 'Hatsune Miku: An Uncertain Image'. *Digital Creativity* 28 (4): 318–31. https://doi-org.abc.cardiff.ac.uk/10.1080/14626268.2017.1381625

Kalpokas, I. 2021. 'Problematising Reality: The Promises and Perils of Synthetic Media'. *SN Social Sciences* 1 (1). https://doi.org/10.1007/s43545-020-00010-8

Kamble, A., and C. Chaudhari, 2024. 'Beyond Faces: A Conceptual Framework for Responsible Use of Deepfake Algorithm in Advertising'. *International Conference on Intelligent Systems and Advanced Applications (ICISAA)*, 1–6. doi: 10.1109/ICISAA62385.2024.10829340

Kania-Lundholm, M. 2019. 'Digital Mourning Labor: Corporate Use of Dead Celebrities on Social Media'. In *Death Matters*, edited by T.

Holmberg, A. Jonsson and F. Palm. Palgrave Macmillan, Cham. https://doi.org/10.1007/978-3-030-11485-5_9

Kapcár, A. 2015. 'The Origins of Necromancy or How We Learned to Speak to the Dead'. *Sacra* 13 (2): 30–58.

Kasket, E. 2019. *All the Ghosts in the Machine: Illusions of Immortality in the Digital Age*. Robinson.

Kasstan, J. R., G. Pearson and V. Brooks. 2023. *Rethinking Research Ethics in the Humanities: Principles and Recommendations*. doi.org/10.34737/w36yq.

Kaur, A., A. Hoshyar, X. Wang and F. Xia. 2024. 'Beyond Deception: Exploiting Deepfake Technology for Ethical Innovation in Healthcare'. In *Proceedings of the 1st International Workshop on Multimedia Computing for Health and Medicine (MCHM'24)*. Association for Computing Machinery, 70–8. https://doi.org/10.1145/3688868.3689196

Keightley, E., and M. Pickering (eds). 2013. *Research Methods for Memory Studies*. Edinburgh University Press.

Kennedy-Eden, H., and U. Gretzel. 2021. 'My Heritage in My Pocket: Mobile Device and App Use by Genealogy Tourists'. *Information Technology & Tourism* 23 (3): 327–50.

Kennedy, H. 2018. 'Living with Data: Aligning Data Studies and Data Activism Through a Focus on Everyday Experiences of Datafication'. *Krisis: Journal for Contemporary Philosophy* 38 (1): 18–30.

Kennedy, H., and R. L. Hill. 2018. 'The Feeling of Numbers: Emotions in Everyday Engagements with Data and Their Visualisation'. *Sociology* 52 (4): 830–48.

Kidd, J. 2014. *Museums in the New Mediascape: Transmedia, Participation, Ethics*. Routledge.

Kidd, J. 2019. 'With New Eyes I See: Embodiment, Empathy and Silence in Digital Heritage Interpretation'. *International Journal of Heritage Studies* 25 (1); 54–66. (10.1080/13527258.2017.1341946).

Kidd, J., and A. Rees. 2021. 'A Museum of Deepfakes? Potentials and Pitfalls for Deep Learning Technologies'. In *Museum Media(ting): Emerging Technologies and Difficult Heritage*, edited by T. Stylianou-Lambert, A. Heraclidou and A. Bounia. Berghahn Books.

Kidd, J., and E. Nieto McAvoy. 2019. 'Immersive Experiences in Museums, Galleries and Heritage Sites: A Review of Research Findings and Issues'. [Discussion paper]. Creative Industries' Policy and Evidence Centre (PEC).

Kidd, J., and E. Nieto McAvoy. 2023. 'Deep Nostalgia: Remediated Memory, Algorithmic Nostalgia, and Technological Ambivalence'. *Convergence* 29 (3).

Kidd, J., and E. Nieto McAvoy. 2025. 'Debating Synthetic Media: AI, Ethics, and the Creative Industries'. *Cultural Trends*.

Kidd, J., E. Nieto McAvoy and A. Ostrowska. 2021. *Implications of the COVID-19 Digital 'Pivot' in Museums and Galleries: Lessons from Practitioners*. AHRC Policy and Evidence Centre, Cardiff University. Available at: https://www.pec.ac.uk/discussion-papers/pivot-to-digital-how-museums-and-galleries-responded-to-covid-19

Kidd, J., E. Nieto McAvoy and A. Ostrowska. 2022. 'Negotiating Hybridity, Inequality, and Hyper-Visibility: Museums and Galleries? Social Media Response to the COVID-19 Pandemic'. *Cultural Trends* 33 (1): 19–36. (10.1080/09548963.2022.2122701).

Kidd, J., Nieto McAvoy, E., Jones, B. and John, A. 2025. *The Responsible AI Afterlives Workbook*. Available at https://www.syntheticpasts.com/aiafterlivesworkbook [Accessed 19th March 2026].

Kitchin, R. 2014. 'Big Data, New Epistemologies and Paradigm Shifts'. *Big Data & Society* 1 (1).

Kitchin, R. 2017. 'Thinking Critically about and Researching Algorithms'. *Information, Communication & Society* 20 (1): 14–29.

Kitchin, R. 2023. *Digital Timescapes: Technology, Temporality and Society*. Polity.

Knauft, Bruce M. 2017. 'What Is Genealogy? An Anthropological/Philosophical Reconsideration'. *Genealogy* 1 (1): 5. https://doi.org/10.3390/genealogy1010005

Kneese, T. 2023. *Death Glitch: How Techno-Solutionism Fails us in this Life and Beyond*. Yale University Press.

Konstantakis, M., J. Aliprantis, A. Teneketzis and G. Caridakis. 2018. 'Understanding User Experience Aspects in Cultural Heritage Interaction'. In *Proceedings of the 22nd Pan-Hellenic Conference on Informatics (PCI'18)*, 267–71. Association for Computing Machinery. https://doi.org/10.1145/3291533.3291580

Kopelman, S., and P. Frosh. 2023. 'The "Algorithmic as if": Computational Resurrection and the Animation of the Dead in Deep Nostalgia'. *New Media & Society* 27 (4): 2393–413. https://doi.org/10.1177/14614448231210268

Kretsedemas, P. 2017. 'Genealogy: Inaugural Editorial'. *Genealogy* 1 (1). https://doi.org/10.3390/genealogy1010001

Kubota-Hiramoto, T. 2018. 'New Dimensions in Testimony. Interactive 3-D Exhibit'. *The Oral History Review* 45 (2): 346–8. https://doi.org/10.1093/ohr/ohy056

Kukutai, T., and J. Taylor (eds). 2016. *Indigenous Data Sovereignty: Toward an agenda* (Vol. 38). ANU Press. https://www.jstor.org/stable/j.ctt1q1crgf

Lambert, A., B. Nansen and M. Arnold. 2018. 'Algorithmic Memorial Videos: Contextualising Automated Curation'. *Memory Studies* 11 (2): 156–71.

Laqueur, T. 2015. *The Work of the Dead: A Cultural History of Human Remains.* Princeton University Press.

Laqueur, T. 2023. 'The Pocahontas Exception'. *London Review of Books* 45 (7). https://www.lrb.co.uk/the-paper/v45/n07/thomas-laqueur/the-pocahontas-exception

Latour, B., and A. Lowe. 2010. 'The Migration of the Aura, or How to Explore the Original through its Facsimiles'. In *Switching Codes: Thinking Through Digital Technology in the Humanities and the Arts*, edited by T. Bartscherer and R. Coover, 275–98. Chicago University Press.

Latzko-Toh, G., C. Bonneau and M. Millette. 2016. 'Small Data, Thick Data: Thickening Strategies for Trace-based Social Media Research'. In *The SAGE Handbook of Social Media Research Methods*, edited by L. Sloan and Quan- A. Haase. SAGE.

Le, T., and R. Jin. 2024. 'The Beginning of Cyber-Necromancy: Replacing Deceased Loved Ones with AI Agents'. https://osf.io/8eb76/download/?format=pdf

Le Goff, J. 1992. *History and Memory.* Columbia University Press.

Leatham, X. 2024. 'Creepy AI Tool Narrates Audiobooks in the Style of Deceased Actors Including Judy Garland and Sir Laurence Olivier – and it's Eerily Realistic'. *The Guardian.* 5 July. https://www.dailymail.co.uk/sciencetech/article-13604125/Judy-Garland-Laurence-Olivier-books-AI.html.

Leaver, T. 2018. 'Co-Creating Birth and Death on Social Media'. In *A Networked Self and Birth, Life, Death*, edited by Zizi Papacharissi, 35–49. Routledge.

Leaver, T. 2019. 'Posthumous Performance and Digital Resurrection: From Science Fiction to Startups'. In *Residues of Death: Disposal Refigured*, edited by T. Kohn, M. Gibbs, B. Nansen and L. van Ryn. Routledge.

Leaver, T., T. Highfield and C. Abidin. 2020. *Instagram: Visual Social Media Cultures.* Polity.

Lee, J. 2020. 'Algorithmic Uses of Cybernetic Memory: Google Photos and a Genealogy of Algorithmically Generated Memory'. *Social Media and Society* 1: 1–12.

Lee, D. 2019. 'Deepfake Salvador Dalí Takes Selfies with Museum Visitors'. Available at https://www.theverge.com/2019/5/10/18540953/salvador-dali-lives-deepfake-museum (Accessed 15 January 2020).

Lees, D. 2023. 'Deepfakes and Documentary Film Production: Images of Deception in the Representation of the Real'. *Studies in Documentary Film* 18 (2): 108–29.

Lees, D., T. Bashford-Rogers and M. Keppel-Palmer. 2021. 'The Digital Resurrection of Margaret Thatcher: Creative, Technological and Legal Dilemmas in the Use of Deep Fakes in Screen Drama'. *Convergence* 27 (4): 954–73.

Lell, H. M. 2022. 'What Does "Dignity" Mean? Different Meanings in a Jurisprudential Analysis from a Distant Reading'. *International Journal of Law, Language & Discourse* 10 (2): 55–76.

Leslie, D., C. Rincón, M. Briggs, A. Perini, S. Jayadeva, A. Borda, S. J. Bennett, C. Burr, M. Aitken, M. Katell, C. Fischer, J. Wong and I. Kherroubi Garcia. 2023. *AI Ethics and Governance in Practice: An Introduction*. The Alan Turing Institute.

Lewis, J. E., A. Abdilla, N. Arista, K. Baker, S. Benesiinaabandan, M. Brown, M. Cheung, M. Coleman, A. Cordes, J. Davison, K. Duncan, S. Garzon, D. F. Harrell, P.-L. Jones, K. Kealiikanakaoleohaililani, M. Kelleher, S. Kite, O. Lagon, J. Leigh, M. Levesque, K. Mahelona, C. Moses, I. Nahuewai, K. Noe, D. Olson, 'Ō. Parker Jones, C. Running Wolf, M. Running Wolf, M. Silva, S. Fragnito, and H. Whaanga. 2020. *Indigenous Protocol and Artificial Intelligence Position Paper*. Concordia University Library. https://doi.org/10.11573/spectrum.library.concordia.ca.00986506

Li, J., X. Zheng, I. Watanabe and Y. Ochiai. 2024. 'A Systematic Review of Digital Transformation Technologies in Museum Exhibition'. *Computers in Human Behavior* 161 (December): 108407. https://doi.org/10.1016/j.chb.2024.108407

Liebermann, Y. 2021. 'Born Digital: The Black Lives Matter Movement and Memory after the Digital Turn'. *Memory Studies* 14 (4): 713–32.

Liew, K. K., N. Pang and B. Chan. 2015. 'Remembering Digitally: New Media and the Communicating of New Memories'. *Continuum* 29 (4): 509–10. https://doi.org/10.1080/10304312.2015.1051801

Light, B., J. Burgess and S. Duguay. 2016. 'The Walkthrough Method: An Approach to the Study of Apps'. *New Media and Society* 20 (3).

Lindemann, N. F. 2022. 'The Ethics of "Deathbots" '. *Science and Engineering Ethics* 28: 60. https://doi-org.abc.cardiff.ac.uk/10.1007/s11948-022-00417-x

Lindgren, S. (ed.). 2023. *Handbook of Critical Studies of Artificial Intelligence*. Edward Elgar Publishing.

Lipovetsky, G. 2005. *Hypermodern Times*. Polity Press.

Liu, J. 2023. 'Virtual Presence, Real Connections: Exploring the Role of Parasocial Relationships in Virtual Idol Fan Community Participation'. *Global Media and China* 10 (4): 490–511. https://doi.org/10.1177/20594364231222976

Liv, N., and D. Greenbaum, 2020. 'Deep Fakes and Memory Malleability: False Memories in the Service of Fake News'. *AJOB Neuroscience* 11 (2): 96–104, DOI: 10.1080/21507740.2020.1740351

Lizardi, R. 2016. *Mediated Nostalgia: Individual Memory and Contemporary Mass Media*. Lexington Books.

Loftus, E. F. 2005. 'Planting Misinformation in the Human Mind: A 30 Year Investigation of the Malleability of Memory'. *Learning & Memory* 12 (4): 361–6.

Loftus, E. F., and J. E. Pickrell. 1995. 'The Formation of False Memories'. *Psychiatric Annals* 25 (12): 720–5.

Lonetree, Amy. 2012. *Decolonizing Museums: Representing Native America in National and Tribal Museums*. University of North Carolina Press.

Lou, C., S. T. J. Kiew, T. Chen, T. Y. M. Lee, J. E. C. Ong and Z. Phua. 2022. 'Authentically Fake? How Consumers Respond to the Influence of Virtual Influencers'. *Journal of Advertising* 52 (4): 540–57. https://doi.org/10.1080/00913367.2022.2149641

Lowenthal, D. 1990. *The Past Is a Foreign Country*. Cambridge University Press.

MacCormack, P. 2025. *Death Activism: Queer Death Studies and the Posthuman*. Bloomsbury.

MacKenzie, A., and A. Munster. 2019. 'Platform Seeing: Image Ensembles and Their Invisualities'. *Theory, Culture & Society* 36 (5): 3–22. https://doi.org/10.1177/0263276419847508

Magni, F., J. Park and M. M. Chao. 2024. 'Humans as Creativity Gatekeepers: Are We Biased Against AI Creativity?' *Journal of Business and Psychology* 39: 643–56.

Maras, M.-H., and A. Alexandrou. 2019. 'Determining Authenticity of Video Evidence in the Age of Artificial Intelligence and in the Wake of Deepfake Videos'. *Psychology of Women Quarterly* 23(3): 427–35.

Manca, S. 2021. 'Digital Memory in the Post-Witness Era: How Holocaust Museums Use Social Media as New Memory Ecologies'. *Information* 12 (1): 31. https://doi.org/10.3390/info12010031

Manca, S., M. Passarelli and M. Rehm. 2022. 'Exploring Tensions in Holocaust Museums' Modes of Commemoration and Interaction on Social Media'. *Technology in Society* 68: 101889. 10.1016/j.techsoc.2022.101889.

Manovich, L. 2020. *Cultural Analytics*. MIT.

Manovich, L. 2023. 'AI Image Media through the Lens of Art and Media History'. In *IMAGE. Zeitschrift für interdisziplinäre Bildwissenschaft*, Band 37, 19. Jg., 2023 (1): S. 34–41.

Markham, T. 2020. *Digital Life*. Polity Press.

Massimi, M., and A. Charise. 2009. 'Dying, Death, and Mortality: Towards Thanatosensitivity in HCI'. In *CHI '09 Extended Abstracts on Human Factors in Computing Systems (CHI EA '09)*. Association for Computing Machinery, 2459–68. https://doi.org/10.1145/1520340.1520349

Matthews, J., and Nairn, A. 2023. 'Holographic ABBA: Examining Fan Responses to ABBA's Virtual "Live" Concert'. *Popular Music and Society* 46 (3): 282–303, doi: 10.1080/03007766.2023.2208048

Mbembe, A. 2002. 'The Power of the Archive and Its Limits'. In *Refiguring the Archive*, edited by Carolyn Hamilton, Verne Harris, Jane Taylor, Michele Pickover, Graeme Reid and Razia Saleh, 19–27. Springer Netherlands. https://doi.org/10.1007/978-94-010-0570-8_2

McCammon, M. 2022. 'Tweeted, Deleted: An Exploratory Study of the US Government's Digital Memory Holes'. *New Media and Society* 24 (3): 741–59.

McCosker, A. 2024. 'Making Sense of Deepfakes: Socializing AI and Building Data Literacy on GitHub and YouTube'. *New Media & Society* 26 (5): 2786–803. https://doi.org/10.1177/14614448221093943

McKelvey, F., J. Redden, J. Roberge and L. Stark. 2024. '(Un)stable Diffusions: The Publics, Publicities, and Publicizations of Generative AI'. *Journal of Digital Social Research* 6 (4): 1–12. doi: 10.33621/jdsr.v6i440453

McLeod, K. 2015. 'Living in the Immaterial World: Holograms and Spirituality in Recent Popular Music'. *Popular Music and Society* 39 (5): 501–15. https://doi-org.abc.cardiff.ac.uk/10.1080/03007766.2015.1065624

McStay, A. 2018. *Emotional AI: The Rise of Empathic Media*. SAGE.

Meese, J., B. Nansen, T. Kohn, M. Arnold and M. Gibbs. 2015. 'Posthumous Personhood and the Affordances of Digital Media'. *Mortality* 20 (4): 408–20. https://doi.org/10.1080/13576275.2015.1083724

Mejias, U. A., and N. Couldry. 2024. *Data Grab: The New Colonialism of Big Tech and How to Fight Back*. WH Allen.

Merrill, S. 2025. 'Hybrid Methodologies for Studying Social and Cultural Memory in the Postdigital Age'. In *The Remaking of Memory in the Age of the Internet and Social Media*, edited by Qi Wang and Andrew Hoskins. Oxford Academic. https://doi.org/10.1093/oso/9780197661260.003.0015

Merritt, E. 2025. 'Against Efficiency'. *American Alliance of Museums*. https://www.aam-us.org/2025/03/12/against-efficiency/

Meta. 2023. 'Meta Platform Terms'. Available at: https://developers.facebook.com/terms/dfc_platform_terms/ (Accessed 2 May 2023).

Michaelian, K., and J. Sutton.2013. 'Distributed Cognition and Memory Research: History and Current Directions'. *Review of Philosophy and Psychology* 4 (1): 1–24.

Mignolo, W. D. 2010. 'Epistemic Disobedience and the Decolonial Option: A Manifesto', *Subaltern Studies: An Interdisciplinary Study of Media and Communication*, 44–66.

Mihailova, M. 2021. 'To Dally with Dalí: Deepfake (Inter)faces in the Art Museum'. *Convergence* 27 (4): 882–98.

Millière, R. 2022. 'Deep Learning and Synthetic Media'. *Synthese* 200: 231.

Milne, G. 2020. *Smoke nad Mirrors: HOw hype obscures the future and how to see past it*. Robinson.

Miltner, K. M., and T. Highfield, 2017. 'Never Gonna GIF You Up: Analyzing the Cultural Significance of the Animated GIF'. *Social Media and Society* 3 (3): 1–11.

Mitchell, M. 2019. *Artificial Intelligence: A Guide for Thinking Humans*. Pelican.

Modest, W., and C. Augustat (eds). 2023. *Spaces of Care—Confronting Colonial Afterlives in European Ethnographic Museums* (1st ed., Vol. 77). transcript Verlag. https://doi.org/10.14361/9783839468487

Moore, S., D. Rosenthal and R. Robinson. 2020. *The Psychology of Family History: Exploring Our Genealogy*. Routledge.

Morgan, F. 2021. *A Nation of Descendents: Politics and the Practice of Genealogy in U.S. History*. University of North Carolina Press.

Morris, M. R., and J. R. Brubaker. 2024. 'Generative Ghosts: Anticipating Benefits and Risks of AI Afterlives (No. arXiv:2402.01662)'. arXiv. https://doi.org/10.48550/arXiv.2402.01662

Morse, T. 2023. 'Digital Necromancy: Users' Perceptions of Digital Afterlife and Posthumous Communication Technologies'. *Information, Communication & Society* 27 (2): 240–56.

Muldoon, J., C. Cant, M. Graham and F. Ustek Spilda. 2023. 'The Poverty of Ethical AI: Impact Sourcing and AI Supply Chains'. *AI & Soc* https://doi-org.abc.cardiff.ac.uk/10.1007/s00146-023-01824-9

Munn, L. 2023. 'The Uselessness of AI Ethics'. *AI Ethics* 3: 869–77. https://doi-org.abc.cardiff.ac.uk/10.1007/s43681-022-00209-w

Münster, S., F. Maiwald, I. di Lenardo, J. Henriksson, A. Isaac, M. Milica Graf, C. Beck and J. Oomen. 2024. 'Artificial Intelligence for Digital Heritage Innovation: Setting up a R&D Agenda for Europe'. *Heritage* 7 (2): 794–816. https://doi.org/10.3390/heritage7020038

Murphy, G., and E. Flynn. 2022. 'Deepfake False Memories'. *Memory*.30 (4): 480–92. doi: 10.1080/09658211.2021.1919715.

Murphy, O., and E. Villaespesa.2020. *AI: A Museum Planning Toolkit*. University of London.

Musa Giuliano, R. 2020. 'Echoes of Myth and Magic in the Language of Artificial Intelligence'. *AI & Society* 35: 1009–24. https://doi-org.abc.cardiff.ac.uk/10.1007/s00146-020-00966-4

Museums Association. 2020. 'Museum Curators among the Most Trusted Professions, Poll Finds'. https://www.museumsassociation.org/museums-journal/news/2020/12/museum-curators-among-the-most-trusted-professions-poll-finds/ (Accessed 24 March 2025).

MyHeritage. 2022a. 'MyHeritage Privacy Policy'. Available at: https://www.myheritage.com/FP/Company/popup-privacy-policy.php (Accessed 22 April 2023).

MyHeritage. 2022b. 'MyHeritage Terms and Conditions'. Available at: https://www.myheritage.com/FP/Company/popup-terms-conditions.php (Accessed 22 April 2023).

MyHeritage. 2023a. 'MyHeritage'. Available at: https://www.myheritage.com (Accessed 22 April 2023).

MyHeritage. 2023b. 'DeepStory – Animate Your Family Photos'. Available at: https://www.myheritage.com/deep-nostalgia (Accessed 22 April 2023).

MyHeritage. 2023c. 'DeepStory – Make Your Family Photos Speak'. Available at: https://www.myheritage.com/deepstory (Accessed 22 April 2023).

MyHeritage. 2023d. 'What are the specific terms and conditions for using AI Time Machine'. Available at: https://www.myheritage.com/help-center?a=What-are-the-specific-terms-and-conditions-for-using-AI-Time-Machinetm---id--S4NX-j0dRUOPg0BUfvY6WQ&lang=BG.

MyHeritage. 2024. 'Introducing LiveMemory™: Bring Your Photos to Life in Video'. https://blog.myheritage.com/2024/11/introducing-livememory-bring-your-photos-to-life-in-video/

Nagy, P., and G. Neff. 2024. 'Conjuring Algorithms: Understanding the Tech Industry as Stage Magicians'. *New Media & Society* 26 (9): 4938–54. https://doi.org/10.1177/14614448241251789

Nakonieczna, E., and J. Szczepański. 2024. 'Authenticity of Cultural Heritage Vis-à-Vis Heritage Reproducibility and Intangibility: From Conservation Philosophy to Practice'. *International Journal of Cultural Policy* 30 (2): 220–37. https://doi.org/10.1080/10286632.2023.2177642

Nansen, B., H. Gould, M. Arnold and M. Gibbs. 2023. 'Media, Mortality and Necro-Technologies: Eulogies for Dead Media'. *New Media & Society* 25 (8): 2163–82. https://doi.org/10.1177/14614448211027959

Nash, R. A., K. A. Wade and D. S. Lindsay. 2009. 'Digitally Manipulating Memory: Effects of Doctored Videos and Imagination in Distorting Beliefs and Memories'. *Memory & Cognition* 37: 414–24. https://doi-org.abc.cardiff.ac.uk/10.3758/MC.37.4.414

Natale, S. 2021. *Deceitful Media: Artificial Intelligence and Social Life after the Turing Test*. Oxford University Press.

NEMO (Network of European Museum Organisations). 2023. 'Trust in Swedish Museums at Record High'. https://www.ne-mo.org/news-events/article/trust-in-swedish-museums-at-record-high/#:~:text=According%20to%20a%20study%20by,compared%20to%20last%20year's%20figures (Accessed 24 March 2025).

NEMO (Network of European Museum Organisations). 2025. 'Council of Europe Adopts New Guidelines on AI and Cultural Policy'. https://www.ne-mo.org/news-events/article/council-of-europe-adopts-new-guidelines-on-ai-and-cultural-policy/#:~:text=NEMO's%20thoughts%20on%20AI&text=Recognising%20the%20unique%20position%20of,them%20into%20a%20regulatory%20framework (Accessed 30 April 2025).

Newell, J., L. Robin and K. Wehner (eds). 2017. *Curating the Future: Museums, Communities and Climate Change*. Routledge.

Ng, J. 2021. *The Post-Screen Through Virtual Reality, Holograms and Light Projections: Where screen boundaries lie*. Amsterdam University Press.

Ng, J. P., and N. Bax. 2023. 'Spooker Trouper: ABBA Voyage, Virtual Humans and the Rise of the Digital Apparition'. *Paragraph* 46: 160–75. ISSN 0264-8334.

Ng, J., and O. Tomkins. 2023. 'The New Virtuality: A Video Essay on the Disappearing Differences between Real and Unreal'. *ScreenWorks*. https://www.screenworks.org.uk/archive/volume-13-1/the-new-virtuality.

Nguyen, D., J. Meese, J. Burgess, J. Thomas, L. Bartolo, N. Carah, D. Carlon, J. Chan, S. Kininmonth, A. Lawrence, R. Lobato, A. Matamoros-Fernández, S. X. Montana-Nino, L. Nelson, J. Qian, A. Snoswell, D. Spina, A. Srinivas, N. Suzor, A. Tamta, P. Wikstrom and J. Williams 2023. *AI and Automated Decision-Making in News and Media: Key Technologies and Emerging Challenges*. ARC Centre of Excellence for Automated Decision-Making and Society, RMIT University.

Niemeyer, K. 2014. *Media and Nostalgia: Yearning for the Past, Present and Future*. Palgrave Macmillan.

Niemeyer, K., and E. Keightley. 2020. 'The Commodification of Time and Memory: Online Communities and the Dynamics of Commercially Produced Nostalgia'. *New Media & Society* 22 (9): 1639–62. https://doi.org/10.1177/1461444820914869 (Original work published 2020).

Nieto McAvoy, E., and J. Kidd. 2024. 'Synthetic Heritage: Online Platforms, Deceptive Genealogy and the Ethics of Algorithmically Generated Memory'. *Memory Mind and Media* 3 (e12): 1–18. https://doi.org/10.1017/mem.2024.10

Nieto McAvoy, E., and J. Kidd. 2026. *AI failure in the Google Gemini Controversy: Synthetic History and Epistemic Disobedience*. Annals of the Fondazione Luigi Einaudi

Nieto McAvoy, E., and S. Allan. 2023. 'Mediations of Cultural Policymaking During COVID-19: British Newspaper Reporting of the Culture Recovery Fund'. *International Journal of Cultural Policy* 30 (6): 794–814. https://doi.org/10.1080/10286632.2023.2268648

Nightingale and Wade. 2022. 'Identifying and Minimising the Impact of Fake Visual Media: Current and Future Directions'. *Memory, Mind & Media* 1 (15): 1–13.

NMDC. 2022. 'Written Evidence Submitted by the National Museum Directors' Council'. https://committees.parliament.uk/writtenevidence/111554/pdf/ (Accessed 24 March 2025).

Noble, D. 1997. *The Religion of Technology: The Divinity of Man and the Spirit of Invention*. Penguin.

Noble, S. U. 2018. *Algorithms of Oppression: How Search Engines Reinforce Racism*. NYU Press.

Nowaczyk-Basińska, K., and P. Kiel. 2024. 'Exploring the Immortological Imagination: Advocating for a Sociology of Immortality'. *Social Science* 13: 83. https://doi.org/10.3390/socsci13020083

Nowell, L. S., J. M. Norris, D. E. White and N. J. Moules. 2017. 'Thematic Analysis: Striving to Meet the Trustworthiness Criteria'. *International Journal of Qualitative Methods* 16: 1–13.

Ntalla, I. 2017. *The interactive museum experience: investigating experiential tendencies and audience focus in the Galleries of Modern London and the High Arctic exhibition*. (Unpublished Post-Doctoral thesis, City, University of London)

Nyholm, S. 2023. *Thies is Technology Ethics*. Wiley-Blackwell.

O'Connor, M., and E. Kasket.2022. 'What Grief isn't: Dead Grief Concepts and Their Digital-Age Revival'. In *Social Media and Technology Across the Lifespan*, edited by T. Machin, C. Brownlow, S. Abel and J. Gilmour. Palgrave Macmillan, Cham. https://doi-org.abc.cardiff.ac.uk/10.1007/978-3-030-99049-7_8

O'Neil. C. 2016. *Weapons of Math Destruction*. Penguin.

OECD (The Organisation for Economic Co-operation and Development). 2024. *OECD Survey on Drivers of Trust in Public Institutions – 2024 Results: Building Trust in a Complex Policy Environment*. OECD Publishing. https://doi.org/10.1787/9a20554b-en

Offert, Fabian, and Thao Phan. 2024. 'A Sign That Spells: Machinic Concepts and the Racial Politics of Generative AI'. *Journal of Digital Social Research* 6 (4): 49–59. https://doi.org/10.33621/jdsr.v6i440462

Öhman, C., and L. Floridi. 2017. 'The Political Economy of Death in the Age of Information: A Critical Approach to the Digital Afterlife Industry'. *Minds & Machines* 27 (4): 639–62.

Öhman, C., and L. Floridi. 2018. 'An Ethical Framework for the Digital Afterlife Industry'. *Nature Human Behaviour* 2 (4): 318–20. https://doi.org/10.1038/s41562-018-0335-2

Öhman, C. 2024. *The Afterlife of Data: What Happens to Your Information When You Die and Why You Should Care*. University of Chicago Press.

Öhman, C. J., and D. Watson. 2019. 'Are the Dead Taking Over Facebook? A Big Data Approach to the Future of Death Online'. *Big Data & Society* 6 (1). https://doi.org/10.1177/2053951719842540

Oscar, S. 2023. 'Curious Spectatorship in the Age of Deepfakes'. *Digital Creativity* 34 (3): 230–47. doi: 10.1080/14626268.2023.2248964

PAI. 2023. 'PAI's Responsible Practices for Synthetic Media: A Framework for Collective Action'. https://syntheticmedia.partnershiponai.org/

Parikka, J. 2012. 'What is Media Archaeology?' In *Machinology*. https://jussiparikka.net/2012/12/16/what-is-media-archaeology-beta-definition-ver-0-9/

Parikka, J. 2023. *Operational Images: From the Visual to the Invisual*. University of Minnesota Press.

Paris, B. 2021. 'Configuring Fakes: Digitized Bodies, the Politics of Evidence, and Agency'. *Social Media + Society* 7 (4). https://doi.org/10.1177/20563051211062919

Parry, R. 2013a. 'The Trusted Artifice: Reconnecting with the Museum's Fictive Tradition Online'. In *Museum Communication and Social Media: The Connected Museum*, edited by Kirsten Drotner and Kim Christian Schrøder, 17–32. Routledge.

Parry, R. 2013b. *The End of the Beginning: Normativity in the Postdigital Museum. Museum Worlds.*

Pennebaker, J. W., B. Rim and D. Paez (eds). 2013. *Collective Memory of Political Events: Social Psychological Perspectives*. Psychology Press.

Perry, S., Roussou, M., Economou, M., Young, H., and Pujol Tost, L. 2018. 'Moving Beyond the Virtual Museum: Engaging Visitors Emotionally'. In *23rd International Conference on Virtual Systems & Multimedia (VSMM), Dublin, 2017*, 1–8. IEEE. https://doi.org/10.1109/VSMM.2017.8346276

Pickering, L., and H. Kara 2017. 'Presenting and Representing Others: Towards an Ethics of Engagement'. *International Journal of Social Research Methodology* 20 (3): 299–309. https://doi-org.abc.cardiff.ac.uk/10.1080/13645579.2017.1287875

Pilkington, D. 2024. 'Myopic Memory: Capitalism's New Continuity in the Age of AI'. *Memory, Mind & Media* 3 (24): 1–10. doi:10.1017/mem.2024.21

Poell, T., D. Nieborg and J. van Dijck. 2019. 'Platformisation'. *Internet Policy Review* 8 (4): 1–13.

Poole, S. 2017. 'Ghosts in the Garden: locative gameplay and historical interpretation from below'. In *International Journal of Heritage Studies* 24 (3): 300–14. https://doi-org.abc.cardiff.ac.uk/10.1080/13527258.2017.1347887

Powell, H. 2018. 'Introduction to Part 1: Digital Emotion'. In *Emotions and Social Media: Emotion, Mediation, Anxiety and Contagion*, edited by T. D. Sampson, S. Maddison, and D. Ellis. Rowman and Littlefield.

Prescott, A., K. Headon, V. Hoyle, H. Graham, R. Brigham, L. Brigham, E. Tilley, R. Richards, A. Minnion and S. Ledger. 2020. *Communities, Archives and New Collaborative Practices*. Policy Press. http://ebookcentral.proquest.com/lib/kcl/detail.action?docID=6110736

Prey, R., and R. Smit. 2018. 'From Personal to Personalized Memory: Social Media as Mnemotechnology'. In *A Networked Self and Birth, Life, Death*, edited by Z. Papacharissi, 209–23. Routledge.

Prior, N. 2017. 'On Vocal Assemblages: From Edison to Miku'. *Contemporary Music Review* 37 (5–6): 488–506. https://doi-org.abc.cardiff.ac.uk/10.1080/07494467.2017.1402467

Puig de la Bellacasa, M. 2017. *Matters of Care: Speculative Ethics in More than Human Worlds: 41* (3rd ed. edition). Univ Of Minnesota Press.

Puschmann, C., and A. Powell. 2018. 'Turning Words Into Consumer Preferences: How Sentiment Analysis Is Framed in Research and the News Media'. *Social Media + Society* 4 (3). https://doi.org/10.1177/2056305118797724

Quadflieg, S., K. Neuburg and S. Nestler (eds). 2022. *(Dis)Obedience in Digital Societies: Perspectives on the Power of Algorithms and Data*. Transcript.

Rassool, C. 2015. 'Re-storing the Skeletons of Empire: Return, Reburial and Rehumanisation in Southern Africa'. *Journal of Southern African Studies* 41 (3): 653–70. https://doi.org/10.1080/03057070.2015.1028002

Raun, T. 2018. 'Connecting with the Dead: Vernacular Practices of Mourning through Photo-Sharing on Facebook'. In *Mediated Intimacies*, edited by R. Andreassen, M. Nebeling Petersen, K. Harrison and T.Raun. Routledge.

Reading, A., and T. Notley. 2015. 'The Materiality of Globital Memory: Bringing the Cloud to Earth'. *Continuum* 29 (4): 511–21.

Recuber, T. 2023. *The Digital Departed: How We Face Death, Commemorate Life, and Chase Virtual Immortality*. NYU Press.

Redden, J. 2022. 'Data Harms'. In *Data Justice*, edited by L. Dencik, A. Hintz, J. Redden, and E. Treré, 59–72. Sage.

Rees, G. 2019. 'How the Technology behind Deepfakes can Benefit all of Society'. *The European Sting*. https://europeansting.com/2019/11/27/how-the-technology-behind-deepfakes-can-benefit-all-of-society/

Reid, G. 2002. '"The History of the Past Is the Trust of the Present": Preservation and Excavation in the Gay and Lesbian Archives of South Africa'. In *Refiguring the Archive*, edited by Carolyn Hamilton, Verne Harris, Jane Taylor, Michele Pickover, Graeme Reid and Razia Saleh, 193–208. Springer Netherlands. https://doi.org/10.1007/978-94-010-0570-8_12

Rettberg, J. 2023. *Machine Vision: How Algorithms are Changing the Way We See the World*. Polity.

Richardson-Walden, V. G., and M. Makhortykh. 2024. 'Imagining Human-AI Memory Symbiosis: How Re-Remembering the History of Artificial Intelligence Can Inform the Future of Collective Memory'. *Memory Studies Review* 1: 323–42.

Ricoeur, P. 2004. *Memory, History, Forgetting*. University of Chicago Press.

Rini, R. 2019. 'Deepfakes and the Epistemic Backstop (Working Draft)'. https://philpapers.org/archive/ RINDAT.pdf (Accessed 15 June 2022).

Rini, R., and L. Cohen. 2022. 'Deepfakes, Deep Harms'. *Journal of Ethics and Social Philosophy* 22 (2): 143–61.

Ritter, C. S. 2022. 'Rethinking Digital Ethnography: A Qualitative Approach to Understanding Interfaces'. *Qualitative Research* 22 (6): 916–32. https://doi.org/10.1177/14687941211000540

Robards, B., and S. Lincoln. 2017. 'Uncovering Longitudinal Life Narratives: Scrolling Back on Facebook'. *Qualitative Research* 17 (6): 715–30.

Rodríguez Reséndiz, H., and J. Rodríguez Reséndiz. 2024. 'Digital Resurrection. Challenging the Boundary between Life and Death with Artificial Intelligence. *Philosophies* 9: 71. https://doi.org/10.3390/philosophies9030071

Roediger, H. L., and J. V. Wertsch. 2008. 'Creating a New Discipline of Memory Studies'. *Memory Studies* 1 (1): 9–22.

Romele, A. 2024. *Digital Habitus: A Critique of the Imaginaries of Artificial Intelligence*. Routledge.

Rossi, M. 2010. *Fabricating Authenticity: Modeling a Whale at the American Museum of Natural History, 1906–1974*, Vol. 10, 338–61. Isis. International Review Devoted to the History of Science and Its Cultural Influences.

Routledge, C. 2016. *Nostalgia: A Psychological Resource*. Routledge.

Ruckenstein, M. 2023. *The Feel of Algorithms*. University of California Press.

Rueda, J., T. Ausín, M. Coeckelbergh, J. I. del Valle, F. Lara, B. Liedo, J. Llorca Albareda, H. Mertes, R. Ranisch, V. Lúcia Raposo, B. C. Stahl, M. Vilaça, and Í de

Miguel. 2025. 'Why Dignity Is a Troubling Concept for AI Ethics'. *Patterns* 6 (3). https://doi.org/10.1016/j.patter.2025.101207

Ruffer, N., J. Knitza and M. Krusche. 2020. '#Covid4Rheum: An Analytical Twitter Study in the Time of the COVID-19 Pandemic'. *Rheumatology International.* 40 (12): 2031–7.

Rumsey, A. S. 2016. *When We Are No More: How Digital Memory Is Shaping Our Future*. Bloomsbury.

Safavi, G., and S. Ghazinoory. 2024. 'Creative Bits: Challenges of Applying Industry 4.0 in Digital Creative Industries'. *Multimedia Tools and Application* 84: 15897–923. https://doi-org.abc.cardiff.ac.uk/10.1007/s11042-024-19701-y

Salvaggio, E. 2023. 'How to Read an AI Image: Toward a Media Studies Methodology for the Analysis of Synthetic Images'. *Image Journal* 37. https://image-journal.de/how-to-read-an-ai-image/

Salvaggio, E. 2024. 'Infrastructures of Memory: Between Archives and Datasets'. https://cyberneticforests.substack.com/p/infrastructures-of-memory (Accessed 30 April 2025).

Savin-Baden, M., and D. Burden. 2018. 'Digital Immortality and Virtual Remains'. *Postdigital Science and Education* 1: 87–103.

Savin-Baden, M., and V. Mason-Robbie (eds). 2020. *Digital Afterlife: Death Matters in a Digital Age*. Chapman and Hall/CRC. https://doi.org/10.1201/9780429322198

Sayers, N. 2020. *The Promise of Nostalgia*. Routledge.

Sanderhoff, M. 2014. *Sharing is Caring: Openness and Sharing in the Cultural Heritage Sector.* Statens Museum for Kunst, Copenhagen.

Scharlach, R., B. Hallinan and L. Shifman. 2023. 'Governing Principles: Articulating Values in Social Media Platform Policies'. *New Media & Society* 26 (11): 6658–77.

Schincariol, A., H. Otgaar, C. M. Greene, G. Murphy, P. Riesthuis, I. Mangiulli and F. Battista. 2024. 'Fake Memories: A Meta-Analysis on the Effect of Fake News on the Creation of False Memories and False Beliefs'. *Memory, Mind & Media* 3: e17. doi:10.1017/mem.2024.14.

Scholz, T. (ed.). 2012. *Digital Labor: The Internet as Playground and Factory.* Routledge.

Schuh, J. 2024. 'AI As Artificial Memory: A Global Reconfiguration of Our Collective Memory Practices?'. *Memory Studies Review* 1 (2): 231–55. https://doi.org/10.1163/29498902-202400012

Schumann, F. 2022. 'Using Voyant Tools for Data Mining Social Media Comments about a Destination: A Guam Study'. *Journal of Hospitality & Tourism* 20 (2): 106–18.

Shamim, S. 2024. 'Why Google's AI tool was slammed for showing images of people of colour', *AlJazeera*. https://www.aljazeera.com/news/2024/3/9/why-google-gemini-wont-show-you-white-people

Sen, A. 2021. 'Art and Artificial Intelligence: How "Deepfakes" Can Help Create Authentic Museum Experiences!' *ArtWorldZen*, 1 June. https://medium.com/art-world-zen/art-and-artificial-intelligence-how-deepfakes-can-help-create-authentic-museum-experiences-65d8aa7da29c

Sherlock, A. 2013. 'Larger Than Life: Digital Resurrection and the Re-Enchantment of Society'. *The Information Society* 29 (3): 164–76.

Silbey, J., and W. Hartzog. 2019. 'The Upside of Deep Fakes'. *Maryland Law Review.* 78 (4): article 8.

Simon, N. 2010. *The Participatory Museum*. Museum 2.0.

Sisto, D. 2020. *Online Afterlives: Immortality, Memory, and Grief in Digital Culture.* MIT Press.

Sisto, D. 2021. *Remember Me: Memory and Forgetting in the Digital Age*. Polity.

Sloan, L. 2017. 'Who Tweets in the United Kingdom? Profiling the Twitter Population Using the British Social Attitudes Survey 2015'. *Social Media and Society* 3 (1): 1–11.

Small, Z. 2023. 'Dream of talking to Vincent van Gogh? AI tries to resurrect the artist in NY Times'. https://www.ekathimerini.com/nytimes/1227083/dream-of-talking-to-vincent-van-gogh-ai-tries-to-resurrect-the-artist/.

Smit, R. 2020. 'Connective Memory on *Justice for Mike Brown*'. In *Social Movements, Cultural Memory and Digital Media: Mobilising Mediated Remembrance*, edited by S. Merrill, P. Daphi, and E. Keightley, 85–108. Palgrave Macmillan.

Smit, R., A. Heinrich and M. Broersma. 2018. 'Activating the Past in the Ferguson Protests: Memory Work, Digital Activism and the Politics of Platforms'. *New Media & Society* 20 (9): 3119–39.

Smit, R., T. Smits and S. Merrill. 2024. 'Stochastic Remembering and Distributed Mnemonic Agency: Recalling Twentieth Century Activists with ChatGPT'. *Memory Studies Review* 1: 1–22.

Smith, L. 2020. *Emotional Heritage: Visitor Engagement at Museums and Heritage Sites*. Routledge. https://doi.org/10.4324/9781315713274

Smith, L., and G. Campbell. 2017. '"Nostalgia for the Future": Memory, Nostalgia and the Politics of Class. *International Journal of Heritage Studies* 23 (7): 612–27. https://doi.org/10.1080/13527258.2017.1321034

Snelson, C. L. 2016. 'Qualitative and Mixed Methods Social Media Research: A Review of the Literature'. *International Journal of Qualitative Methods* 15 (1). https://doi.org/10.1177/1609406915624574

Snow, J. 2021. 'These Historical Artefacts are Totally Faked'. *Wired*. https://www.wired.com/story/fake-artefacts-ai/

Sofka, C., I. N. Cupit and K. R. Gilbert. 2012. *Dying, Death, and Grief in an Online Universe*. Springer Publishing.

Solomon, T. 2024. 'The AI-Powered Ask Dalí and Hello Vincent Installations Raise Uncomfortable Questions about Ventriloquizing the Dead'. *ARTnews*. https://www.artnews.com/art-news/issue/salvador-dali-vincent-van-gogh-ai-installations-ethics-1234714954/

Sontag, S. 2008. *On Photography*. Penguin.

Srnicek, N. 2016. *Platform Capitalism*. Polity.

St. John, P. 2020. 'The Untold Story of How the Golden State Killer Was Found: A Covert Operation and Private DNA'. *Los Angeles Times*, December 8. Available At: Https://Www.Latimes.Com/California/Story/2020-12-08/Man-In-The-Window (Accessed 26 April 2023).

Stallard, M., and J. de Groot. 2020. '"Things Are Coming Out That Are Questionable, We Never Knew About": DNA and the New Family History'. *Journal of Family History* 45 (3): 274–94. https://doi.org/10.1177/0363199020906853

Stanyek, J., and B. Piekut, 2010. 'Deadness: Technologies of the Intermundane'. *The Drama Review* 54 (1): 14–38.

Stark, L. 2019. 'Affect and Emotion in digitalSTS'. In *DigitalTS: A Field Guide for Science & Technology studies*, edited by J. Vertesi, D. Ribes, C. DiSalvo, L. Forlano, S. J. Jackson, Y. A. Loukissas, D. K. Rosner and H. R. Shell, 117–35. Princeton University Press.

Stark, L. 2023. 'Breaking Up (with) AI Ethics'. *American Literature* 95 (2). doi: 10.1215/00029831-10575148

Stiegler, B. 2009. *Technics and Time*, Vol. II: *Disorientation*, translated by S. Barker. Stanford University Press.

Stiegler, B. 2011. *Technics and Time,* Vol. III: *Cinematic time and the question of malaise*, translated by S. Barker. Stanford University Press.

Stoler, A. L. 2002. 'Colonial Archives and the Arts of Governance: On the Content in the Form'. In *Refiguring the Archive*, edited by Carolyn Hamilton, Verne Harris, Jane Taylor, Michele Pickover, Graeme Reid and Razia Saleh, 83–102. Springer Netherlands. https://doi.org/10.1007/978-94-010-0570-8_7

Stokes, P. 2021. *Digital Souls: A Philosophy of Online Immortality*. Bloomsbury Academic.

Stone, C. B., and A. Zwolinski. 2022. 'The Mnemonic Consequences Associated with Sharing Personal Photographs on Social Media'. *Memory, Mind & Media* 1: e12. doi: 10.1017/mem.2022.6.

Striphas, T. 2015. 'Algorithmic Culture'. *European Journal of Cultural Studies* 18 (4–5): 395–412.

Styx, L. 2024. 'How Are Museums Using Artificial Intelligence?' *MuseumNext*, 12 May. https://www.museumnext.com/article/artificial-intelligence-and-the-future-of-museums/

Sujon, Z., and H. T. Dyer. 2020. 'Understanding the Social in a Digital Age'. *New Media & Society* 22 (7): 1125–34. https://doi.org/10.1177/1461444820912531

Sumiala, J. 2013. *Media and Ritual: Death, Community and Everyday Life*. Routledge.

Sumiala, J. 2022. *Mediated Death*. Polity.

Sutherland, T. 2023. *Resurrecting the Black Body: Race and the Digital Afterlife*. University of California Press.

Tackett, J. 2021. *Deep(er) Nostalgia: Formulating Tech's In-Control Valley and Uncanny Asymptote. Los Angeles Review of Books*. https://www.lareviewofbooks.org/article/deep-nostalgia/

Taffel, S. 2021. *Digital Media Ecologies: Entanglements of Content, Code and Hardware*. Bloomsbury.

Tanner, G. 2023. *Foreverism*. Polity.

Thiel, S., and J. C. Bernhardt (eds). 2023. *AI in Museums: Reflections, Perspectives and Applications* (1st ed., Vol. 74). transcript Verlag. https://doi.org/10.14361/9783839467107

Tiribelli, S., S. Pansoni, E. Frontoni and B. Giovanola. 2024. 'Ethics of Artificial Intelligence for Cultural Heritage: Opportunities and Challenges'. *IEEE Transactions on Technology and Society* 5: 293–305. https://doi.org/10.1109/TTS.2024.3432407

Trillò, T., B. Hallinan, A. Green, B. Kim, S. Mizoroki, R. Scharlach, P. H. Park, P. Frosh and L. Shifman. 2023. '"I Love this Photo, I Can Feel their Hearts!" How Users Across the World Evaluate Social Media Portraiture'. *Journal of Communication* 73 (3): 235–46. https://doi.org/10.1093/joc/jqad009

Troeger, J., and Bock, A. 2022. 'The Sociotechnical Walkthrough – A Methodological Approach'. *Studies in Communication Sciences* 22 (1): 43–52.

Tsai, S., 2019. 'Augmented Reality Enhancing Place Satisfaction for Heritage Tourism Marketing'. *Current Issues in Tourism* 23 (9): 1078–83. https://doi.org/10.1080/13683500.2019.1598950

Ufarte-Ruiz, M.-J., F.-J. Murcia-Verdú and J.-M. Túñez-López. 2023. 'Use of Artificial Intelligence in Synthetic Media: First Newsrooms Without Journalists'. *Profesional De La información* 32 (2): e320203. https://doi.org/10.3145/epi.2023.mar.03

UKRI. 2023. 'Framework for Responsible Research and Innovation'. https://www.ukri.org/who-we-are/epsrc/our-policies-and-standards/framework-for-responsible-innovation/

Vaccari, C., and A. Chadwick. 2020. 'Deepfakes and Disinformation: Exploring the Impact of Synthetic Political Video on Deception, Uncertainty, and Trust'. *Social Media and Society* 6 (1): 1–13. https://doi.org/10.1177/2056305120903408

van den Hoonaard, W. C., and A. Hamilton. 2016. *The Ethics Rupture: Exploring Alternatives to Formal Research-Ethics Review*. University of Toronto Press.

van Dijck, J. 2007. *Mediated Memories in the Digital Age*. Stanford University Press.

van Dijck, J. 2017. 'Connective Memory: How Facebook Takes Charge of Your Past'. In *Memory Unbound: Tracing the Dynamics of Memory Studies*, edited by L. Bond, S. Craps and P. Vermeulen. Berghahn Books.

van Dijck, J. 2020. 'Governing Digital Societies: Private Platforms, Public Values'. *Computer Law & Security Review* 36.

van Dijck, J., T. Poell and M. de Waal. 2018. *The Platform Society*. Oxford Academic.

Véliz, C. (ed). 2023. *The Oxford Handbook of Digital Ethics*. Oxford University Press.

Viidalepp, A. 2022. 'The Semiotic Functioning of Synthetic Media'. *Informacios Tarsadalom* 22 (4): 109–18.

Villaespesa, E., and O. Murphy. 2021. 'This is Not An Apple! Benefits and Challenges of Applying Computer Vision to Museum Collections'. *Museum Management and Curatorship* 36 (4): 362–83. https://doi.org/10.1080/09647775.2021.1873827

Vincent, J. 2023. 'AI art tools Stable Diffusion and Midjourney targeted with copyright lawsuit'. *The Verge*, 16 January. Available at: https://www.theverge.com/2023/1/16/23557098/generative-ai-art-copyright-legal-lawsuit-stable-diffusion-midjourney-deviantart (Accessed 1 May 2023).

Vinchon, F., T. Lubart, S. Bartolotta, V. Gironnay, M. Botella, S. Bourgeois-Bougrine, J.-M. Burkhardt, N. Bonnardel, G. E. Corazza, V. Glăveanu, M. Hanchett Hanson, Z. Ivcevic, M. Karwowski, J. C. Kaufman, T. Okada, R. Reiter-Palmon and A. Gaggioli. 2023. 'Artificial Intelligence & Creativity: A Manifesto for Collaboration'. *The Journal of Creative Behavior* 57: 472–84. https://doi.org/10.1002/jocb.597

Voinea C. 2023. 'On Grief and Griefbots'. https://blog.practicalethics.ox.ac.uk/2023/11/on-grief-and-griefbots/

Voon, C. 2016. 'Could the Nefertiti Scan Be a Hoax—And Does that Matter?' *Hyperallergic*, 9 March. http://hyperallergic.com/281739/could-the-nefertiti-scan-be-a-hoax-and-does-that-matter/

Walker, R. 2022. 'Artificial Intelligence for Health and Care Is Not Inevitable: Introduction and Critical Vocabulary'. In *Nursing a Radical Imagination*, edited by Jess Dillard-Wright, Jane Hopkins-Walsh and Brandon Brown. Routledge.

Walter, M., T. Kukutai, S. R. Carroll and D. Rodriguez-Lonebear (eds). 2022. *Indigenous Data Sovereignty and Policy* (1st edition). Routledge.

Walter, T. 2015. 'Communication Media and the Dead: From the Stone Age to Facebook'. *Mortality* 20 (3): 215–32. DOI: 10.1080/13576275.2014.993598.

Wang. Q. 2008. 'On the Cultural Constitution of Collective Memory'. *Memory* 16 (3): 305–17.

Warzel, C. 2018. 'Believable: The Terrifying Future Of Fake News'. *BuzzFeed News*. https://www.buzzfeednews.com/article/charliewarzel/the-terrifying-future-of-fake-news#.ydWEVENBd

Weedon, C., and G. Jordan. 2012. 'Collective Memory: Theory and Politics'. *Social Semiotics* 22 (2): 143–53.

Westerlund, M. 2019. 'The Emergence of Deepfake Technology: A Review'. *Technology Innovation Management Review* 9: 40–53. https://doi.org/10.22215/timreview/1282

Westling, J. 2019. 'Are Deep Fakes a Shallow Concern? A Critical Analysis of the Likely Societal Reaction to Deep Fakes'. *TPRC47: The 47th Research Conference on Communication, Information and Internet Policy 2019 (24 July)*, 1–29. Available at SSRN: https://ssrn.com/abstract=3426174 or http://dx.doi.org/10.2139/ssrn.3426174.

Willever-Farr, H. L., and A. Forte. 2014. 'Family Matters: Control and Conflict in Online Family History Production'. In *Proceedings of the 17th ACM Conference on Computer Supported Cooperative Work & Social Computing (CSCW'14)*, 475–86. Association for Computing Machinery. https://doi.org/10.1145/2531602.2531737

Willson, M. 2017. 'Algorithms (and the) Everyday'. *Information, Communication & Society* 20 (1): 137–50. DOI: 10.1080/1369118X.2016.1200645

Wilson, J. L. 2005. *Nostalgia: Sanctuary of Meaning*. Bucknell University Press.

Wingström, R., J. Hautala and R. Lundman. 2022. 'Redefining Creativity in the Era of AI? Perspectives of Computer Scientists and New Media Artists'. *Creativity Research Journal* 36 (2): 177–93. https://doi.org/10.1080/10400419.2022.2107850

Worcman, K., and J. Garde-Hansen. 2016. *Social Memory Technology: Theory, Practice, Action*. Routledge.

Yadlin-Segal, A., R. Tsuria and W. Bellar. 2020. 'The Ethics of Studying Digital Contexts: Reflections from Three Empirical Case Studies'. *Human Behavior & Emerging Technologies* 2: 168–78. https://doi.org/10.1002/hbe2.183

Yates, S., and E. Carmi. 2024. *Digital Inclusion: International Policy and Research*. Palgrave Macmillan.

Yip, A., and S. Kenderdine. 2018. 'The Proliferation of Aura: Facsimiles, Authenticity and Digital Objects'. In The *Routledge Handbook of Museums, Media and Communication*, edited by Kirsten Drotner, Vince Dziekan, Ross Parry, and Kim Schrøder, 274–89. Routledge.

Zaidi, S., and S. Allahdad. 2023. 'Analyzing Recent (2019) Kashmir Socio-Political Issue: A Voyant Sentiment Analysis of Tweets'. *Linguistics and Literature Review* 9 (2): 21–46.

Zerubavel, E. 2011. *Ancestors and Relatives: Genealogy, Identity, and Community*. Oxford University Press.

Zibner, J. 2019. 'Artificial Intelligence: A Creative Player in the Game of Copyright'. *European Journal of Law and Technology* 10 (1): 1–20.

Zuboff, S. 2019. *The Age of Surveillance Capitalism: The Fight for a Human Future at the New Frontier of Power*. Profile Books.

Zylinska, J. 2023. *The Perception Machine: Our Photographic Future Between the Eye and AI*. MIT Press.

Index

www.ingramcontent.com/pod-product-compliance
Ingram Content Group UK Ltd.
Pitfield, Milton Keynes, MK11 3LW, UK
UKHW021908150926
475560UK00003B/246

9 781350 437524